INDIA-SRI LANKA PARTNERSHIP IN THE 21st CENTURY

INDIA-SRI LANKA PARTNERSHIP IN THE 21st CENTURY

Editor
ADLURI SUBRAMANYAM RAJU

PUBLICATIONS

KALPAZ PUBLICATIONS
DELHI-110052

India-Sri Lanka Partnership in the 21st Century

Rs. 690

ISBN: 81-7835-544-2

Published in 2008 in India by
Kalpaz Publications
C-30, Satyawati Nagar,
Delhi-110052
E-mail: kalpaz@hotmail.com

Lasser Type Setting by: Rudra Computer Graphics, Delhi
Printed at : Vishal Kaushik Printers Delhi - 110093

The People of India and Sri Lanka

Contents

Contents

Acknowledgements

It is my foremost duty to express my sincere gratitude to late Prof. Isaac Sequeira, former Director of Indo-American Centre for International Studies (IACIS), Hyderabad, for his encouragement and help in organizing the seminar. But for his wholehearted support the seminar would not have materialized.

I would be failing in my duty if I do not acknowledge the monetary support given by the University Grants Commission (UGC), New Delhi, in organizing the seminar. I express my deep sense of indebtedness to Prof. V. N. Rajasekharan Pillai, the then Vice-Chairman of UGC, who was instrumental in making the seminar a success. I also express my gratitude to Sri Lankan Airlines and Berghof Foundation for Conflict Studies, Colombo and its Director, Ms.Kanaka Abeygunawardana, for co-sponsoring the seminar.

I would like to acknowledge the contribution and support of IACIS staff, particularly Srinivas Rao, Anitha Badrinath, Ann Kumaraswamy, Ahalya, Nagabhushanam, Prasad and Hanumanth Rao.

I express my gratitude to H. E. Sumith Nakandala, Sri Lankan Ambassador to Nepal, Prof. P.V. Rao, Centre for Indian Ocean Studies, Osmania University, and my friends-J.L.N. Rao and G.B. Reddy, who helped and stood by me in times of need. I am thankful to Prof. T. Nirmala Devi, Director, Centre for SAARC Studies, Andhra University, who encouraged and supported me in completing this volume. I thank all the contributors for their help.

I wish to thank my parents, my wife and my daughters-Mahitha and Samhitha for their encouragement and cooperation.

List of Contributors

J. Kedareswari, Director, Department of Archeology and Museum, Hyderabad

H.E. Ms. Nirupama Rao, joined the Indian Foreign Service in 1973. She held various positions on different capacities. She served as the High Commissioner of India to Sri Lanka during 2004-2006. She was a Fellow at the Centre for International Affairs at Harvard University where she specialized on Asia Pacific Security. Recently appointed as Ambessador to China

P. Sahadevan is Associate Professor and member of the Core Group for the Study of National Security at the School of International Studies, Jawaharlal Nehru University, New Delhi. He is the author of three books and published several papers.

Amb. S.J.C Chhatwal, former High Commissioner to Sri Lanka and former Chairman of UPSC, New Delhi.

P. P. Devaraj, Chairman of Foundation for Community Transformation, Colombo.

V.Suryanarayan is a specialist in South and South East Asian studies. He was associated with the Centre for South and South East Asian Studies, University of Madras. He has published several books and papers. He is a regular contributor to the Hindu and the Frontline.

Shahul H. Hasbullah is faculty in Geography at the University of Peradeniya, Sri Lanka. He has authored/edited several works. He was a Visiting Fulbright Scholar at the Institute for the Study of International Migration of the Georgetown University in 2002 and was Guest Researcher at Norwegian University of Technology in 1998.

Cmde. R.S. Vasan IN (Retd) has held many important appointments both ashore and afloat. Since retirement, he has been writing extensively and contributing to journal and many think tanks. Presently, he is the Additional Director, Projects and Development in the Observer Research Foundation, Chennai.

Vijay Sakhuja is former Indian Navy officer and currently Senior Research Fellow at the Observer Research Foundation, New Delhi, India. He has authored a book titled *Confidence Building From The Sea: An Indian Initiative* and is the recipient of Vice Admiral S L Sethi Maritime Media Award, 2002.

A.Subramanyam Raju is former Honorary Academic Fellow at the Indo-American Centre for International Studies, Hyderabad. Recently hired as Associate Professor of Political Science in centre for SAARC Studies at Andhra University. He has published seven books and several articles.

Manoj Soni, Vice-Chancellor of M.S.Baroda University, Baroda. He specializes in International Relations Studies. In addition to several articles and research papers, his major publication is a 1998 published book on the Post-Cold War International Systemic Transition entitled as *Understanding the Global Political Earthquake* by Ashgate Publishing Company, England.

K. Ishaq is faculty in the Department of Management at South Eastern University of Sri Lanka, Olluvil, Sri Lanka.

Indra Nath Mukherji, Professor, South Asian Studies, School of International Studies, Jawaharlal Nehru University in New Delhi. He has authored two books and co-authored and edited several others and published more than 80 articles. He is currently Member, Editorial Board, *South Asia Economic Journal,* Member, Editorial Board, *Journal of Himalayan Studies,* Member, Group of Experts BIMST-EC, under aegis of Ministry of Commerce, Government of India.

M.Ganeshamoorthy is faculty in the Department of Economics at the University of Colombo, Sri Lanka

Somindra Kishen Hazari was President of India-ASEAN-Sri Lanka Chamber of Commerce and Industry, Chennai. He is currently Managing Director of SHOSOVA Properties Ltd.,

Chennai and President for India – Indonesia Business Association – South India Chapter.

N. Sathiya Moorthy, Journalist and Political Analyst, is the Honorary Director of the Chennai Chapter of the Observer Research Foundation (ORF), the Delhi-based policy think-tank.

Santasilan Kadirgamar was retired lecturer from Jaffna College, Universities of Colombo and Jaffna. He was Japan Foundation Fellow and Researcher at the Tokyo University of Foreign Studies 1983-84 and until 2000 lectured at the Meiji Gakuin University and also briefly at the University of Tokyo. He has published two books and papers.

G.S.Rao, Director of National Institute of Tourism and Hospitality Management (NITHM), is involved in the establishment of the institute and associated with Training, Consultancy and other tourism development related activities of Government of Andhra Pradesh.

Shailesh Sikha, Consultant, National Institute of Tourism and Hospitality Management, Telecom Nagar, Gachibowli, Hyderabad, – India.

Introduction

A. Subramanyam Raju

India and Sri Lanka were ruled by the British prior to their independence in 1947 and 1948 respectively. Geographically both are contiguous and culturally close. The island state of Sri Lanka is barely thirty kilometers away from India's southern coastal tip. People of these two countries share many similarities in terms of dress, food habits, manners, customs and ways of life. Politically both the countries have a common interest in keeping the region free from conflict. In spite India sharing border with all its neighbouring countries in South Asia, its relationship with Sri Lanka has been relatively more cordial than with other countries in the region.

In addition to their cordial relationship, there is misunderstanding and mistrust between the two resulted in many ups and downs in their mutual relationship. The issue of Tamils of Indian origin and maritime issues between the two countries created turbulence. The civil war of 1983 further aggravated the situation. The interests of the fishermen of both the countries also got affected. Apart from the disturbances caused by the illegal movement of the Tamil groups, there began frequent incidents of attack on fishermen, smuggling of illicit weapons, drugs, pirate activities and assault on security forces by the Tamil guerrillas.

India and Sri Lanka signed a Free Trade Agreement in 1998. This agreement set an example for others in the region to promote a greater economic cooperation in the region. It might have paved the way for the South Asian countries to have an agreement on South Asian Free Trade Agreement (SAFTA) in Pakistan in 2004 and later it was ratified at Dhaka summit in 2005. Half of India's investment in the South Asian region is invested in Sri Lanka and as such the island state has emerged as a close economic partner of India. However, it was reported that much of the trade between them is unofficial. Both the countries realize that restrictions on trade between the two are detrimental to their economic growth and prosperity. They also realize that relaxation of the restrictions, abolition of tariffs and lifting restrictions on free movement of manufactured goods and services minimize the illegal trade between the two countries.

There is a greater need to enhance mutual cooperation on maritime security. Such cooperation may include measures such as joint naval patrolling, controlling of smuggling and pirate activities and strengthening communication networks. Apart from such measures, there is great potential for enhancing and institutionalizing economic cooperation in the exploration and exploitation of sea resources in the Indian Ocean waters. A few steps have already been initiated by both countries to extend cooperation in some of the above areas. Yet, a more organized thrust is needed to boost and to strengthen institutionalize bonds between the two countries.

Neither country can ignore the security of the other. Sri Lanka cannot ignore the problems of Tamil Nadu when it talks about its relationship with India. Similarly India cannot ignore the internal problems of Sri Lanka when it seeks to improve its relations with the latter.

In this context, the Indo-American Centre for International Studies (Hyderabad) organized a three day international seminar entitled *Indo-Sri Lanka Partnership in the New Century* on 30, 31 January-1 February 2006. Main objective of the seminar was to probe into various mechanisms, which may improve cooperation between the two countries and internal stability within the states. Experts – policymakers, scholars, bureaucrats, entrepreneurs and NGO's from both the countries involved in the debate to develop strategies with a view to shaping better future for both the countries. The papers provide a perspective in debating the emerging issues of greater concern to India and Sri Lanka in the dynamic world of the twenty first Century.

Overview of the Volume

There are eighteen papers, which are divided into six sections.

Section-1: Historical Interfaces Between India and Sri Lanka

J.Kedareswari, in her paper on "India and Sri Lanka: The Buddhist Connection", describes that Buddhism entered the island during the high period of Mauryan rule in India in the third Century B.C. Buddhism was to serve as an umbilical cord between the main land and the island and connection was to last for more than a thousand years. During this period Buddhist philosophy and Buddhist art flowed from India to Sri Lanka. The Indian source was to greatly influence the Island making it a lasting religion of this land. The paper focuses on this connection drawing record from archeological evidence and literature.

Section-2: Indo-Sri Lanka: Political Relations

Nirupama Rao, in her paper "Glimpses of Indo-Sri Lanka Relations" (inaugural address), stresses the importance of relations between India and Sri Lanka. Further, she maintains that the cooperation between the two countries is very cordial and would strengthen further. She traces the historical and cultural linkages between Sri Lanka and South India. She maintains that closer connectivity and consonance in economic interaction between Sri Lanka and South India will increasingly be a fact of life in this century.

In his paper "India's Policy of Non-Intervention in Sri Lanka", P. Sahadevan describes the two distinct phases in India's policy towards the Sri Lankan ethnic conflict. The first phase, covering seven years (1983-90), saw India's proactive politico-military intervention for peacemaking. The second phase since 1990 is marked by India's decision not to intervene directly in the conflict. The paper focuses on the second phase of the Indian policy. It seeks to focus on the determinants of India's policy of non-intervention, the changing national and regional contexts in which the policy is pursued and some of the core elements of the new policy. The paper analyses India's options in the current situation by taking cognizance of the trends in the conflict process, the task of peacemaking and the cost and benefit of Indian intervention or non-intervention.

Section-3: Ethnic, Repatriates and Refugee Issues in Indo-Sri Lanka Relations

S.J.S Chhatwal's paper, "Ethnic Crisis in Sri Lanka – A Peaceful Solution", analyzes various Sri Lankan governments' policies that have tried to solve the ethnic problem within a unitary framework of the constitution without a success. Whenever a Sinhalese political party is in power, proposed legislation to give a certain degree of autonomy to the Tamils, the opposition Sinhalese party opposed it so that the credit to solve the ethnic problem peacefully would not go to the political party in power. The same process was repeated, when the opposition Sinhalese party came into power! Therefore, it is imperative that first Sinhalese majority (74%) should arrive at a consensus as to what degree of autonomy they are prepared to give to Tamils. At the same time, the degree of autonomy proposed has to be meaningful and viable so that the Tamil groups from India can go back to their land and people and make it acceptable.

P.P.Devarj, in his paper, "A Cinderella Community in Transition: The Indian Origin Tamils of Sri Lanka", maintains that India has moved away from its past policies regarding the Overseas Indian communities numbering well over twenty millions living in many parts of the world. Non Resident Indians and Persons of Indian Origin (PIO) have been accorded recognition and their roots and links with India have been accepted and given esteem. The PIO card scheme, which allowed persons of Indian Origin a twenty-year visa and other facilities, has been enhanced as an overseas Indian Citizenship scheme, which provides lifetime visa and other facilities. This paper examines the position of the PIO community in Sri Lanka, its demographic profile, interactions, participation, representation and rights.

V. Suryanarayan's paper, "Integration and Assimilationof Sri Lankan Repatriates in Tamil Nadu", provides a critical analysis of the problems associated with the rehabilitation and integration of Sri Lankan repatriates in Tamil Nadu. After analyzing the political background to the India-Sri Lanka agreements, the paper proceeds to examine the effectiveness of various rehabilitation schemes. It describes the marginalisation and pauperization of the overwhelming majority of repatriates and how they started moving to Kotagiri and Kodaikanal ending up as bonded labourers. The concluding part highlights how repatriation came to an end and how the repatriates have become an integral part of the Tamil Nadu society.

S. H. Hasbullah's paper, "Facilitating the Return of Sri Lankan Refugees in India", examines how to facilitate the return of Sri

Lankan refugees from India. It looks into the issue of whether there is a conducive environment for a large number of refugees from India to return to their former homes in the war-affected areas of the north and east. The paper also investigates and reports the possibility of having a plan of a return of refugees from India in phases.

Section-4: Maritime Cooperation between India and Sri Lanka

In his paper "Role of Maritime Forces in Disaster Management", R.S. Vasan examines the experience of the Indian navy and the coast guard in tackling the post Tsunami situation both within the country and also in the neighbourhood in the Indian Ocean. While there were many success stories, there is a need to put the entire operations in a proper perspective to draw up lessons for the future. The shortage of the right kind of vessels that would provide large lift capability and platforms with sufficient vertical envelopment capability would need to be overcome.

Vijay Sakhuja's paper, "India and Sri Lanka: Assessing Maritime Security Relationship", describes that India has always had a stake in Sri Lanka's security. It remains concerned about the prevalent gunrunning, drug smuggling, sea piracy and terrorism in the Palk Bay. Indian naval ships have also carried out patrolling in south Sri Lanka waters too. The most important facet of the growing joint activity is that both Sri Lanka and India have now entered into a phase of building an extraordinary relationship to ward off destabilizing actors and contribute to regional stability.

A.Subramanyam Raju, in his paper "Maritime Issues between India and Sri Lanka describes that both the countries signed bilateral agreements in June 1974 and March 1976 to demarcate their maritime boundaries. In spite of demarcation of their boundary, there are some issues that are coming in the way of cooperation between the two. The paper examines Indo-Sri Lankan maritime relations with the focus on the problems of fishermen, threat from sea tigers, land bridge between the two countries, Sethusamudram ship canal project and its implications on Indo-Sri Lankan relations.

Section-5: Indo-Sri Lanka Economic Relations

Manoj Soni's paper, "India and Sri Lanka: From Political Fissures To Economic Bridges", divides into three parts. The first part of the paper identifies and addresses the broad areas of political divergence and conflict. In the second part it focuses on the possible areas of convergence and the third part explains why this convergence is important against the larger issue of South Asian resurgence.

K.Ishaq, in his paper "Strategic Marketing Formulation for the Domestic Manufacturers Through the Operation of Regional Corporation in the Context of Globalisation", examines how the domestic manufacturers should concentrate in evaluating their strengths and weaknesses and threats and opportunities in the regional market. It also discusses the various possibilities and advantages to establish an institutional framework between the Sri Lankan and Indian manufacturers to ensure their independent and dependent role in the regional market.

Indra Nath Mukherji's paper, "Indo-Sri Lanka Free Trade Agreement: Can Trade Agreement among Unequal Partners Work?, highlights how the agreement provided for a differentiated menu offers by each country that addressed the concerns of the different stakeholders. The differentiated offers took note of the unequal capabilities of each country so that the smaller country was not placed on a level playing field with its larger neighbour. The free trade agreement was stimulated by the flow of Indian investment into Sri Lanka to take advantage of the latter's congenial investment climate not only to meet the country's domestic demand but also to cater to India's market in its southern region. This led to a more rapid increase in India's imports as against its exports thereby reducing its trade imbalance with that country. It also led to trade diversification of Sri Lanka's exports to India.

M. Ganeshamoorthy's paper, "Free Trade Agreement between India and Sri Lanka: The way forward for improvement", argues that Sri Lanka produces a limited number of commodities for the Indian market whereas India supplies a wide range of goods for the Sri Lankan markets. This may be partly due to the inability to access information regarding regional markets in India for potential exports from Sri Lanka. This situation is clearly reflected in the current composition of the Sri Lankan exports, which are largely consumed by the Indian urban dwellers. In contrast, Indian products have penetrated deeply into both urban and rural markets in Sri Lanka. This paper thus attempts to investigate market potential in India for the Sri Lankan produce while identifying the major obstacles that hinders the possible improvement of bilateral trade between the two nations under this agreement.

Somindra Kishen Hazari, in his paper "Ground Level Problems Encountered in importing Sri Lankan Goods into India Under the FTA", discusses various problems including delays in clearance, costs escalation due to the delays, cost benefit under FTA negated due to the delays/demurrage costs, Indian bureaucracy demanding documents which are not specified under the FTA. Further, he highlights the issues such as misuse of FTA amongst a section of importers in India, ignorance of Sri Lankan facilities some of which are far better / superior than that of India, lack of awareness of the FTA stipulated thirty five per cent value addition, Indians efforts in dumping goods and services while Sri Lanka has only a few goods to offer.

Section-6: India-Sri Lanka Partnership

N. Sathiya Moorthy's paper "The 'why', and the 'how' of India-Sri Lanka Partnership" maintains that given Sri Lanka's continued dependence on other nations for importing goods, India could provide the same at low manufacturing and transportation costs than any other nation. The advent of FDI-culture in India has ensured the manufacture of global brands in regions closer to Sri Lanka, makes these branded goods can be cheaply imported by Sri Lanka. The reverse can also be true as manufacturing of certain products may become less attractive for India in the coming years. Sri Lanka, in such a scenario, would be the best source of imports. Overall, there is now a growing acceptance in India about Sri Lanka's geo-strategic importance, going beyond New Delhi's restricted security concerns.

Santasilan Kadirgamar's paper, "Indo-Sri Lanka Cooperation in Education", traces the close and intimate ties the people of Sri Lanka had have with India in the field of higher education from the middle of the nineteenth century. The paper makes a critical evaluation of educational policies adopted in Sri Lanka in the post-independence years, especially in the universities and the vital lessons that can be learnt from the Indian experience. The development of multiple facets of education will require greater cooperation with India. Any effort in improving communicative skills in English language will require hundreds of the Indian teachers.

Finally G.S. Rao & Shailesh Sikha's paper, "Sustaining Tourism through Cultural Cooperation", argue that tourism has evolved out of the need of the people to travel. Tourism and its effect have provided linkages between the cultures. Considering religions linkages, more opportunities and greater possibilities in understanding about each other through spiritual tourism. Be it the case of the flow of Buddhist Philosophy to Sri Lanka or the relative reference of Lanka in the epic Ramayana, travel has had assumed a significant influence on the cultures of both the countries. The paper also seeks to explore the cases of best practices in tourism and in adapting cultural cooperation in tourism.

SECTION-I
HISTORICAL INTERFACE BETWEEN INDIA AND SRI LANKA

1

India and Sri Lanka: The Buddhist Connection

J.Kedareswari

On the south side of the continent of Asia lies the subcontinent of India. Hanging from the Southern tip of this country like a great pearl drop – is Sri Lanka referred to as the 'Pearl of the Eastern Seas', linked with the mainland by a chain of low coral reef and sand banks known as Adam's Bridge.

This geological connection and geographical proximity was to historically connect the mainland with the island and Buddhism – the great Historical Religion, faith and Philosophy was to serve as an umbilical cord not only bonding the two nations but also moulding and nourishing the island's cultural pattern and civilization.

The island of Sri Lanka has a continuous track record of settled and civilized life for over two millennia, Sri Lanka possesses a continuous historical tradition preserved in written form of Buddhist chronicles. The core of this tradition, Mahavamsa and Culavamsa constitutes a literary record of the establishment and growth of Sinhalese political power and of the Buddhist faith on the island.

According to the earliest Sinhalese tradition, recorded in the Mahavamsa, the first Indian colonists in Ceylon was Vijaya, son of Simha – Bahu king of Lala in India who ruled for thirty eight years from 483-445 B.C. who ruled from Tamhapanninagara (Sinh. Tammannanuvara)

According to tradition the founder of the dynasty landed from the Indian main land and married the daughter of a native chief, with whose aid he mastered the whole island and parceled it out among his followers, some of whom formed petty kingdoms. Vijaya was succeeded by Panduvasudeva (Sinh. Panduvasdev) son of king Sumitta of Lala, brother of Vijaya who ruled for thirty years and succeeded by his second son Abhaya after whose abdication his nephew Pandu Kabhaya came to reign from 377-307 for fifty years and made Anuradhapura the seat of his government and it was probably under him that this ancient city developed which had streets sixteen miles long.

According to *Mahaparinibbana sutta* and also Ceylonese Pali text *Daladanamsa* after the great demise of the Lord Buddha, there was a dispute about the division of the relics among the kings.

Prior to this, a certain *Arhat* named Khema Thera collected the left canine tooth of the Lord Buddha and handed it over to the king Brahmadatta who was ruling the Kalinga kingdom. After the great battle between Kalinga and Magadha for the tooth relic, king Brahmadatta asked his grandson, Dantakumara to hand over the relic to the ruling king of Sri Lanka, Mahasena for safety and enshrinement in a stupa. As per the instructions, Dantakumara reached diamond sands, Paritala village near Amaravati and boarded the ship at Tambalithi (Talagadadivi) in Majerika visaya in the Krishna river basin near Machilipatnam in Krishna District and reached Sri Lanka. The tooth relic worshipped today by the Sinhalese at Anuradhapura was literally transported from the Indian soil during the 5th–4th C.B.C. Thus it appears that the early roots of Buddhism in Sri Lanka can be dated back to Buddha's life.

During the propagation of Buddhism to far flung places the Great Mauryan Emperor Asoka (269-232B.C.) sent a Buddhist mission headed by his son Mahendra to Ceylon. The Sinhalese tradition supports this and about 300 yards to the west from the foot of the Mihimtale hill, famous in the history of Ceylon Buddhism, as the scene of the first meeting between Tissa, the king of Ceylon and Mahida sent by Asoka to preach the religion of Sakyamuni.

The Kataragama copper inscriptions refer to the Kshatriya clan whose seat was Kajaragama who were present when the Bodhi tree was brought to Anuradhapura by Sanghamitra and planted there, beginning of the Vriksha Ghana - one of the eight off-shoots of this Bodhi tree was planted at Kajaragama.

It thus appears that by the 2nd C.B.C., the Sinhalese had accepted Buddhism totally and this faith helped to produce unity and consciousness on which subsequent political and economic strength was founded.

From 1st to 5th Century A.D., Amaravati Art, the Greatest Art, form of the Asian sub-continent contributed greatly to the sustenance of the emerging Sinhala Art.

Prior to this infact, the occurrence of bell-shaped Asokan pillars with animal figures in Sri Lanka suggest the influence of Mauryan Art. However the Mathura and Gandhara art forms seem to have had little or no influence on Sinhala Art.

Archaeologists are of opinion that the carvings on both Abhayagiri and Jetavana shrines have been subject to Andhra influence. It was stated earlier that in the establishment of these two centers there existed very strong relations between Andhra and Sri Lanka. The space between the figures in these carvings and the presence of a certain amount of refinement in them, are considered to be the main Andhra features. The Buddha image was introduced to Sri Lanka in the 2nd Century B.C. during the reign of King Dutugamunu and that it developed gradually to be carved on stone from the time of King Gotabhaye. The plastic vigor of the Buddhist art in the region was indeed the Buddhist art of the Satavahana-Ikshvaku phase as passed through Ceylon.

The changes in the life of the social economy of the Andhra region due to Indo-Roman trade must have reached upto Sri Lanka. As a matter of fact this was the natural route for overseas trade. Owing to commercial and religious affiliations, the influence of the art of the Andhra Empire was enormously wide spread not only the style of Amaravati extended to Ceylon, but Buddhist image in the Andhra style of the 2nd –3rd Centuries A.D. have been found as far away as Dang Huang in Champa (Modern Indo-China). In fact after the decline of Buddhism in India in the Medieval period after rapid destruction by the Muslims, the newly Buddhist art form took recourse to Ceylonese Buddhist art form for rejuvenation, which was in fact preserved for till date, the tradition that they had received from the famous Buddhist sites of the Andhra region.

Amaravati Art as we know, was divided into four phases. And the two Amaravati Marbles depicting Queen Maya's Dream displayed at the Colombo Museum and the second depicting Prince Siddhartha's Great Renunciation – *Mahabinishkramana* – at

Girihandu, Ambalantota testify to the flow of Buddhist Art history from the coast of Andhra Desa to Ceylon and from there to the South Asian countries, as Ceylon was a great entry port and enjoyed both eastern and western trade.

The relationship between India and Sri Lanka thus became closer through religious pursuits. Inscriptions have provided the names of a number of Buddhist sects inhabiting the Andhra region. Of these the Mahasanghikas and their offshoots dominated the scene but there was one sect named Mahavihara- Vasin which was from Sri Lanka.

The cultural religious contacts between the two countries was mutually interactive. Bodhisri, a Lay worshipper from Govagama from an inscription at Nagarjunkonda who donated an apsidal stupa shrine and a monastery for Ceylonese monks in the main complex at Chula Dhammagiri at Nagarjunkonda. Some what taken in time the Mahavihara vasin monastery meant for Theravadin sect from Ceylon adopted the practice of raising Chaityagrihas for regular worshipping, image shrine was added to this.

A Brahmi inscription of the time of Sri Mathariputra VIrapurushadatta, the second Ikshvaku king, dated in 14th regnal year corresponding to A.D. 286, records the building of a *Chaitya griha* within the Chuladharmagiri *Vihara* on the Sriparvata hill (Site-43) east of the Ikshvaku city called Vijayapuri.[2] This was meant for the teachers of Ceylon who were engaged in the pursuit of spreading the *dharma* to various countries. The *Theravddins* from Tamraparnidvipa greatly influenced the *Samghas* at Sriparvata and converted to the faith those who belonged to *Kasmira-Gandhara-China-Chilata, Tosali, Avaramta, Vamga, Vanavasa, Yavana, Damila, Palura* and *Tambapamnidvipa.*

The text read:

Part of Line 1: (Bhada) ta raja cha riydnam kasmira Gandhara— China-

Chilata- Tosali- Avaramta — Vamga — Vanavasi — Yavana — Damila —Palura — Tambap – amnidipa - pasadakanam theriydnam Tambapamnikanam suparigahe.

Part of Line 2: Siripavate Vijayapuriya-puva-disa-bhage vihare chula-dhamma-girlyam chetiya-gharam sapata-

samtharam Sachetlyam-Sava niyutam karitam Uvasikaya Bodhisirlya. These countries are also found mentioned in the *Mahavamsa* among the territories, which had been converted to Buddhism after the third Council. The mention of China, besides Ceylon and other places, in this record is of seminal importance for us and clearly points to the pilgrimage of certain acharyas to such far-flung countries in their pursuit of proselytizing.

Another important thing that attracted the Ceylonese monks to the Chuladharmagiri *vihara* on Sriparvat, in particular, was the *Bodhivriksha Prasada*, i.e. the Bodhi-tree pavilion, which was necessary adjunct. It is well known that Asoka through Mahendra got a branch of Bodhi tree (from Bodhgaya) planted in Ceylon. After this great event, the entire island of Ceylon became a stronghold of Buddhism. Could it be that another branch of *Bodhivriksha* was planted at Sriparvata as early as in Ceylon? Whatever it may be, the Simhala *vihara* at Sriparvata was justly famous internationally for its *Bodhivriksha prasada* during the 3rd Century A.D. as clearly noted from the sculptured and inscribed *Buddhapada* consecrated at another monastery as well. In this record even the names of the Ceylonese *acharyas* are stated.

The Lihinimalai (Kandy district) inscriptions state that the great King Kanitha Tissa(A.D.226-244) or Ceylon made certain perpetual gifts to the Bodhi house and refectory attached to the Sriparvata monastery. He also caused to be built an *uposatha* house and a big refectory for benefit of the community of the bhikkus frequenting the Sipavata- vihara. This clearly corroborates the evidence available at the Chuladhammagiri (Nallarallabodu, site-43) and the monastic site-38, which was established by Mahaviharavasins, a Ceylonese Theravadin sect, from where the above-inscribed Buddhapada was reported. The Ceylonese were orthodox Theravadins but soon yielded to the worship of Buddha image and constructed votive stupas as well at Nagarjunakonda.

It is said that during the region of Mahanama (468-490 A.D), Buddhaghosha visited Ceylon and commenced his commentaries on the Buddhist canon. Though it was believed that Buddhaghosha was born in Maghada yet there is a consensus among scholars that he hailed from Andhra particularly Dhanyakataka region. In the colophons of his work he mentions a few eminent people like Joti Pala of Kanchipura, Buddhamitta of Mayurasuttapattana. He terminates the colophon of Visuddhimagga with a reference that he should be called a person of "Moranda Khetaka" the literal meaning of which is village of peahen's eggs.

Some scholars have identified Moranda Khetaka with Kota Nemalipuri and Gandlur in Palnad of Guntur district (which means in Telugu Fort of Peahen's eggs). It is at a distance of fifty miles from Nagarjuna Konda and fifty eight miles from Amaravathi. It may be remembered that Krishna valley is studded with several Buddhist sites. According to R.Subramanyam and S.P.Nainar, Buddha Ghosa's birth place is Nemalipuri and Gandlur, the twin villages, where old vestiges of Buddhist establishments are still seen. Sukumar Dutt strongly advocates this view and after thoroughly examining all the available sources he comes to the conclusion that Buddhaghosa is from Andhra, probably from farmers community. The internal evidence found in his works confirms that Buddha Ghosa hails from Andhra. If the above hypothesis is correct then it is a matter of great pride that this towering personality revered as the greatest sage in all the countries following Theravada Buddhism, was born in Andhra desa.

A scholar of vast and varied learning, a writer of rigorous diligence and precision, Buddah Ghosa produced Visuddhimagga, an encyclopedic work summarizing the essence of Tipitakas. Wading through Attakathas in Simhala language accumulated over ages, he made it his life's mission to translate them into Pali interpreting and clarifying the voluminous commentarical literature. A wall painting, i.e. a mural at Kalania temple in Colombo depicts a scene Bhadantacariya Buddha Ghosa, presenting his magnum opus, Vissuddhi Magga (Path of Purification) to Sanghapala of Maha ihara Anuradhapura, Sri Lanka during the reign of Mahanama (5th C. AD.).

Gummadidurru (Ramireddypalli)

It is 10 kms away from Madhira railway station on Vijayawada -Hyderabad line in Krishna district. It is 9 kms to the east of the famous *stupa* at Jaggayyapeta. Excavations have brought to light a *Mahastupa,* votive *stupas* an apsidal *chaityagriha,* relic caskets, Buddha images in stone, seals inscribed with Buddhist creed and other inscribed slabs belonging to the period from 2nd century A.D. to medieval times.

Text:

1. *Svasti Acarya Mougalya yanasya priya-sisyasya Acarya.*
2. *(Dha)ramma-devasya sisyena sramaneka Rahulena Bhagavath*
3. *Pratima Pratista pita Sarvva Satva manuttarayi.*
4. *Avapataye yadattra punyam Sarvvam Caitya - Sahghasya.*

Mean: It records the consecration of the image of the Lord by a Sramana, named Rahula, a disciple of Acarya Dharmmadeva, a favourite disciple of Acarya (Maugglayana).

Note: It is in Sanskrit language dated to 8th-9thA.D. The inscription is engraved on the pedestal of Buddha image, which has an effigy of the donor.

Sriparvata-Vijayapuri (Nagarjunakonda in Sri Lankan Epigraphs)

It is very interesting to note that the earliest reference to the hill Sriparvata (Sipavata) is found from the epigraphs discovered at Lithinimalai, Kandy district, Sri Lanka, dated to the regnal period of King Kanittha Tissa (226-244 A.D.).

There is a reference to *Sihalavihara* i.e. monastery of Simhala in an inscription of Sri Mathariputra Virapurisadatta of the Ikshvaku king dated to the 14th regnal year. It also mentions a *Chaityagriha* over the Chuladhammagiri located on Sriparvata, for the stay of Buddhist monks and teachers coming from Sri Lanka.

Besides the above information, the material evidences unearthed from the *Jetavanavihara* of Anuradha Pura in Sri Lanka suggests the existence of cultural contacts with the Andhra region right from the early centuries of the Christian era.

Text:

1. *Sidam mala-tisa-maharaji Naka-Malayaha*
2. *huvahaka bujana kalahi ratiya h o na-*
3. *(ya de) vaya karavi kadara-maraya arada vaviganavaya*
4. *(na)va-(ga)ma kotu daka-patiya kara kadaya si-pa-*
5. *vata-veherahi bota-gehi dini mahapakavata-*
6. *hi ca dini niyadaya*

Mean: Success! In the reign of the king Kanittha Tissa, a tank (named) Kadara-maraya was constructed by Devaya the *ratthika,* when Naka Mulaya was ruling the *huvaka* (province), and formed a new village, gave the water-revenue (thereof), having, remitted the taxes (to which it is liable) to the Bodhi-house of the *Sipavata* monastery. It was a fixed asset to the great refectory *(Mahapakavat).*

Text:

1. *Si Mala-Tisa-maharaji me P(o)hota-gara Karaya*
2. *(Giri) Gama-vavi ca Mala-ketaka ca Curaviya ca me Tini Ta-*
3. *nahi do-patiya kara dadaya dini Sipavataviharahi*
4. *bikusagahata mahapaka- vatahi dini*

Mean: Success! The king Kanittha Tissa caused this *Uposatha-* house to be constructed, and granted the two categories of revenue, having remitted the taxes (there on) these three lands, namely, the tank of *(Giri)gama,* the tract of fields named *Malaketake* and *coraviya* (tank) to the great refectory *(Bhojanasala),* for the benefit of the community of *bhikkus* in the monastery of Sriparvata.

Note: The inscriptions from Lithinimalai, mention *Sipavvat,* the name of a hill. Obviously, is a contractive form for *Siri* and *Pavata* is Sri Parvata(hill). Thus Sriparvata can be identified with the present Nagarjunakonda (Sriparvata-Vijayapuri).

Gadaladeniya rock inscription in Kandy district from Sri Lanka refers to the great Sthavira Dharmma Kirtti who laid the foundation of a shrine of Buddha at Gadaladeniya, constructed, or rather repaired, a two storied image house at Sri Dhanyakataka (i.e. Amaravati) in India. This statement is also confirmed by the Saddarmaratnakara, which gives a more detailed account of Dharmma Kirtti's works of religious devotion at Amaravati. This inscription also records that, the work of Dharmma Kirtti at Amaravati is not the only instance of the Ceylon Buddhists of 14th Century striving to revive the dying flame of South Indian Buddhism. The great minister Sena Lamkadhikara, who was contemporary of Dharmma Kirtti, is said to have dispatched men and money to Kanchi and established a Buddhist shrine in that city.

Buddhism seemed as an umbilical cord, but when Ceylon was fully nourished and emerged as a Theravada Centre, the religion declined in the mother country where it was born and now it provides sustenance to the mother country. In fact the recently founded only Buddhist Monastery at Hyderabad Ananda Buddha Vihara in Mahendra Hills sends its monks for higher training in the Buddhist Cannons to Sri Lanka.

Recently the department of Archaeology & Museums has had the privilege of having the first cultural exchange with the Sri Lankan government in the form of exchange of publications, and the books donated by the department of Archaeology, government of the Democratic Socialist Republic of Sri Lanka to the government of Andhra Pradesh.

SECTION-II
INDO-SRI LANKA: POLITICAL RELATIONS

2

Glimpses of Indo-Sri Lankan Relations

Nirupama Rao

This is an apt venue to reflect on this relationship. The people of Southern India have had ancient cultural and religious links with the people of Sri Lanka. Today, Sri Lanka and the states of Southern India are poised on the threshold of a new, mutually beneficial partnership based on commerce, investment and people-to-people links.

India is Sri Lanka's closest neighbour. Its links go back to the origins of time. We have a close political relationship to which they have added a rapidly growing economic relationship in the past decade. India's development partnership with Sri Lanka, anchored primarily in project assistance through credit lines and the 'Aid to Sri Lanka' programme as well as training and skill development programmes, is also entering a new phase of maturity and consolidation. When the tsunami struck both the countries on 26 December 2004, India launched its biggest emergency relief effort to stand by Sri Lanka in that hour of mutual distress and suffering. Given the natural sense of affinity and empathy between our peoples it was only natural that we came together in the face of this unprecedented disaster. We were determined that the community of grief we shared should not become a community of despair. The recent successful visit of president Mahinda Rajapaksa to India bears ample testimony to the intensive and wide-ranging bilateral relations that our two countries enjoy. Indeed, it would be no exaggeration to say that Indo-Sri lankan relations now serve as a role model for the entire region.

The India-Sri Lanka bilateral free trade area (FTA) that came into being in April 2000 has been a huge success story with two-way trade crossing $1.9 billion. Interestingly, trade has expanded in a more balanced manner and the trade deficit has narrowed down to less than half of what it was earlier. This has happened because the India-Sri Lanka FTA encouraged Indian companies to invest in Sri Lanka especially in export-oriented industries for export to India and to third country. With these investments expanding supply capabilities, Sri Lanka is now able to export a number of goods that were not previously exported. India has notably emerged as one of the most important sources of foreign direct investment in the island. The FTA with India has also contributed to improving the overall climate for foreign direct investment in the country as a production base for export to India. A number of Sri Lankan companies too have become active players in India market – Brandix, a prominent garment manufacturer, is investing in Visakhapatnam - and the Sri Lankan tourism and civil aviation sectors have benefited immensely from Indian visitors. Therefore, the interdependence of the two economies is increasing. To mention some more instances – Ceylinco Consolidated developing real estate with Sri Ram Group in Bangalore, Ceylon Biscuits – Bakeman Patiala opening of bank branches in Chennai and BOI opened first office abroad in Bangalore.

Both countries are determined to realize the enormous potential that exists for further economic and commercial cooperation. Emboldened by the achievements of the FTA both the countries have agreed to expand the scope of economic cooperation by including investment and services in the framework of a Comprehensive Economic Partnership Agreement (CEPA). A Joint Study Group (JSG), set up by the two governments to study different aspects of CEPA, submitted its report in October 2003. Negotiations are currently in progress for concluding the CEPA, hopefully by the end of this year. Encouraged by the success of the bilateral FTA and its beneficial impact even at the micro, enterprise level, Pakistan too has signed a FTA with Sri Lanka. As more countries across the region realize the win-win potential of such agreements their confidence in the South Asia Free Trade

Area (SAFTA) process would strengthen. Thus the importance of India-Sri Lanka trade lies not only in the numbers but also in the message it sends to policy makers and the business community across the region on the potential of win-win partnerships.

Civil aviation and tourism have been another success story. There are now more than hundred flights per week between India and Sri Lanka. As new airports come up in Hyderabad and Bangalore in the near future, and as the plans of the Sri Lankan government in the civil aviation sector are realized, this traffic will grow. It is striking that Colombo is closer to Chennai and Bangalore than these cities are to New Delhi. Indian tourists are now among the topmost arrivals in Sri Lanka and are in any event the highest spenders. Tourist inflows from India have in fact cushioned some of the post-tsunami shocks in this critical sector. Sri Lankans are rediscovering India and its Buddhist sites, including in Andhra Pradesh thanks to the admirable efforts of AP Tourism. Southern Indian states can work with Sri Lanka to promote combined circuits and luxury cruises. Special facilities and packages can be drawn up on each side. For example, a Ramayana Trail could be developed and marketed for Indian tourists visiting Sri Lanka. Connectivity in the field of surface transport is an underdeveloped link. The challenge is not just physical infrastructure. We also need to transcend traditional ways of looking at this issue. However, the accelerating momentum of people to people contacts is already changing perceptions.

Our bilateral development cooperation has entered an important stage with the agreement on small development projects, which would act as a platform for exchange of development expertise at the grass roots level. We are working specifically on supplementing agricultural incomes through dairy development, technical and vocational training to create employment opportunities, rural roads, IT in rural areas and also health infrastructure in poorer areas such as the upcountry. India is also deeply interested in projects that benefit the people of the north and east. During the visit of president Mahinda Rajapaksa to India we have agreed to help Sri Lanka draw up a master plan for the development of Trincomalee and its surrounding region. There are opportunities here for Indian companies and institutions. Separately and importantly, there are opportunities to learn together and to share. Southern states such as Andhra Pradesh can contribute immensely to Sri Lanka's development by sharing their experience in areas such as e-governance.

Given the geographical proximity of India and Sri Lanka their security is inseparable. Developments with regard to the ethnic issue in Sri Lanka have often been of interest to people of South India given not only because of the ties of kinship and culture with Sri Lanka but also because insecurity and instability in Sri Lanka has a direct impact on Southern Indian states. India supports the unity, territorial integrity and sovereignty of Sri Lanka. We are for a peaceful and negotiated settlement of the ethnic issue. Today while not being directly involved in the peace process, India consults closely with the government of Sri Lanka, the facilitators (Norway) and different strands of democratic opinion in Sri Lanka. We appreciate Sri Lanka's efforts to build a national consensus on a negotiated solution within a united Sri Lanka and on the basis of maximum devolution. We stand ready to share with Sri Lanka our own experience of unity in diversity, plural democracy and devolution. We are also with Sri Lanka in rejecting war and conflict and in opposing terrorism, which constitutes the biggest threat to democratic societies today. Violence in any form undermines prospects for peace and reconciliation. This is why recent developments in Sri Lanka have been of concern. We are happy that the parties have agreed to resume dialogue. We hope that this creates the necessary conditions for negotiations on more substantive issues.

The destinies of India and Sri Lanka are intertwined. Closer connectivity and consonance in economic interaction between Sri Lanka and the dynamic sub region of South India will increasingly be a fact of life in this century. More than ever our cooperation is a factor for regional stability and prosperity. Our partnership in the new century will be anchored in close political dialogue, stronger economic and commercial cooperation and greater people-to-people contacts. Southern Indian states will play a major role in this exciting story.

3

India's Policy of Non-Intervention in Sri Lanka

P. Sahadevan

India has often faced a policy dilemma in responding to the Sri Lankan ethnic conflict. Indeed, its dilemma has become acute since the mid-1990s when successive governments in Colombo led by two mainstream Sinhalese parties—United National Party (UNP) and Sri Lanka Freedom Party (SLFP)—have constantly sought India's direct politico-military intervention. Having redefined India's interest and role in the conflict in the wake of a massive failure of Indian diplomacy and military in the 1980s, successive governments in New Delhi have resisted the temptation and pressure for intervention. However, the demand from Sri Lanka's political class and the Indian opinion-makers has not ceased. The question that lingers in India's mind is: whether to directly involve again in the conflict or continue to remain a non-participant while being interested in conflict resolution? The desire and bipartisan invitation of the UNP and SLFP leaders for New Delhi's proactive role in the conflict indicates that India is still seen as an important factor in restoration and maintenance of peace on the island. This paper examines India's current policy posture against the backdrop of its role in the 1980s.

India: A Much Maligned Participant (1983-1990)

India's policy since 1990 has drawn much from its experience in the 1980s when it actively participated in the conflict in various capacities—militant supporter, mediator and peacekeeper—which entailed both political and military strategies.[1] In the process, it emerged as a dominant external actor, which sought to promote its self-and-regional interests while trying to resolve the conflict that had drawn into its vortex many extra-regional forces. In the end, for India, its participation became unexpectedly a costly affair as it lost more than one thousand soldiers in the Indian Peacekeeping Force (IPKF) war against the Liberation Tigers of Tamil Eelam (LTTE) which rejected the July 1987 India-Sri Lanka peace accord. In addition, the operational cost of war ran into millions of rupees.[2] Worse, ultimately, the Indian role became much maligned. It was not only the Sinhalese but also the Sri Lankan Tamils who vehemently disparaged and disapproved the Indian intervention to the utter dismay of the Indian establishment and public opinion.

As India's reluctance now to undertake a direct role in the Sri Lankan conflict is partly influenced by its bitter experience in the past, it is necessary to point out certain peculiarities of its earlier participation in the conflict in terms of its objectives, behaviour and strategies. Although India was an affected country because of violence against the Sri Lankan Tamils (which caused widespread repercussions in its internal politics and for its national security and, therefore, became an interested third party in the ethnic conflict), the impression in Sri Lanka and abroad was that it carved out a participant role for itself in order to promote its agenda for regional hegemony. When India first decided to intervene in the conflict way back in 1983, it was a unilateral step. The larger Sinhalese community and the Sri Lankan government remained steadfastly opposed to India's direct role but the Sri Lankan Tamils wholeheartedly welcomed it. Both communities held different perceptions and opinions about India and developed competing high expectations from its role. Whereas the Sinhalese perceived India as pro-Sri Lankan Tamils and, therefore, anti-Sinhalese, the Sri Lankan Tamils considered India as a crucial source of support to fight the hegemonic Sinhalese majoritarianism and change the entire structure and nature of the Sri Lankan state. Worse, the Sinhalese leadership and the Sri Lankan government feared that India was out to disintegrate the country and, therefore, it needed an external diplomatic and military support to defeat the nefarious designs of the Indian government. The regional security environment was vitiated by the Sri Lankan government's strategic gestures to the West and its efforts to cultivate the anti-Indian forces with the aim of undermining India's national security and regional interests.[3] India's strong response by rejecting Sri Lanka's security policy and, at the same time, supporting the Sri Lankan Tamil cause had tremendously aggravated the insecurity of the Sri Lankan state. Thus the Indian role in the conflict was seen as a partisan affair to promote its self-interest as well as the ethnic interest of the Sri Lankan Tamils.

But the July 1987 accord which prime minister Rajiv Gandhi and president J.R. Jayewardene had signed did not get the approval of the Sri Lankan Tamil community in general and the LTTE in particular. Soon India was perceived to be antagonistic. It was unwise on India's part to arrogate to itself the authority to sign the peace accord on behalf of the Sri Lankan Tamils on the assumption that they would be forced to accept the Indian policy. In the process India failed to understand the complex Sri Lankan Tamil society and divergent goals of militant organisations which challenged the Sinhalese hegemony. The IPKF war to secure support and legitimacy for the peace accord had eventually led to India's alienation. For many in Sri Lanka, India became an unwanted interventionist and the IPKF was characterised as an army of occupation.[4]

India's multiple activities in the conflict testify to its varied interests and goals. If its covert military support to the militants and overt military intervention were guided by its strong desire to protect the interests of both the Sri Lankan Tamils and Sri Lankan government, it had a definite defensive motivation of promoting its own interests. Similarly, its peacemaking role had protective-defensive goals. Thus the concentration of too many goals as a guiding force created a structure of pressure on India to act in desperation so that the interests of all three parties (governments of India and Sri Lanka, and Sri Lankan Tamils) to the conflict were promoted. The inference that can be drawn from India's strategies is that external actors in violent ethnic conflict face enormous difficulties in producing multiple results to the satisfaction of all the participants. Dissatisfaction of even one can be enough to derail the entire peace process.

India's deep interest in wining security concessions from Sri Lanka was a major cause for its unpopularity. The letters exchanged between Rajiv Gandhi and Jayewardene in July 1987 spelt out the extent to which both countries could address each other's security concerns.[5] Sri Lanka agreed to consult India on employment of foreign military personnel, review its agreements with the Voice of America, involve India in restoration of oil tank farm and keep the foreign powers off Trincomalee port. On its part, India promised not to make its soil available for terrorist activities, supply arms and give military training to the Sri Lankan security forces. But the general impression was that India, a regional power, coerced the strife-torn small country to make extensive unilateral security concessions and offered its military help to the Sri Lankan army with a view to restricting the island's external defence links. The security arrangement was seen as a demonstration of India's desire for regional hegemony, subjecting Sri Lanka to be a dependent of India for its security and survival. Some Sinhalese hardliners argued that by conceding to India's security demands Sri Lanka had compromised on its independence and sovereignty.[6] The disapproval of the peace accord and security concessions was made widespread through a systematic smear campaign by some political parties and Sinhalese chauvinistic groups.

The lessons that India has learnt from its intervention are very harsh and hard to forget. India has realized its limitations and constraints in effecting changes in the course of events and influencing the behaviour of actors in its turbulent neighbourhood. Many feel that the Indian policy was ill conceived, unrealistic and adventurous. It was driven by an over-confident leadership which put the entire nation to bear a heavy cost without any tangible achievement.

The Changing Contexts

India's non-interventionist policy should be seen not only in the context of the failure of its earlier policy but also the changing security perceptions of the Indian leadership in the post-cold war period. Unlike in the 1980s when the Sri Lankan leaders tried to use the island's strategic location to manoeuvre against India, the post-cold war period has signified the loss of the country's strategic importance in regional politics. This has effectively removed India's apprehensions and security concerns over, for instance, the status of Tricomalee harbour, resulting in convergence of security interests between the two countries. Now violence and disorder in the island remain India's major security concern and not Sri Lanka's foreign and security policy. It must be emphasised that the new generation of Sri Lankan leaders, unlike their hawkish predecessors, has been pragmatic about their India policy. For the first time, they find India an asset rather than a threat to Sri Lanka's security. In changing their mindset India's non-interventionist policy has initially played a major role. For the past one-decade, India-Sri Lanka relations have recorded improvements in economic and security areas. The free trade agreement (1998) and the leasing of oil tanks to the Indian Oil Corporation are the notable indicators of growing economic interactions.[7]

India has a positive image in Sri Lanka's south. Having changed their perception of India being a big bully and threat to their country's sovereignty, many Sinhalese seek its direct involvement in the conflict, preferably in the form of a large-scale military assistance. Their expectation is that such a role would eventually help defeat or at least contain the LTTE. It is for this reason that the Sri Lankan Tamils, barring those who fiercely oppose the LTTE, are disturbed by India's growing friendship with Sri Lanka. They want India, as in the past, to be solely by their side to achieve their equal rights. Knowing well the adverse implications of India-Sri Lanka friendship for its liberation movement, the LTTE is keen to neutralise 'the India factor' in the conflict by seeking friendship with the Indian government. Thus there is an element of competition between the majority and minority communities in wining India's open support against each other. However, since the early 1990s the Indian government has maintained loose neutrality while keeping its interest in the conflict.

Principles of New Policy

India's new Sri Lanka policy vis-à-vis the ethnic conflict combines its old stands with the new realities. At the core of it is a reiteration of the Indian government's commitment to protect Sri Lanka's 'unity, sovereignty and territorial integrity'.[8] There is no compromise on the existing fundamentals of the Sri Lankan state whose break-up, as sought by the LTTE, is unacceptable to India. At the same time, maintaining the political status quo at the structural and institutional level, as desired by the Sinhalese majoritarian ideology, is not viable. Permanent peace in Sri Lanka requires institutional restructuring aimed at creating ethnic equality; a power-sharing arrangement to satisfy the 'aspirations of all the Sri Lankan communities', especially those of the Sri Lankan Tamils and the Sri Lankan Muslims, is considered as the most desirable democratic option.[9] This pro-minority position underlining the need for devolution of powers is to counter the majority community's entrenched position on ethnic democratic centralism. For conflict resolution India suggests a broader multiethnic approach that will establish a vibrant multicultural polity. While strongly opposing the national hegemony (of the Sinhalese), India does not want to support any attempt at creating a regional hegemony (of the Sri Lankan Tamils).[10]

India's insistence on a political process to achieve peace has clearly rejected war. At the height of the hostilities between the Sri Lankan army and the LTTE in the 1980s and the 1990s, the Indian position always favoured political negotiations. The IPKF war (1987-90), though highly undesirable, was considered as a means to achieve peace—it was a war for peace. Now, India does not want to endorse the same strategy in view of its resultant cost in terms of death and destruction. Since war does not increase the prospects of peace, it is considered as a futile strategy. The alternative to war is peace process on which India has now radically changed its views and position. It strongly prefers a home-grown solution to the conflict, reached through a serious negotiation process involving all the ethnic stakeholders.[11] Yet, unlike in the past, it is not interested in sitting in the driver's seat as a mediator or facilitator of the peace process. At the same time, it is not opposed to greater international involvement in peacemaking. India's approval of the Norwegian facilitation supported by the United States, Japan and the European Union indicates some revision of its traditional policy of preventing external involvement in South Asia. In willingly allowing such an international role, India is clear that no one is allowed to make a political capital at the cost of its regional and international interests. India's opposition to Japan's desire to play a proactive facilitation role along with Norway with the aim of improving its international political image should be seen in this context.

Recognising India's importance for permanent peace, the Sri Lankan government and the Norwegian facilitators have taken New Delhi into confidence while engaging the LTTE in negotiations.

They periodically briefed the Indian leaders about the outcome of several rounds of talks and sought their advice on the conduct of the peace process. India is pleased with such frequent informal consultations in New Delhi. This is advantageous to both India and Sri Lanka. India is assured that nothing is done behind its back to undermine its interests and due recognition is given to its regional power status. For the Sri Lankan government, its constant touch with India is to indicate the latter's continued interest in the conflict and to convey a tough message to the LTTE that if necessary, India will not hesitate to intervene in the future. In other words, by keeping the 'India factor' alive in the ethnic conflict, the Sri Lankan leaders want to moderate, as far as possible, the LTTE's ruthless behaviour and tough negotiating position. For the international actors involved in peace-making and peace-building in Sri Lanka, India's strong support to the peace process amounts to giving legitimacy to their activities.

On the LTTE, India's policy has been unambiguous. The government has banned the organisation and refused to have any contacts with it. The Indian leaders have ignored the friendly overtures of the LTTE and turned down its request in 2002 for transit and medical facilities for its theoretician Anton Balasingham in Tamil Nadu on humanitarian grounds. In the same year the government refused to share platform with the LTTE at the donor conferences organised by Norway, the US and Japan. Even though India does not press hard for the extradition of LTTE leader V. Prabhakaran to stand trail in the Rajiv Gandhi assassination case, he is legally a wanted man in India. This is a mater of serious concern for the LTTE, which not only wants to change its terrorist image but also win back India's recognition, if not its support. Sri Lanka finds in India's opposition to the LTTE a strong external factor to modify the behaviour of the outlawed outfit.

India's insistence on democracy and pluralism as cardinal principles of conflict resolution is in a way to challenge the position of the LTTE which believes in one-party dictatorship at best and wants to create an exclusionary political framework in which the non-LTTE political formations or militant groups are not included. Known for its vibrant democratic tradition, the Sri Lankan Tamil society located in the island's northeast has acquired an authoritarian political culture. Democratic political structures are completely destroyed and dissent is considered by the LTTE as a crime. The punishment for dissenters ranges from endless detention to unpublicised cruel execution. While arguing for a participatory democracy in which all the groups with political differences participate, India wants the LTTE to stop forthwith all political killings. This brings out the issue of human rights. It is not only the Sri Lankan security forces that have involved in serious violations of human rights of the minorities but also the LTTE, which has, apart from the Sri Lankan Tamils, targeted at the Sinhalese and the Muslims. By making protection of human rights as an important component of its policy, India is keen to change the LTTE's ruthless behaviour.

India has never openly opposed the LTTE's demand for an interim civil administration in the northeast province. Nor did it openly disapprove or criticise the LTTE's recent proposal for a full-fledged interim self-governing authority (ISGA) even though some of its provisions clearly appeared outrageous in the sense that they, if accepted, would not only undermine the legal authority of the Sri Lankan government but also create security challenges to India. To avoid an impression that it was trying to influence the island's internal opinion on the ISGA issue and, at the same time, to convey its concerns over the LTTE's demand, India has taken a stand that any "interim arrangement should be an integral part of the final settlement".[12] India expects that both adversaries—the Sri Lankan government and the LTTE—adopt a reasonable stand on the issue of interim administration for northeast.

Options for India

Should India directly play a proactive role in the Sri Lankan conflict? While the Indian foreign policy establishment is sure about what it wants to do in Sri Lanka, there are two views among the opinion makers. Some prefer India to erase its bitter memories of the past and intervene in the conflict. Their argument is mainly based on considerations of India's 'geographical proximity' and 'regional power status'. Given the fact that geographically India is very close to Sri Lanka and the peoples of both countries share trans-border ethnic affinities, it cannot remain indifferent to or insulate itself from the developments in the island. It is also argued that being a regional power, India is duty bound to protect national interests of its neighbours while promoting and preserving its own national and regional interests. Many think that the crowded international role for peacemaking and peace-building in Sri Lanka since 2001 will tend to undermine India's regional power status. The lacuna in these arguments of the pro-interventionists has been that they are not clear about the nature of Indian role—military or political or both.

The other opinion is that India should continue the new policy of non-intervention, and it is truly pointless in undertaking an interventionist role when there is a heavy cost that it has to bear in the process. For the anti-interventionists, India's experience in the 1980s is pertinent to judge what it can do in Sri Lanka given the present power configuration of the adversaries in the conflict. They do not support the geographical proximity argument but insist on realism to be the guiding principle of India's Sri Lanka policy. Given these two divergent but less articulated positions, what should be the option for India?

Any Indian role in the conflict can be either political or military. It cannot be both at the same time. A political role will largely entail peacemaking between the adversaries. This means that India will have to repeat the role it had undertaken in the mid-1980s when it enjoyed tremendous leverage over both the Sri Lankan government and LTTE. Even then its efforts became a total failure. What went wrong is a matter of well-recorded history. The point is that given the complex nature of the conflict, India cannot be sure of making its failure in the 1980s into a belated success for the following reasons. First, despite their declaration of interest in a negotiated political solution, both the Sri Lankan government and LTTE take tough negotiating positions and appear unwilling to compromise.[13] All their expressions of desire for peace are beset with doubts and uncertainties. It is more so with regard to the LTTE, which has not totally given up its *eelam* goal. Second, the difficulty in evolving a Sinhalese consensus is a mater of discouragement for any Indian political role in the future. In the past, exertion of pressure by India on the Sri Lankan government to accept its peace proposals became counter-productive. It is worth remembering that the Sinhalese hardliners then called India a regional bully, trying to divide the small country. There is a clear danger of this allegation being repeated if India, by undertaking a peacemaking role, tries to impose a federal solution. If at all the Indian government enjoys some leverage over the Sri Lankan government, it cannot assume to have the same on the larger Sinhalese society. Given the historical antecedents and high expectations of the people, India can be easily made a villain under the influence of chauvinistic groups and hard-line political parties which draw a political capital out of the issues of war and peace. In the absence of a bipartisan approach in the Sinhalese polity, which India will find it difficult to evolve, no political solution can be successfully implemented. The same can be said about the LTTE, which may not accept, as in the past, an India-mediated peace accord if it fails to satisfy the group's maximalist position. It may brand a reasonable peace package reached under Indian pressure as an unfair or ignominious deal. India should not think that it has leverage over the LTTE any longer. It must be noted that the group has survived as a formidable militant force even in adverse situations marked by tight international control and alienation.

This takes us to the second question viz. should India undertake a military role in the island? The Sri Lankan government will be pleased if India willingly extends its military support against the LTTE. In fact a large section of the Sinhalese society is appreciative of India's unpublicised military assistance to their government, which includes a limited sale of military hardware, intelligence-sharing and naval cooperation against the LTTE in the Palk Strait. But the Sinhalese hard-liners expect a larger Indian support and cooperation. In the past, such a desire was expressed when the Sri Lankan army suffered military reverses at the hands of the LTTE. Surely, any Indian military role or institutionalised bilateral defence cooperation with Sri Lanka will evoke scathing criticisms and opposition from the LTTE.[14] Certainly, India will be able to ignore the LTTE, but not the displeasure of Tamil Nadu and the Sri Lankan Tamil society. Presumably, on this issue, the ordinary Sri Lankan Tamils like to agree with the LTTE views. If the LTTE is worried about its military survival in the event of India extending a direct military support to the Sri Lankan army, the major concern of the Sri Lankan Tamils in the northeast province is that a militarily strong Sri Lankan government will not accept even a reasonable federal solution under the pressure of the emboldened Sinhalese chauvinists who are, at present, somewhat compelled to accept political negotiations merely because of the rising cost of the war. For a number of Sri Lankan Tamils who otherwise dislike the LTTE's belligerent behaviour, ruthlessness and lack of commitment to a political solution, India still remains the most important source of external support to win their legitimate equal political rights. They do not want India to deviate from its stated policy and commitment to work towards fulfilling their legitimate aspirations within a united and multicultural Sri Lanka. For India, ignoring the sentiments of the Sri Lankan Tamils will be an outright contravention of its well-stated policy of promoting and preserving their ethnic interests.

Apart from the fact that an Indian military role will tend to be partial (in support of the government), there is also a question about the nature of military intervention. Will India prefer to directly involve physically? Or, will it merely extend military assistance? Any direct military involvement will entail a repetition of its earlier war (1987-90), which India should be sensible enough to avoid because of its impending high cost and probable futility in achieving its objectives. Another huge investment by India in terms of men and materials or sacrifice for the cause of Sri Lanka's sovereignty will be difficult to justify in India. At the same time, extension of a limited Indian military support to the Sri Lankan government will be inconsequential as far as changing the LTTE's behaviour is concerned. Whatever may be its nature and scale, India's direct military role will tend to make it eventually unpopular among the Sinhalese and the Sri Lankan Tamils alike. India will not be able to fully satisfy the Sinhalese in the end. At the same time, the Sri Lankan Tamils will reject its role from the beginning.

Realising the constraints and costs of its direct intervention, an ideal Indian policy should combine 'non-intervention' with 'active interest' in the conflict. Its decision not to intervene directly should not mean that it is disinterested in the conflict process and its outcome. The assumption is that India should be able to control the conflict process and influence the adversaries without physically getting involved if it remains responsive to the developments and actively associates itself with those who regularly interact with the Sri Lankan government and the LTTE.[15] While counselling and, if necessary, coercing the two adversaries through tough policy statements, directives and postures, India should strengthen the hands of Norway so that its facilitation role becomes absolutely credible and effective. Needless to say, the presence of the international community in Sri Lanka provides a conduit for India to influence the behaviour and position of both adversaries. A pragmatic Indian policy should be based on what prime minister Nehru said in the Constituent Assembly on 8 March 1948:

"(L)ess we interfere in international conflicts, the better unless our own interest is involved, for this reason that it is not in consonance with our dignity just to interfere without any effect being produced. Either we should be strong enough to produce some effect or we should not interfere at all. I am not anxious to put my fingers in every international pie. Unfortunately sometimes one cannot help it. One is dragged in to it..."

In some way, India's current policy conforms to the Nehruvian prescriptions.

References

1 Both from Indian and Sri Lankan points of view, many studies have critically analysed India's involvement in Sri Lanka. Some of the notable works from an Indian perspective are J.N. Dixit, *Assignment Colombo,* New Delhi: Konark, 1998; S.D. Muni, *Pangs of Proximity: India and Sri Lanka's Ethnic Crisis,* New Delhi: Sage Publications, 1993; P.S. Suryanarayana, *The Peace Trap: An Indo-Sri Lankan Political Crisis,* New Delhi: Affiliated East-West Press, 1988; Shankar Bhaduri, (et.al)., *The Sri Lankan Crisis,* New Delhi: Lancer International, 1990; and S.C. Sardeshpande, *Assignment Jaffna,* New Delhi: Lancer Publishers, 1992. The Sri Lankan views are explained in K M. de Silva, *Regional Power and Small State Security: India and Sri Lanka, 1977-90,* New Delhi: Vikas Publishing House, 1996; Rohan Gunaratna, *Indian Intervention in Sri Lanka: The Role of India's Intelligence Agencies,* Colombo: South Asian Network on Conflict Research, 1993; Shelton U. Kodikara (ed)., *Indo-Sri Lanka Agreement of July 1987,* Colombo: University of Colombo, 1989; and John Gooneratne, *A Decade of Confrontation: Sri Lanka and India in the 1980s,* Pannipitiya, Sri Lanka: Stamford Lake (PVT) Ltd, 2000.

2 It is said that more than 1200 soldiers (including a good number of officers) were killed and over 2500 wounded. India spent about $180 million on the operation.

3 In desperation to win US support, the Jayewardene administration allegedly extended refuelling and recreation facilities to visiting US naval ships. It sought to make itself closer to Western strategic interests by granting a contract for leasing oil storage tanks in the strategically important Trincomalee harbour to a Singapore-based US company. The contract was subsequently revoked when India exposed the manipulation in selecting the tender. Furthermore,

Sri Lanka entered into an agreement with the US in December 1983 to set up a powerful Voice of America (VOA) station on the island. India's apprehension was that the station would be used by the US Navy in the Indian Ocean. Not only these, Jayewardene sought Britain's direct role in the ethnic conflict by giving a fresh lease of life to the 1947 Sri Lanka-UK defence agreement.

4 President Premadasa himself led the anti-IPKF campaign. Having thoroughly got disillusioned with the presence of the Indian forces in the island, he sought to neutralise the internal political criticism by implementing his 1988 election promise that he would ensure the withdrawal of the IPKF on being voted to power. But it was not easy at all for him to convince the Indian government to de-induct its forces before implementing the accord. Therefore, he opened the doors for negotiations with the LTTE in 1989-90.

5 For the text of the letters see India, Ministry of External Affairs, *Foreign Affairs Record (FAR), 1987*, vol. 33, no. 7, July 1987, pp. 255 - 257

6 It is worth quoting the SLFP leader, Sirimavo Bandaranaike, who said that "Indians have achieved much more than they dreamed of achieving", and Sri Lanka became "an Indian protectorate" through the agreement. *The Telegraph*, 7 August 1987.

7 India and Sri Lanka signed a free trade agreement in December 1998, which became operational from 15 December 2001. By this agreement India committed itself to make duty-free 102 items immediately and give fifty per cent duty concession on 400 items which would become duty-free in three years. Bilateral trade has registered a significant expansion in the last five years, reaching $ one billion. Sri Lanka's trade deficit with India is also decreasing. In 2002 the trade increased by forty eight per cent. India's exports increased from US $ 600 million in 2000 to $ 831 million in 2002 (37.5 per cent), and Sri Lanka's exports to India from $ fifty eight million to $ 167 million (136.9 per cent). The trade balance has declined from 85:1 in 2001 to 49:1 in 2002. See http://www.meaindia.nic.in. Both countries have been in talks to conclude a Comprehensive Economic Partnership Agreement (CEPA). The Joint Study Group set up for this purpose has presented its recommendations to the prime ministers of the two countries. It is said that the CEPA will cover services and investment. It will take the two countries to a "qualitatively new level of engagement by intensifying and deepening bilateral economic interaction, building on the advantages of close political and geographical proximity".

Statement issued at the end of prime minister Ranil Wickremasinghe's visit to India in October 2003. *Ibid.* In June 2002, the Indian Oil Corporation and the Ceylon Petroleum Corporation signed a MoU under which the former is allowed to engage in retail oil trade in the island as well as to manage and operate, on a long lease, the Tricomalee oil tanks.

8 Every joint statement issued by the governments of India and Sri Lanka since the mid-1990s has made a reference and reassurance to protect Sri Lanka's sovereignty. See http://www.meaindia.nic.in

9 The present United Progressive Alliance (UPA) government's common minimum programme explicitly states that it will support peace talks that fulfil the legitimate aspirations of Tamils and religious minorities within the territorial integrity and solidarity of Sri Lanka. However, various India-Sri Lanka official joint statements issued during the National Democratic Alliance (NDA) government in the past and the UPA government at present have not given any special importance to Tamils and religious minorities. Instead they have made a general reference to 'fulfilment of aspirations of all sections of the Sri Lankan society' as the common position of both countries. See http://www.meaindia.nic.in

10 India's insistence on democracy, pluralism, openness, inclusiveness and transparency in the peace process should be seen in this context. See India-Sri Lanka joint statement issued at the end of president Mahinda Rajapakshe's visit to India in December 2005, http://www.mea.gov.in/cgi-bin/db2www/meaxpsite/coverpage.d2w/coverpg?sec=ss&filename=speech/2005/12/30js

11 This is emphasised in many of the India-Sri Lanka joint statements. See, for instance, the statement issued during the visit to India of the Sri Lankan foreign Minister, Mangala Samaraweera,from 30 November to 1December 2005. http://peaceinsrilanka.com/peace2005/Insidepage/printV/GOSLpv /011205PV.htm

12 See the official document on India-Sri Lanka Relations, http://www.meaindia.nic.in

13 This is evident from the current position of both the government and LTTE on the Oslo Declaration of 5 December 2002, signed by Balasingham, G.L. Peiris and Vidar Helgesen (Norwegian deputy minister of foreign affairs and head of the facilitation team). Responding to the LTTE chief's call for a political solution based on the principle of internal self-determination in the areas of

historical habitation of the Tamil-speaking peoples, both delegations to the third round of talks agreed to explore a federal solution acceptable to all communities as the basis of permanent peace. Now, both parties have backtracked on their commitment. Whereas the government headed by Mahinda Rajapakse is interested in a unitary solution, the LTTE has refused to abandon its *eelam* goal. See the text of the Oslo declaration in *The Hindu*, 21 November 2004.

14 Anton Balasingham said that "A military pact with India would encourage the Sinhalese political leadership to take a hard-line belligerent attitude towards the Tamils and eventually destroy the mutual trust between the estranged communities which is a crucial factor necessary for the consolidation and promotion of peace". cited in Jehan Perera, "Indo-Lanka Relations: Recent Trends", in Dev Raj Dahal and Nishchal Nath Panday, *Comprehensive Security in South Asia*, New Delhi: Manohar, 2006 , p. 102.

15 Becoming one of the Co-Chairs of the Sri Lanka Donor Group (SLDG), along with Norway, the US, Japan and the European Union, can be the first step. But it requires a redefinition of India's relations with the LTTE, something which is politically difficult for the UPA government in Delhi to undertake now.

SECTION-III
ETHNIC, REPARTRIATES AND REFUGEE ISSUES IN INDO-SRI LANKA RELATIONS

4

Ethnic Crisis in Sri Lanka: A peaceful solution

J.S.C Chhatwal

Sri Lanka, which was earlier known as Ceylon, came under British rule in 1833. After independence, Sri Lankan Tamil minority had hoped that they would be treated equally with the Sinhalese majority. After all, they had struggled shoulder to shoulder with the Sinhalese majority for the freedom of the country. This was, unfortunately, not to be. The Tamil minority there faced discrimination against them after independence. Therefore, there was no surprise that Tamil minority started a struggle to get equal status and rights from the Sri Lankan government. For a very long time, the Tamil struggle for equality in Sri Lanka was peaceful.

To understand the struggle of Tamils in Sri Lanka, one has to have some background understanding of the Tamil community there. There are two categories of Tamils in Sri Lanka. Ceylon Tamils (sometimes also referred to Jaffna Tamils) and Indian Tamils. Ceylon Tamils are as old settlers in Sri Lanka as the Sinhalese community itself – both having migrated from India thousands of years back. Ceylon Tamils are by and large an educated community of professionals mostly settled in the north of the country and in the three eastern provinces. They belong to higher castes of the caste system of Tamil Nadu in India. On the other hand Indian Tamils are comparatively recent migrants to Sri Lanka from India – their migration to Sri Lanka having started only in the end of the nineteenth century. To begin with and still Indian Tamils are mostly tea plantation workers in the central highlands of Sri Lanka. They were recruited by the British to work on the tea estates owned by them in Ceylon. They were manual workers, uneducated and in search of living. They belong to lower castes of the caste system of Tamil Nadu. During the British period a large number of professional and administrative jobs were manned by Ceylon Tamils in Sri Lanka. Ceylon Tamils with professional qualifications like doctors, engineers and administrators also migrated to a number of European countries, USA, Canada and countries like Malaysia, Australia, Singapore etc. The vast majority of Tamils in Sri Lanka belong to the category of Ceylon Tamils (around four million) while Indian Tamils number around one million. During the British rule and even today there is little social intercourse between these two categories of Tamils in Sri Lanka. Ceylon Tamils have always regarded themselves superior to Indian Tamils because of their education, background, vocation and castes.

In 1956, the Sri Lanka government enacted the Sinhalese language would be the official language of the country. This was made applicable even to areas where Tamils were in a majority. This resulted in a situation in which Tamils were required to transact every business with the government from the lowest to the highest level in Sinhalese, a language, which they did not know. This was the biggest discriminatory step against Tamils since independence in 1948. However, to get their grievances redressed, Tamils continued their peaceful struggle. The result of this peaceful struggle was the Selvanayakam-Bandaranaike Pact of 1957. This pact, however, was not implemented by Sri Lanka government because of the opposition to the pact by Sinhalese Buddhist clergy. In 1958 there were anti-Tamil riots and the government-sponsored colonialisation of traditionally Tamil in the east continued. Again in 1965 the Selvanayakam-Senanayke Pact to remove at least some discriminations against Tamils was signed. This pact also remained on paper only. J.R. Jayawardane who became president of the country after this pact was signed, opposed it and the pact had to be abrogated. In the series of anti-Tamil measures, in 1970 Sri Lanka government enacted a law that Tamil students have to secure much higher marks than their Sinhalese counterparts to get admission to professional courses such as medical, engineering colleges. In the same year, Sri Lanka security forces forced their way into the venue of World Tamil Conference in Jaffna and opened fire killing nine Tamils. In 1972 the Constitution of Sri Lanka was amended to make Buddhism the official religion of Sri Lanka. In 1981, the world-renowned Jaffna library was burnt down in which lakhs of volumes of Tamil literature were reduced to ashes. (Incidentally, Jaffna has been a major center of Tamil culture over the ages. The largest library of Tamil literature and culture and the first medical college with Tamil language as the medium of instruction, was established in Jaffna and not in Tamil Nadu or anywhere else in India). Also in 1981 with the efforts of moderate Tamil leaders an agreement was reached with Sri Lanka government to form District Development Councils (DDCs) to redress the Tamil grievances. This experiment was basically to get local autonomy to Tamils. However, this also like other pacts signed earlier, remained on paper only. In actual practice no worthwhile powers were delegated to the DDCs and no finances were made available to them by Colombo. It is in these circumstances that the Tamil struggle which to begin with was for the redressal of their grievances in day to day life. Asking for local autonomy only, took the shape of demanding a Tamil Homeland by merging the Jaffna peninsula in the north and the three provinces on the eastern coast.

The LTTE was established in 1975 and had its following from amongst Ceylon Tamils. The Indian Tamils throughout their existence in Sri Lanka have been led by moderate leadership (Such as late S. Thondaman). They took up their grievances with Sri Lanka government separately from Ceylon Tamils, irrespective of which Sinahalese party was in power in Colombo. Even at the height of the ethnic crisis and even during Sri Lanka government's operations against LTTE, there was always an Indian Tamil representative in Sri Lankan cabinet and most of the time the same person who was a minister in the earlier government of the opposition Sinhalese party.

In 1983, when the author was high commissioner in Colombo, 64 Tamil political prisoners were killed in Vallikadai prison in a so-called riot. In July 1983 as required under diplomatic practice, the author had informed Sri Lanka foreign office that he would be proceeding on two months home leave. He has every reason to believe that some Sri Lanka agency had already hatched a heinous plan to do away with these sixty four Tamil prisoners. The author was hardly away for two days in Delhi on home leave where these Tamil prisoners were massacred in the prison, taking advantage of the fact that the high commissioner was away in India. When the news of this tragedy reached Delhi, he rushed back to Colombo. On contacting Sri Lanka government, the author was told that these sixty four Tamil prisoners were killed in a "Riot" with Sinhalese prisoners in the same jail. When asked as to the number of casualties suffered by Sinhalese prisoners in this riot, he was told that the Sinhalese prisoners suffered no casualties! It was clear that there was no riot as such in the prison in which these Tamil prisoners were killed. On the contrary these Tamil prisoners were butchered by a Sri Lanka agency from outside the prison with the knowledge of Sri Lanka authorities. It was at this stage, i.e., in July 1983 that Tamil struggle in Sri Lanka took a violent turn and LTTE came in the forefront to achieve Ealam for Tamils in Sri Lanka.

The Indo-Sri Lanka Accord was signed in 1987, as a result of which Indian Peace-Keeping Force (IPKF) was sent to Sri Lanka. With hindsight it is now clear that the 1987 accord was basically flawed in the sense that it was not signed between the two parties directly concerned, i.e., the Sri Lanka government and the LTTE. Before the signing of the accord, the LTTE Supremo, V. Prabhakaran was asked to come to Delhi. He was shown the text of the accord, to which it is believed that he did not agree. However, India and Sri Lanka still went ahead and signed the accord. Prabhakaran returned to Jaffna from Delhi on 1 August 1987.

To begin with, relations between the IPKF and LTTE were correct. However, these relations took a dramatic turn for the worst when seventeen LTTE top cadres who were apprehended by the Indian navy while crossing over to Tamil Nadu, Committed suicide by swallowing cyanide capsules when they were being handed over to Sri Lanka army by IPKF on 3 October 1987. According to some watchers of Indo-Sri Lanka relations after the signing of 1987 accord, there was an unwritten agreement that Indian coastal guard will turn a blind eye to such crossings by LTTE cadres from Sri Lanka to Tamil Nadu and back. Whether these LTTE cadres should have been apprehended by the Indian Coast guard or not, the fact remains that ever since these LTTE cadres were taken into custody by the Indian side, LTTE had been pleading vehemently that these cadres should not be handed over to Sri Lanka army. This was the turning point in relationship between LTTE and IPKF,

Despite all the difficulties created for IPKF both by the LTTE and Sri Lanka government (soon after the 1987 accord, Premadasa who was against this accord became the president of Sri Lanka), by 1988 IPKF had succeeded in creating fairly peaceful conditions both in Jaffna and in the eastern provinces. Elections were held in this area and a moderate Tamil leader was chosen as the chief minister of this Tamil homeland. However, with Premadasa in the driving seat on Sri Lanka side, no steps were taken to devolve the agreed powers to the elected rulers of this Tamil homeland. For one and a half year after the establishment of the Tamil homeland there was a chief minister, a set of ministers but no devolution of powers to them whatsoever. As if this was not bad enough, president Premadasa joined hands with LTTE to attack IPKF wherever they were present in Sri Lanka. It is no longer a secret that Premadasa supplied continuously in a clandestine manner arms and ammunition to LTTE to fight against IPKF. The irony was that Premadasa dispatched these arms in Tata trucks, which were presented earlier as a gift from India to Sri Lanka! Such was the role of Premadasa, which eventually resulted in the ignominious exit of IPKF from Sri Lanka in 1990. Prior to Indo-Sri Lanka accord and the sending of IPKF to Sri Lanka, India's position in Sri Lanka was that of a referee in the Sinhalese –Tamil ethnic conflict. Both sides had a healthy respect for India. After IPKF's presence in Sri Lanka from 1987 to 1900, India started getting hated both by Tamils and the Sinhalese, which, unfortunately, continued for quite some time.

In recent times, Sri Lanka formally asked India twice to help them in their serious internal problems. In 1971, Sri Lanka asked for Indian forces to solve the situation of insurgency created by their Janata Vimukhi Perumuna – JVP, an extremist Sinhalese organization. The Indian forces landed at Colombo airport and helped Sri Lanka Army to put down this insurgency by their extremists. What did India get in return? In December of the same year i.e. 1971, when Pakistan declared war against India over the happenings in Bangladesh, Pakistani air force planes carrying re-inforcements to east Bengal were given refueling facilities by no other country than Sri Lanka. The next request for help was in 1987 for sending IPKF to Sri Lanka to deal with the situation created by LTTE in the north and east of the country. The IPKF kept the LTTE busy while the Sri Lanka government had the sufficient military power to crush the insurgency once again by their JVP in the south. What did India get again? The president of Sri Lanka (Premadasa) allied in a clandestine manner with LTTE to fight against the IPKF resulting in eventual exit of IPKF from Sri Lanka in 1990. IPKF suffered no less than 1,200 casualties and 3,500 wounded. This figure is more than the casualties and wounded India suffered in the Kargil war against Pakistan. In financial terms the cost to India for the IPKF in Sri Lanka was to the tune of Rs. 10 crores a day for their entire duration of stay in Sri Lanka.

The ethnic conflict in Sri Lanka is a political problem. There is no military solution possible to this conflict despite all the military strength that Sri Lanka government can muster and despite all the arms and ammunition, which LTTE can smuggle from abroad.

The northern tip of Sri Lanka is hardly twenty kms away from the shores of Tamil Nadu, where no less than sixty million Tamils reside. India cannot remain indifferent to what happens in Jaffna or in the eastern provinces of Sri Lanka because the Tamils in Tamil Nadu have historical and cultural relations with the Tamils in Sri Lanka. These geographical and ground realities cannot be washed away in Indo-Sri Lanka relations. India as a good neighbor has to help Sri Lanka in resolving the ethnic crisis in a peaceful manner. This is not only in the interest of India and Sri Lanka but also in the overall interest of the whole of South Asia. There is no harm in accepting the Tamil Nadu factor in our relations with Sri Lanka. After all India is not the only country which takes into consideration a domestic factor in its relations with a neighboring country. Actually, with the information and communication revolutions, taking the domestic factors into consideration in framing foreign policy has now become an imperative all over the world. At the same time, this does not mean that Tamil Nadu should ever be in a position to dictate India's relations with Sri Lanka. It is a folly for anyone to think that India is interested in Sri Lanka only because of the Tamil Nadu factor. This should be clear from the fact that when anti-Tamil riots took place in Sri Lanka in July 1983; in the discussion in our Parliament the first ten Speakers to voice their concern over the happenings in Sri Lanka were non-Tamils.

This should make it amply clear that India as a whole is interested and concerned over the happenings in its neighboring country namely Sri Lanka.

Having accepted that there is no alternative to a negotiated peaceful solution to the ethnic conflict in Sri Lanka; the pillars of this solution should be on the basis of the outline given by Mrs. Chandrika Bandaranaike Kumaratunga in her address in New Delhi in April 2002. Once the principles outlined in her address are followed, a viable and meaningful autonomy package can emerge for the Tamil minority in Sri Lanka, which they can sell to their people. Such a package will, of course, be within the sovereignty and unity of Sri Lanka. To achieve this the present ceasefire has to be strengthened and time-bound negotiations have to begin. Open-ended negotiations after the recent experience of the current ceasefire of February 2002 and only six rounds of talks in a period of four years do not inspire confidence. Further to inspire confidence both in Sinhalese and Tamils of Sri Lanka, any agreement arrived at between them will have to be guaranteed by an outside power like Norway with the support of US and EU. Needless to say that such a guarantee is essential as all pacts signed between the Sinhalese majority and the Tamil minority in Sri Lanka for over half a century now, have failed to be implemented on the ground.

5

A Cinderella Community in Transition : The Indian Origin Tamils of Sri Lanka

P.P. Devraj

Looking at the satellite photograph of the region covering India and SriLanka one is made acutely aware of the slight tilt SriLanka has towards its proximate neighbour India. This is both a geographic reality and in a way, it symbolizes the affinity and inclination SriLanka has for India. Nature has bound the two countries together in a special relationship.

The unique and distinctive relationship between Sri Lanka and India has not been without its vicissitudes. Notwithstanding the historical exchanges, the cultural and religious linkages there have been occasions when the relations between the two countries have been marred by suspicions and apprehensions. There have been misunderstandings and misinterpretations of intentions.

However, the issues that were the causes of divergence between the two countries have ceased to have any relevance today. Much water has flown under the bridge since those days. Today a new era has opened and a fresh look is necessary in regard to all problems. There has to be a paradigm shift in the understanding of Indo-Sri Lanka relationship.

Trade between India and SriLanka has increased phenomenally after the free trade agreement was signed between the two countries. Indian investments in SriLanka have grown and Srilankan firms have also established their presence in India.

The position taken up by Sri Lanka that solution to the ethnic problem should take place within the framework of a unitary state could not be given support by India as it would have been in conflict with the evolutionary federal growth in India and also there were the constraints of coalition politics which has firmly come to stay in India.

At the request of Sri Lanka, India had played a mediatory role in the ethnic conflict in Sri Lanka in the eighties, resulting in the Indo- Ceylon accord of 1987. This accord started with the acknowledgement that Sri Lanka was a multi ethnic, multi cultural pluralistic country. It is within this framework that the provincial council system was created in Sri Lanka. However, the experiences India had in actively involving itself in the resolution of the ethnic conflict had perhaps made it more cautious and thus an unwillingness to play any active direct role in the Sri Lankan peace process. However, India expressed its willingness to share experiences with Sri Lanka in regard to the accommodation of the rights of various communities within the multi ethnic, multi cultural and pluralist framework of India.

India is not only a regional power with bilateral and multilateral relations within the region but also a country whose global role is expanding. The horizons of its economic cooperation are continuously extending to new areas. India has become an important player in the global arena.

All these developments have brought about far reaching changes in the policies adopted by India in many respects including its approach to the People of Indian Origin (PIO) living in various parts of the world. Unlike the position taken earlier India has now recognized that it has a responsibility to the PIO living in the other countries and that due regard must be given to the emotional & cultural connections PIO's have to the country of their ancestors.

Scholars had described the PIO community as a Cinderella community as this community had been ignored both by the Indian and Sri Lankan governments despite many agreements signed about them. With its changed policies India has now started taking greater interest in the welfare of the PIOs of Sri Lanka along with its developing cooperation with Sri Lanka. The extension of the OCI (overseas citizenship of India) to Sri Lanka PIOs was an important development. Earlier Sri Lankan PIOs were excluded from the PIO card scheme. India is also providing support to upgrading the health and education standards of the Indian origin Tamil plantation workers. This has earned the appreciation of the government of Sri Lanka and all Sri Lankans.

It is in the background of these changes and far reaching new developments that this paper seeks to analyze the identity, interactions, rights and participation of the Indian Origin Tamils IOTs of Sri Lanka, one of the four major communities of the island. The position and aspirations of the IOT community have not found a place so far in the political discourse connected with the peace process in Sri Lanka. Although Sri Lankan leaders have repeatedly stated that in a final solution to the ethnic conflict in Sri Lanka the interest of all communities will be looked after. So far the issues of one of the four major communities of the island have been not even mentioned.

Writing in 1965, S.U. Kodikara, a former Sri Lankan deputy high commissioner, in Chennai, made the observation that "recent divergences and conflict between India and Ceylon have largely centered around the South Indian element in Ceylon's population and these (referred to as the Indo-Ceylon question) stands out as the most significant aspect of Indo-Ceylon relations since independence".[1]

The South Indian element referred to by Kodikara was the community of the descendants of migrants from the Tamil districts in Southern India who came to Sri Lanka in the wake of the phenomenal demand for labour that arose after the British had established control over the entirety of Sri Lanka in 1815 following which they started large scale coffee cultivation. Starting with small quantities in the beginning by 1880, 500,000 tons of coffee exported from Sri Lanka. After coffee was struck by a blight tea cultivation started, tea was a crop that needed a regular settled labour force more than coffee. Although even during coffee cultivation, Tamil plantation workers had become settled in the country with introduction of tea this became consolidated. Workers also settled in the rubber plantations, which were established during this period.

Plantation development brought about a rapid growth in the country. Government expenditure on roads, post and railways helped to create a modern transport and communication systems linking areas, which had hitherto been isolated. Urban centers also developed particularly the city of Colombo emerged as a major commercial and shipping center. The increased wealth in the country brought about a major educational advance. In 1839 there were 140 schools with 8751 pupils. By 1874 the number increased to 838 schools and 1878 to 1278 schools from 1839-1878 the number of pupils had increased tenfold to 87750. An English educated elite and a large white-collar employee class educated in the English medium were created in the country. With large exports of tea and rubber Sri Lanka became integrated with the world market.

The remarkably rapid growth experienced by the country and the consolidation of the plantation industry necessitated the permanent settlement of large number of the Indian Tamil worker's in the country. By the turn of the nineteenth century, IOTs had emerged as the largest minority community in the country.

It should be noted that although plantation workers formed the bulk of the Indian Tamil community there were also others such as urban workers, traders etc. In recent years there has been migration of plantation workers to urban areas and the urban components of the IOT population has increased. Furthermore, as a result of displacement during ethnic violence there had been a movement of plantation workers in some areas to become small time rural farmers. (see annexure 2)

After 1920 British government in India was pressurized by the Indian nationalist movement represented by the Indian National Congress with the demand that those who had gone from India to other countries in the British empire should not be discriminated *visa* vi other British subjects in those countries. This demand was shaped by the personal experiences of Mahatma Gandhi in South Africa. In 1921, the imperial conference held in London passed a resolution that the rights of the Indian emigrants lawfully domiciled in other countries of the empire would be recognized and guaranteed. Sri Lanka was bound by this resolution and committed to give full rights to the Indian Tamil community, which had lawfully settled in the country.

In a follow up to the 1921 Imperial conference resolution the Indian Emigration Act of 1922 was passed. This act prohibited emigration to destinations, which denied the immigrant Indian population equal rights, with local population. This formed the basis of the agreement between India and Ceylon in order to allow emigration of Indian workers to Sri Lanka to continue.

However when Donoughmore constitutional reforms and extension of universal adult franchise was introduced in 1931 the majoritorian leaders abandoned the undertaking given in 1923 and wanted provisions to be included to exclude a large number of IOTs from getting franchise. Although the Donoughmore commissioners had originally proposed more reasonable conditions for registration of Indian origin persons as voters, under pressure from the majoritorian Sinhala leaders and on the instructions of the secretary of State for colonies of the British government they agreed to accept the new stipulations proposed by the majoritorian leaders for franchise qualification.

Under these restricted provisions, 100,000 persons of Indian origin were registered as voters in 1931. With increasing awareness by 1939, 225,000 Indian origin persons were registered as voters. Worried by this increase in the number of IOT voters majoritorian leaders took steps to reduce this number of IOT voters. A new condition was introduced only in regard to IOT applicants. Oral interview was made compulsory for them. Many persons were not aware of the new condition, as it was not adequately publicized. Through systematic discrimination, the number of voters of Indian origin persons was reduced from 225,000 to 168,000 in 1941. It was these 168,000 persons who exercised their vote in 1947 election and elected seven members to a 105-member parliament. If no discrimination of practice the number of IOT voters would have been much higher than 225,000 and they would have been able to elect larger number of member of parliament. This would have helped Sri Lanka to take a more accommodative position in regards to minorities and the country would have developed much faster.

During the period of the Donoughmore constitution, two elections were held. In each of these elections two members were elected to the state council by the IOT workers. In the second state council one of the representatives Perisundaram functioned as a minister.

There were many developments in the 1930s like the economic crisis and the emergence of the Marxist movement. In

1939 Jawarhalal Nehru visited Sri Lanka and held discussions with the government of Sri Lanka and with the representatives of Indian origin persons, in regard to the problems faced by the Indian origin persons. In 1939, various organizations of the Indian origin persons came together to form the Ceylon Indian Congress.

In 1940/41 an Indo-Ceylon exploratory conference popularly known as Senanayake–Bajpai discussions were held to discuss the future status of persons of Indian origin. Although a formula was worked out and a joint statement was made the discussions were inconclusive and it was decided to put off further discussion till after the end of the war which had already broken out.

In 1947 Sri Lanka was given dominion status and a new constitution was enacted.

It will be interesting to note as to how the masters of 'Divide & Rule Policy' the British acted at this time. The joint chief of staff committee of the British government in its assessment on June 30 1947 noted:

A threat to the territorial integrity of Ceylon is likely to come only from India. The danger of India (particularly congress India) interfering with Ceylonese internal politics and provoking dissension among the powerful Indian minority is a real one. The danger is superimposed on the problems of racial differences; anti-European feeling communism and labour unrest, which by themselves are liable at any time to cause internal disorder.

The British cabinet delegation which represented the British government at the independence celebrations in Sri Lanka in February 1948 stated in its report to the British government that:

Relations with India played a leading part in Ceylon policy. The Prime Minister (of Ceylon) told me that he regarded the Indian problem as one of the prime dangers facing Ceylon (the other is the left movement). In part Ceylon fears Indian pressure and for this reason wants a close military tie up with us...

The defense establishment in London had tried its best to convince the British government of the advantage of detaching the Andaman islands from India and retain them under British sovereignty as naval and air bases. Lord Mountbatten strongly objected to this as he knew the real situation. The British General staff turned to Colombo and ensured that the independence of the island was linked to the grant of defense bases there.

Conscious of British strategic concerns D.S.Senanayake agreed to sign the defense and external affairs agreement and Dominion status was granted to Sri Lanka in 1947. In turn Britain retracted from its position of getting minorities agreement before independence. The newly elected government was allowed to decide on the issue of rights of Indian origin persons. The .plea made by the leaders of the Indian Tamil community to settle their rights issue at the time of independence itself was ignored. As a plantation origin, poet C.V.Veluppillai stated the IOT plantation workers were "born to suffer".

In the critical phase of the negotiations for constitutional reform, the British attempted to maintain an outward semblance of non-partisanship towards the various contending groups, but they accepted Senanayake as the sole representative of the Sri Lankan people and found cooperation with him attractive and as securing British interests. They chose to unquestioningly accept his assurances that the minorities would be treated in a liberal manner. Based on available evidence it can be said that the British traded the issue of citizenship rights to Indian origin persons in return for favorable guarantees to their strategic and economic interests.

The worst fears that were harboured about the future rights of the Indian Tamil workers came true. Immediately after taking charge of the new independent government Senanayake moved to introduce draconian citizenship laws and then to disenfranchise the entire community of Indian origin persons advancing the argument that only citizens are entitle to franchise.

In accordance with the agreement reached at the Indo-Ceylon exploratory conference of 1940/41 the issue of the status of the people of Indian origin was taken up for discussions between India and Sri Lanka both of whom had become independent. The discussion began in 1947.

Despite several meetings and a very lengthy correspondence between prime ministers Nehru and Senanayake there was no agreement on the substantive issues. In a mood of disappointment and frustration Nehru declared at the end "If you do not want these Indians, we will take then back. What difference will seven or eight lakhs make in a country of four hundred million people. What Nehru expressed in a mood of disappointment was taken as a signal by Senanayake to go ahead with the proposed legislation on Sri Lanka citizenship. The upshot was the enactment of the Ceylon citizenship act of 1948, which virtually excluded persons of Indian origin from citizenship. In 1949, Indian & Pakistani (residents) citizenship was enacted. If the qualifications were draconian the procedures for implementation were even more so. Finally when implementation procedures and the processing of applications were completed in 1964 only about 134,000 persons were registered as citizens under this act. Even during the implementation of that act it was recognized that it was not satisfactory and cannot resolve the problem. In 1953, discussions were held between Nehru and Senanayake. When Sir John Kotelavala became prime minister another discussion took place in 1954 but these discussions and agreements did not bring results. In 1964 when the implementation under Indian and Pakistani Citizen (residents) act was completed there were an estimated 975,000 persons who had not obtained citizenship. They were categorized as stateless persons.

In the aftermath of the Sino-Indian border conflict, India under the prime ministership of Lal Bahadur Shatri was anxious to mend fences with its neighbours. In his discussions with the government of Sri Lanka he departed from the earlier principle adopted by Nehru and instead agreed to divide the people of IOT in Sri Lanka on the basis of numbers in the first agreement between Bandaranaike and Shastri that India would grant citizenship to 525,000 persons and absorb them in India. Sri Lanka agreed to grant citizenship to 300,000 persons. The balance 150,000 persons were left to discuss at later date. In 1974 Bandaranaike and Indira Gandhi reach an agreement to divide the 150,000 equally between the two countries. Later experience showed how unrealistic these an unprincipled agreement and the implementation was failure. It only resulted in putting the people concern in two enormous difficulties and suffering.

Under changed political circumstances Sri Lanka enacted legislation in 1986 to grant citizenship to all stateless persons who had not become citizens of either country. At that time only about 330,000 persons had left for India. As a result of the 1986 law a total of 469,000 (1964 figure) persons and their natural increase were granted Sri Lankan citizenship. This brought to an end the stateless problem. However, there was still the problem of those who had applied for and obtained Indian citizenship but continued

Table 1 Distribution of the Sri Lankan population by ethnic group in District as given by the official census report of 2001.

District	Total Population	Ethnic Groups (Percentage)				
		Sinhalese	Sri Lankan Tamils	Sri Lanka Moors (Muslims)	Indian Tamils	Others
Colombo	2234289	76.59	10.96	9.18	1.2	2.1
Gampaha	2066096	91.08	3.12	3.89	0.4	1.5
Kalutara	1060800	87.09	1.28	8.75	2.7	0.2
Kandy	1272463	73.95	3.96	13.28	8.4	0.4
Matale	442427	80.24	5.27	8.78	5.3	0.4
Nuwraeliya	700083	40.03	5.92	2.51	51.3	0.2
Galle	990539	94.33	1.17	3.57	0.9	0.0
Matara	761236	94.16	0.65	2.94	2.2	0.0
Hambantota	525370	97.09	.37	1.05	0.1	1.4
Jaffna	490621	0.8	95.2	1.6	2.4	0.0
Mannar	151577	8.2	51.3	26.1	13.0	1.4
Vavuniya	149835	16.6	56.8	6.8	19.6	0.2
Mullaitivu	121667	5.2	75.4	4.7	14.5	0.2
Killinochchi	127263	-	-	-	-	
Batticaloa	486447	3.4	70.8	23.9	1.2	0.7
Ampara	589344	3.439.33	18.70	41.59	0.1	0.3
Trincomalee	340158	33.4	34.3	29.3	2.1	0.9
Kurunegala	1452369	91.74	1.17	6.73	0.2	0.2
Puttalam	705342	73.77	6.90	18.70	0.3	0.3
Annuradhapura	746466	90.78	0.66	8.24	0.1	0.2
Polonauwa	359197	90.3	2.00	7.59	0.0	0.1
Badulla	774555	72.07	4.14	5.22	18.2	0.3
Moneragalle	396173	94.54	1.14	2.03	1.9	0.1
Ratnapura	1008164	86.62	3.41	2.07	7.8	0.1
Kegalle	779774	85.61	1..62	6.63	5.9	0.1
Total	18732255	81.92	4.33	8.0	5.1	0.7

to live Sri Lanka since 1964. This problem was also resolved through Sri Lanka enacting a new legislation to grant them Sri Lankan citizenship in the year 2002. From the originally estimated number of 975,000 stateless persons in 1964 only 330,000 had become Indian citizens and left for India whereas 635,000 persons and their natural increase have become Sri Lankan citizens.

At the completion of the processing of applications under the Indian & Pakistani (residents) citizenship Act, 134,000 IOT had been registered as citizens. The number estimated to be stateless at this time was 975,000. Of this 975,000, 330,000 have left for India and the balance 645,000 have been given Sri Lanka citizenship. If we add to this figure the number who had already been registered as citizens in 1964 (635,000 + 134,000) the total would be 769,000. If the natural increase is added the present population figure would be around (769,000+549,000), 1,318,000. An accurate estimate made by Vijesandran lecturer of Peredeniya University is 1,326,196. However taking into account that there were a number of persons who had been registered under the Ceylon Citizenship Act of 1948 it would be reasonable to estimate the IOT population to be 1.5 million.

(Due to the war situation, full census was conducted only in 18 districts out of the total of 25. In the 5 districts or the northen province Jaffana, Kilinochchi and Mulliathevu were not covered during preliminary and final census. Vavunia & Mannar were covered partially. In the eastern province, Ampara was covered fully. Trincomale and Batticaloa were only partially covered)

The Director of census himself has reported that the official estimate of the IOTs in the population to be incorrect as many had been mistakenly included in the Sri Lankan Tamil category. According to him the correct per centage would be above seven. Vijesandiran, who had made a careful calculation puts the figure at 7.4 only 0.6 percent less than the total Muslim population in the country.

Table 2 gives Indian origin Tamil population as a percentage of the district population (both the census department figures and accurate estimate made by Vijesandiran) IOT distribution in the districts shows that they have large concentrations in some districts and smaller concentrations in other districts. If a sub-district analysis is made it would be found that even in districts where the IOT percentage is small they are concentrated in sub-district levels in larger numbers.

Table 2

District	Total Population	Numbers		As a % of District Population	
		DCS -2001	Estimated by Vijesandiran	DCS -2001	Estimated by Vijesandiran
Colombo	2234289	25,959	155411	1.2	7.0
Gampaha	2066096	7,388	63878	0.4	3.1
Kalutara	1060800	28,769	40802	2.7	3.8
Kandy	1272463	106,341	141428	8.4	11.1
Matale	442427	23,329	41604	5.3	9.4
Nuwraeliya	700083	359,386	391374	51.3	55.9
Galle	990539	8,553	19024	0.9	1.9
Matara	761236	16,983	21387	2.2	2.8
Hambantota	525370	243	1610	0.0	0.3
Jaffna	490621	11,774	*11774*	2.4	2.4
Mannar	151577	15,025	*20160*	9.9	13.3
Vavuniya	149835	29,360	*29068*	19.6	19.4
Mullaitivu	121667	17,641	*16912*	14.5	13.9
Killinochchi	127263	-	-	-	-
Batticaloa	486447	5,837	*5837*	1.2	1.2
Ampara	589344	410	*2357*	0.1	0.4
Trincomalee	340158	7,143	8844	2.1	2.6
Kurunegala	1452369	2,732	17066	0.2	1.2
Puttalam	705342	2,161	43283	0.3	6.1
Annuradhapura	746466	517	4731	0.1	0.6
Polonauwa	359197	147	147	0.0	0.0
Badulla	774555	141,087	168314	18.2	21.7
Moneragalle	396173	7,660	13239	1.9	3.3
Ratnapura	1008164	78,581	108765	7.8	10.8
Kegalle	779774	45,647	59181	5.9	7.6
Total	**18732255**	**855,891**	**1386196**	5.1	7.4

The sub-district level ie divisional secretariat division is the third tier in the administrative system after the central government and district administration. The local government unit (ie Pradeshiya Sabhas) boundaries coincide with that of the divisional secretariat boundaries.

Population distribution is important when it comes to implementation of official languages.

Although the constitution provides for Sinahala and Tamil as languages of administration throughout the country this provision is vitiated by the stipulation that the language of official administration records and languages of courts will be in Sinhala throughout the country except in north east province. This makes it impossible for official language provisions to be implemented in areas other than north east.

There is, however, a provision in the constitution for the president to declare a divisional secretariat area as a bilingual area if he/she is satisfied that in this division there is a substantial number of a language speaking group other than the one in which records had been kept. Up to this time only twenty nine divisional secretariat areas have been declared for bilingual records. This will enable the implementation of official languages provisions in these areas.

During the discussions of the select committee of parliament on constitutional reform in 2000 consensus was reached that if a divisional secretariat division has more than 12.5% of a language group records must be kept in the language of that group also. Since Muslims are also Tamil speaking nearly half the divisional secretariat divisions can be brought under bilingual provisions. (see annexure 1).

Although the census has categorized Indian origin Tamils as a distinct community (Indian Tamils) and they form more than seven per cent of the population, their rights as a community have not figured in state reform discussions. As stated by Uyangoda :

"In Sri Lanka's present debate on power sharing, the main focus continues to remain on political relations between the Sinhalese majority community and the Sri Lankan Tamil community or the State and the Sri Lankan Tamil community. This debate has also given rise to a number of other issues that do not bring into

attention the possibilities of multi-level power sharing arrangements. Firstly, there is a peculiar cartographic imagination often expressed in the idea that Sri Lanka's ethnic conflict is territorially constituted in terms of North-East and the South. Secondly, the two territorial entities of North-East and the South are also often imagined as ethnically undifferentiated social-geographical entities. Muslim communities in the Eastern Province have often challenged this particular political mapping of Sri Lanka, reminding, at times in violent ways, that Muslims represent a third ethnic group in the equation in the settlement to the ethnic conflict. Thirdly, options are understood primarily as constituting a bi-nation future for Sri Lanka in which Sinhalese and Sri Lankan Tamil 'nations' would find a constitutional arrangement of regional autonomy through protracted negotiations among Sinhalese and Tamil political elites". [2]

The Sri Lankan debate on the ethnic conflict is seen mainly as a territorially constituted one. Conveniently ignoring the multi ethnic nature of the country and the non-territorial distribution of some ethnic communities. One of the reasons for the lack of progress in the labyrinthine time and protracted negations on the ethnic issue in Sri Lanka can be attributed to the failure of recognizing the need for power sharing arrangements and participation of all the communities in country.

President Rajapakse has in his election manifesto the "Mahinda Chintana" and also in his speeches emphasized his commitment to human rights. The human right approach is concerned with the rights of national, ethnic, linguistic and religious minorities as part of the universally recognized human rights. The positive, individual rights of minorities are related to the non-discrimination clauses, enshrined in the UN covenants. If the president's commitment to human rights is to have meaning, Sri Lanka has to move towards incorporating a comprehensive charter of rights in the constitution and also ensure independence of the judiciary.

When constitutional reforms were discussed by the select committee of parliament in year 2000 there was consensus on the need to expand the chapter of fundamental rights and freedoms contained in the present constitution. It is possible for Rajapakse to build on this consensus.this will be a major confidence building

Annexure 1: Distribution of IOTs All Tamils and Tamil Speaking Peoples in Selected Divisional Secretariat Divisions

District / Divisional Secretariat	*Indian Origin Tamils*	*Sri Lankan Tamils*	*All Tamils*	*Muslim*	*Tamil Speaking People*	*Total Population*	*Percentage of Tamils*	*Percentage of TSP*
Badulla								
Lunugala	17321	515	17836	1199	19035	32791	54.4	58.0
Haldamula	15486	2015	17501	511	18012	37666	46.5	47.8
Haputale	14902	4642	19544	3187	22731	50295	38.9	45.2
Passara	17372	2287	19659	2153	21812	48783	40.3	44.7
Hali-Ela	21435	6755	28190	3197	31387	87081	32.4	36.0
Ella	11261	1960	13221	1506	14727	42615	31.0	34.6
Welimada	9274	2994	12268	15027	27295	93352	13.1	29.2
Badulla	10921	3183	14104	6083	20187	69971	20.2	28.9
Bandarawela	8250	4872	13122	2939	16061	60063	21.8	26.7
Soranatota	4004	430	4434	291	4725	22658	19.6	20.9
Uva-Paanagama	7939	2177	10116	2233	12349	76282	13.3	16.2
Colombo								
Colombo	7946	117510	125456	1E+05	245565	377396	33.2	65.1

(Contd.)

(Contd.Annexure-1)

District / Divisional Secretariat	*Indian Origin Tamils*	*Sri Lankan Tamils*	*All Tamils*	*Muslim*	*Tamil Speaking People*	*Total Population*	*Percentage of Tamils*	*Percentage of TSP*
Thimbirigasyaya	6022	68162	74184	33190	107374	264767	28.0	40.6
Dehiwela-Mount Lavinia	2060	22737	24797	20357	45154	209787	11.8	21.5
Kolonnawa	1097	12657	13754	19103	32857	160417	8.6	20.5
Galle								
Galle our Gavets	273	1002	1275	29869	31144	104015	1.2	29.9
Gampaha								
Negombo	1459	14834	16293	17191	33484	144551	11.3	23.2
Wattala	2014	24251	26265	8287	34552	161644	16.2	21.4
Kalutara								
Baruwela	422	1223	1645	46477	48122	144251	1.1	33.4
Bulathsinhala	5680	1254	6934	2113	9047	59218	11.7	15.3
Panadura	514	1044	1558	20488	22046	162979	1.0	13.5

(Contd.)

(Contd.Annexure-1)

District / Divisional Secretariat	*Indian Origin Tamils*	*Sri Lankan Tamils*	*All Tamils*	*Muslim*	*Tamil Speaking People*	*Total Population*	*Percentage of Tamils*	*Percentage of TSP*
Mathugama	5525	1290	6815	2524	9339	72872	9.4	12.8
Dodangoda	4904	1852	6756	40	6796	54290	12.4	12.5
Kandy								
Akurana	1473	2058	3531	34893	38424	55366	6.4	69.4
Panvila	15353	93	15446	1195	16641	26687	57.9	62.4
Deltota	7592	2968	10560	7293	17853	29719	35.5	60.1
Pasbage Korela	20210	2358	22568	7807	30375	56934	39.6	53.4
Udapalatha	13523	6415	19938	17359	37297	86136	23.1	43.3
Doluwa	9619	1155	10774	2155	12929	45102	23.9	28.7
Udunuwara	1737	1382	3119	23093	26212	98879	3.2	26.5
Medadumbara	7656	4268	11924	3171	15095	58216	20.5	25.9
Pathadumbara	661	2105	2766	16733	19499	80224	3.4	24.3
Gangawata Korela	9129	12641	21770	16969	38739	161395	13.5	24.0
Ganga Ihala Korela	6723	540	7263	3143	10406	50706	14.3	20.5

(Contd.)

(Contd.Annexure-1)

District / Divisional Secretariat	*Indian Origin Tamils*	*Sri Lankan Tamils*	*All Tamils*	*Muslim*	*Tamil Speaking People*	*Total Population*	*Percentage of Tamils*	*Percentage of TSP*
Poojapitiya	1026	423	1449	8259	9708	53644	2.7	18.1
Kundasale	5321	6766	12087	5701	17788	106473	11.4	16.7
Harispathuwa	503	2414	2917	8308	11225	78207	3.7	14.4
Kegalle								
Mawanella	633	879	1512	28096	29608	100280	1.5	29.5
Yatiyanthota	10357	2097	12454	2432	14886	56838	21.9	26.2
Derniyagala	9990	224	10214	45	10259	44370	23.0	23.1
Dehiovita	9930	1560	11490	3046	14536	73602	15.6	19.7
Bulathsinhala	5822	2438	8260	274	8534	45429	18.2	18.8
Ruwanwella	3457	1037	4494	3324	7818	58231	7.7	13.4
Kurunegalla								
Kuliyapitiya East	6	169	175	13605	13780	46752	0.4	29.5
Rasnayakapura	8	40	48	3188	3236	18763	0.3	17.2
Mawathagama	187	2781	2968	6216	9184	56718	5.2	16.2

(Contd.)

(Contd.Annexure-1)

District / Divisional Secretariat	*Indian Origin Tamils*	*Sri Lankan Tamils*	*All Tamils*	*Muslim*	*Tamil Speaking People*	*Total Population*	*Percentage of Tamils*	*Percentage of TSP*
Mallawapitiya	57	1053	1110	6220	7330	46149	2.4	15.9
Kurunegalla	518	3497	4015	9105	13120	88457	4.5	14.8
Rideegama	414	2385	2799	7903	10702	80408	3.5	13.3
Polgahwela	690	930	1620	5018	6638	58486	2.8	11.3
Panduwasnuwara	45	223	268	7182	7450	69634	0.4	10.7
Matale								
Matale	8749	3975	12724	12690	25414	68826	18.5	36.9
Ukuwela	2889	6522	9411	11733	21144	61663	15.3	34.3
Rattota	5776	6581	12357	1809	14166	49395	25.0	28.7
Amabnganga Korela	2592	1666	4258	61	4319	15542	27.4	27.8
Yatawatta	1043	2220	3263	2014	5277	28676	11.4	18.4
Galewela	966	344	1310	7430	8740	61999	2.1	14.1
Matara								
Kotapola	12469	645	13114	44	13158	63951	20.5	20.6

(Contd.)

(Contd.Annexure-1)

District / Divisional Secretariat	Indian Origin Tamils	Sri Lankan Tamils	All Tamils	Muslim	Tamil Speaking People	Total Population	Percentage of Tamils	Percentage of TSP
Moneagala								
Badalkumbara	3088	1040	4128	1649	5777	36693	11.3	15.7
Moneagalla	3699	2460	6159	334	6493	42575	14.5	15.3
Medaga	8	57	65	3899	3964	32083	0.2	12.4
Nuwaraeliya								
Nuwara-eliya	134554	22266	156820	5850	162670	206944	75.8	78.6
Ambagamuwa	141066	11760	152826	4524	157350	202432	75.5	77.7
Kotmale	36891	3566	40457	6216	46673	96280	42.0	48.5
Walapane	35267	2603	37870	823	38693	106850	35.4	36.2
Hanguranketha	11608	1250	12858	144	13002	87577	14.7	14.8
Puttalam								
Puttalam	406	7699	8105	41260	49365	70915	11.4	69.6
Kalpitiya	178	10514	10692	46310	57002	58923	18.1	96.7

(Contd.)

(Contd.Annexure-1)

District / Divisional Secretariat	*Indian Origin Tamils*	*Sri Lankan Tamils*	*All Tamils*	*Muslim*	*Tamil Speaking People*	*Total Population*	*Percentage of Tamils*	*Percentage of TSP*
Mundel	89	12105	12194	21058	33252	48143	25.3	69.1
Pallama	32	351	383	3363	3746	12908	3.0	29.0
Chilaw	328	6046	6374	4218	10592	37996	16.8	27.9
Madambe	226	1106	1332	2359	3691	20157	6.6	18.3
Nattandiya	143	1691	1834	5569	7403	56064	3.3	13.2
Wennapuwa	268	1676	1944	83	2027	16574	11.7	12.2
Ratnapura								
Kahawatta	6465	2396	8861	1292	10153	42083	21.1	24.1
Godakawela	8718	4374	13092	2432	15524	69263	18.9	22.4
Ratnapura	11347	8253	19600	5623	25223	114640	17.1	22.0
Balangoda	7500	3089	10589	5333	15922	77026	13.7	20.7
Nivithigala	6347	4648	10995	493	11488	58412	18.8	19.7
Kalawana	7747	0	7747	87	7834	48201	16.1	16.3
Impulpe	7113	1389	8502	73	8575	55228	15.4	15.5
Pelmadulla	6520	5455	11975	430	12405	84450	14.2	14.7
Ayagama	2840	741	3581	22	3603	28491	12.6	12.6

measure that can lay the foundation for finding a negotiated solution to the ethnic conflict. It will also help to maintain status quo in the ethnic conflict and help in taking up the power sharing arrangements for north-east after creating demonstrating the bona fides of the government to establish equality among communities.

It will be relevant to quote Nehru's speech at a public reception in Colombo in January 1950. He said "I warn against looking at national problems in a narrow spirit. I want you to think of the future of Ceylon in the largest context of changing Asia. Neither India nor Ceylon can be in isolation today, but should think in terms of the big movements taking place in Asia and the rest of the world." Nehru's prophetic words are more relevant today than ever before.

Although India may be reluctant to get directly involved in the Sri Lankan peace process it cannot avoid helping in finding a holistic and stable solution that will ensure the interests of all communities in Sri Lanka. Regional dimensions and international interests are factors that will have determining role in finding stable peace and development to Sri Lanka.

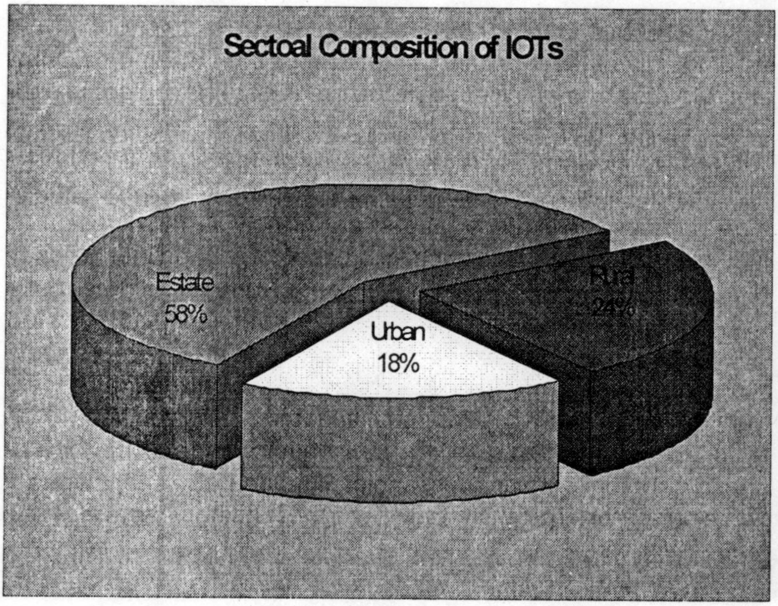

Sectoral Composition of IOT Population

Final solution to ethnic accommodation and democracy have to be found within the framework of international norms and standards of human rights and rights of communities so clearly laid down by UN declarations conventions and covenants.

References

1 S.U. Kodikara, *Indo-Ceylon relationship*, Ceylon : Institute of World Affairs, 1965.

2 Jayadeva Uyangoda's paper submitted at a seminar "Rights and Power Sharing Mechanism for Non Territorial Minorities in Sri Lanka, organized by FES in 2003.

6

Integration and Assimilation of Sri Lankan Repatriates in Tamil Nadu

V. Suryanarayan

The agony and suffering undergone by the Jews during the diaspora and the Palestinians after the second world war had been the subject of international concern. But not the repatriation (or rather expatriation and even in some cases deportation) of the Indian Tamils under the Sirimavo-Shastri Pact and the Sirimavo-Indira Gandhi Pact and their continuing trauma. In fact, the repatriation of Indian citizens to India is one of the largest organised migrations in the twentieth century. As a distinguished Sri Lankan intellectual, Fr. Paul Caspersz, has put it, "Even in a world where there has been so much to hit the headlines, it is surprising that the agreements which heralded the largest organised worker migration in the 20th century have gone largely unnoticed."[1] Unwanted in Sri Lanka and unwelcome in India, these unfortunate people languished in different parts of Tamil Nadu, dispersed all over the state. Ironically, in some parts of Tamil Nadu they were referred to as "Sri Lankan Tamils", a status that they never acquired in Sri Lanka even after many years of residence and service to the island.

Changing Scenarios

Given below are three accounts, which would vividly illustrate the untold problems faced by the repatriates at different points of time, and how as a result of efflux of time the repatriates have got assimilated into the Tamil Nadu society. In January 1983, during author's fieldwork in Sri Lanka, he went to Hatton railway station to interview the repatriates who were coming to Tamil Nadu. It was a heart wrenching sight. Most of the repatriates were born in Sri Lanka, they had no knowledge of the social and economic conditions in Tamil Nadu and what the future had in store for them. Most of them did not want to come to India, but the inhuman policies of the governments in Colombo and New Delhi had converted them into a merchandise to be divided between the two countries in the name of good neighbourly relations. Some of them were carrying small mementoes, for example grinding stone or small soil, as a reminder of their long stay in the island. As the train left Hatton railway station, there was uncontrolled weeping and expression of sorrow.

The second incident relates to Muniamma, an old Sri Lankan repatriate whom I met in the shanties of Kotagiri in August 1987. Muniamma got repatriated to India in 1981 and was provided a business loan amounting to Rs. 5000. In Mandapam few local Tamils posed themselves as good samaritans and swindled her. After wandering in different parts of Tamil Nadu, she finally reached Kotagiri, where she was eking out a bare living by doing household work. Feeling bitter about her life in Tamil Nadu, she exclaimed, "Idu Thai Nada, Nai Nada?" (Is it mother country or dog's country?)

Three years ago, author was associated with the Peradeniya University as a visiting professor. He did extensive fieldwork in the tea country. In a plantation near Hatton, he interviewed Indira, who had spent nine months with her brother, who had settled down in Perambur in Chennai. Her brother got repatriated in 1980; after initial hiccups he had settled down in Perambur, where he was working as a motor mechanic. He had a two-room house, with water supply and electricity and his two children were receiving good education. The son was studying in a teachers training college and the daughter was undergoing training for a nursing profession. Indira told the author, that unlike Hatton, where they were mortally afraid to move around following the Bindunewewa massacre, she could go for late night film shows with her friends in Chennai, without any fear of insecurity. She was very happy that her brother's family got easily assimilated into the Tamil Nadu society and was also moving up the social and economic ladder. She naturally bemoaned the continuing insecurity and economic and social backwardness of her community in Sri Lanka.

Background to Repatriation

Unlike the Sinhalese and Sri Lankan Tamils, the Indian Tamils (they are also referred to as up-country Tamils and estate Tamils) are not indigenous to the island. They are the descendants of the Tamil labourers, who were brought to the island by the British colonialists to provide the much-needed labour for the development of coffee, tea, rubber and coconut plantations. They formed the bulk of labour, which turned the malaria infested forests of Sri Lanka into smiling plantations, earning precious foreign exchange, which sustains the Sri Lankan economy even today.

The agony and suffering undergone by the Indian coolies under the British Raj and the Planters Raj are innumerable and need not be recounted here. The verdant carpet of green in the central parts in the island, which made Sri Lanka the veritable "Island Paradise", was due to the sweat and agony of Indian plantation workers. But the plantation worker was the worst victim of imperialist exploitation and, after independence, of the ultra-nationalist politicians in Sri Lanka. Apply any yardstick – per capita income, living conditions, longevity of life, educational status, status of women – the Indian Tamil is in the worst position today. As the *Economic Review,* published by the People's Bank, summed up few years ago, "After almost 110 years of tea industry, the life of the plantation worker is still characterised by low living conditions, illiteracy, crowded housing and suffering."[2] Even, president Jayewardene admitted as such when he addressed the annual general body meeting of the Ceylon Planters Society in September 1981:

About 150 years ago, citizens from India were brought to this country and had to live as indentured labourers in Lines. They still live in Lines. I hope the very word Lines will be deleted from the dictionary. They were confined to the Lines from their birth to their death. They had no village or house of their own. Their children were going to schools, which were more like cattle sheds and soon they left the schools to join the labour force.[3]

While it is undoubtedly true that the plantation workers went to Sri Lanka under the protective umbrella of the British, it must also be underlined that the Sinhalese leaders and the state council actively encouraged the import of cheap labour from South India. The state council every year allotted funds to subsidise immigration. In the 1920s, when the British government in India threatened to stop immigration of Indian labour into Ceylon, a delegation of prominent Ceylonese went to New Delhi and successfully persuaded the British not to impose such a ban. When finally the ban was imposed it was due to the Indian nationalist pressure on the British government.

Though, in the beginning, the Indian labourers were merely "birds of passage", gradually they began to take roots and became permanent settlers in the island. In 1928, the Donoughmore commissioners estimated that forty to fifty per cent of Indian workers had permanently settled in the island. In 1939, the Jackson report estimated it to be around sixty per cent. The Soulbury report estimated that the degree of permanent settlement was in the region of eighty per cent.

As long as the British ruled, the Indian Tamils had the same legal status as the Sinhalese and the Sri Lankan Tamils, for all were British subjects. As Jawaharlal Nehru wrote in 1948: "One of the conditions for emigration to other countries to which the Government of India have always attached utmost importance... has been that an emigrant labourer shall be given facilities to settle in the country... on equal terms with the members of the indigenous population."[4] Colombo did not subscribe to this point of view. According to W.T. Jayasinghe, former defence and foreign secretary of Sri Lanka, the Indian settlers were Indian nationals. In his book, *The Indo-Ceylon Talks: The Politics of Immigrant Labour,* Jayasinghe has written: "The fact of their Indian nationality was never in question." [5] Colombo wanted to absorb only a small fraction of the Indian population as Sri Lankan citizens. From this perspective, they argued that it is necessary to prescribe rigid tests for proving the permanent, abiding interest of the Indian community. Herein lies the seeds of the "absorbable minimum" put forward by successive Sri Lankan governments. Girija Shankar Bajpai summed up the apparent discrimination: "The Indian who has worked in Ceylon is to be thrown back to India as a squeezed lemon." [6]

Despite the restrictions on franchise, in the 1947 elections held under the Soulbury constitution, the Indian workers elected six representatives of the Ceylon Indian Congress (CIC); where no CIC candidates were fielded, they voted for the Marxist candidates and tilted the balance in Marxist favour in about nine seats. The leftward swing of the plantation workers' votes made the conservative United National Party (UNP) leadership determined to debar the vast majority of Indian Tamils from Ceylonese citizenship after independence. If the government could restrict the citizenship and, therefore, the franchise of the Indians, a large number of Marxist candidates could be eliminated and the UNP could win the Kandyan seats very easily.

The Ceylon Citizenship Act of 1948 and the Indian and Pakistani Residents Act, 1949 not only disfranchised the Indian Tamils, but these acts also made them stateless. When applications were invited, nearly 8,25,000 applied for Ceylon citizenship, which was clear evidence that the overwhelming majority of Indians wanted to permanently stay in Ceylon. But the government granted citizenship to only 1,34,618 applicants. All others were characterised as 'stateless'. It must also be pointed out that the provisions of Citizenship Act were complicated and cumbersome and naturally the plantation workers were not able to produce certificates to the satisfaction of Ceylonese authorities. The Indian Tamils were thus ostracised from the political mainstream of the country. Speaking on the Ceylon Citizenship Act, Pieter Kuneman said in parliament that even Dudley Senanayake would not be able to comply with the clauses because, according to his own admission, he could not trace his father's birth certificates.

If the acts were discriminatory, their implementation was even more tardy and inflexible. By the end of 1953, only 65,714 applications of the total 2,37,034 had been fully investigated and of this number only 7,687 applications, involving 26,360 persons had been allowed. By the end of 1954, a total of 9,672 applications, involving 33,012 persons had been allowed, and by the end of 1955, a total of 37,948 persons covered by 10,875 applications had been registered as Ceylonese citizens. [7]

Sirimavo-Shastri pact

From the very beginning, it was Colombo's implicit assumption that those who failed to qualify for Ceylonese citizenship were unquestionably Indian nationals and that New Delhi should regard them as such. On the contrary, as far as New Delhi was concerned, its policy was to discourage Indians overseas from applying for Indian citizenship. In the protracted negotiations that took place between New Delhi and successive Ceylonese prime ministers, DS Seananayake, Dudley Senanayake, John Kotelawala and SWRD Bandaranaike, Jawaharlal Nehru emphatically maintained that except for those who voluntarily opted for Indian citizenship, the Indian immigrants in the island were the responsibility of Sri Lanka. The era of statelessness thus continued and the problem appeared to be interminable.

Following Nehru's demise in 1964, the time tested and principled policy enumerated above was derailed and sidetracked by prime minister Lal Bahadur Shastri and minister for foreign affairs Swaran Singh. During this period, New Delhi was eager to come out of the "diplomatic isolation in South Asia" following the humiliating defeat in the Sino-Indian conflict in October-November 1962. Shastri wanted fresh efforts to be made to put India-Sri Lanka relations on a sound footing and was willing to find a solution to the problems of the stateless people on the basis of "give and take". As a first step to attain this end, officials in the Sri Lanka division of the ministry of external affairs, who subscribed to Nehruvian principles on the question of the people of Indian origin, were either transferred or sidelined. New Delhi's desire to solve the problem on the basis of "give and take" (which meant more conceding than demanding) becomes evident if one reads CS Jha's book.[8]

The astute politician that Sirimavo Bandaranaike was, she made the best of the New Delhi's changed stance. Ably assisted by Shirley Amarasinghe, the Sri Lankan government clinched the issue in October 1964. The Sri Lankan team pleaded with Shastri and CS Jha that if India could accept 10 million refugees from Pakistan, less than a million from Sri Lanka would not be a heavy burden. Finally the negotiations came to a close in October 1964 with India agreeing to confer citizenship on 5,25,000 people of Indian origin plus their natural increase and Ceylon agreeing to confer citizenship on 3,00,000 plus their natural increase, on the basis of 7:4. By a subsequent agreement in 1974, India agreed to confer citizenship on 75,000 persons; Sri Lanka, in turn also agreed to confer citizenship on 75,000 persons. The entire process was expected to be complete by October 1981. [9]

Few significant features of the Sirimavo-Shastri Pact must be underlined. In author's interview with Thondaman, he repeatedly mentioned that the Ceylon government did not permit him to come to New Delhi to explain his point of view. It is the tragedy of India-Sri Lanka relations that this agreement, which had a bearing on the lives of thousands of people of Indian origin, was finalised by the two governments without taking into consideration the feelings and views of the affected people. All trade unions in the plantation areas, rivals amongst themselves, were unanimous in their opposition to the Sirimavo-Shastri Pact. The Ceylon Workers Congress, the most representative organisation of the Indian workers, vehemently opposed the Pact. The continuing trauma suffered by the people made the organisation revise its stance later and cooperate with the government in its implementation.

The most damning indictment against the Sirimavo-Shastri Pact is the fact that though it lapsed on 31 October 1981, it did not fulfil its objectives. Even after the expiry of the pact, the problem of stateless people continued and the fate of many thousands still hung on the balance. As per the two agreements, a total number of 600,000, plus their natural increase, were to be repatriated to India. The total would amount to 7,50,000. From the very beginning, it was apparent that the majority of the people of Indian origin were reluctant to leave the shores of Sri Lanka. Though Sri Lanka had earmarked 400,000 for Sri Lankan citizenship, the number of applications was as high as 6,25,000. There was a shortfall in the applications for Indian citizenship. Only 4,00,000 had applied during the prescribed period. Subsequently another 87,000, whose applications for citizenship were rejected, also applied for Indian citizenship making a total of 4,87,000.[10] The statistics reveals the wide gap between the wishes of the people concerned and the arbitrary decision of the two governments.

India decides to Terminate the Pacts

The process of repatriation was exceedingly slow. It was expected to commence in 1965, but the Sri Lankan government introduced the enabling legislation only in 1967. As a result, the repatriation commenced only in 1968 and moved slowly throughout the 1970s. The whole exercise was callous, brutal and dehumanising. No principle was enunciated either for the granting of citizenship or for being subjected to repatriation. The agreements merely played around with numbers.

Meanwhile thanks to the initiative taken by Thomas Abraham, Indian high commissioner in Sri Lanka between 1978 and 1982, and 1982, New Delhi began to get sensitised about the inhuman aspects of the agreements.[11] Brought up in Nehruvian traditions and having served in countries, which had large number of people of Indian origin, like Burma, Malaysia and Singapore, Abraham had a natural empathy for these unfortunate children of mother India. He visited almost all the plantations in the island and had detailed discussions with the representatives of the people of Indian origin. It was Abraham who brought to the notice of New Delhi a new dimension of the problem. He brought the 'conundrum of natural increase' to the notice of prime minister Indira Gandhi. By the late 1970s, India had to accept not only the natural increase, but the natural increase of the natural increase also. Indira Gandhi responded, "but this cannot go on for ever." [12] Adding to the dismay of New Delhi was large-scale organised violence in the plantation areas in 1981, engineered by powerful forces in the ruling party and carried out by lumpen sections of Sinhalese population. Their objective naturally was to pressurise the people of Indian origin to leave the island. Abraham immediately proceeded to riot-affected areas, though the Sri Lankan foreign office tried to dissuade him on the plea that the government could not provide him with adequate security. Abraham was shocked with the senseless violence. In one of his memorable statements in Sri Lanka, he declared that if the Sri Lankan government could not restore law and order and provide security to the people of Indian origin, India would have to think of taking its own steps. The chauvinist elements in Sri Lanka accused him of interfering in the internal affairs of the country, but the Indian high commissioner stuck to his principled and courageous stance. The warning had the desired effect and sent shock waves in the Sri Lankan government circles. President Jayewardene acted quickly and the situation was brought under control. Abraham also met MG Ramachandran, then Chief Minister of Tamil Nadu, and apprised him of the developments in Sri Lanka. Ramachandran led an all party delegation to New Delhi and made a strong plea that the Sirimavo-Shastri Pact should not be extended. It was these factors, which compelled New Delhi to take the decision that the pact would terminate on 31 October 1981. No more applications would be received by the Indian high commission for Indian citizenship after that date. It may also be mentioned that the personal equation between prime minister Indira Gandhi and president Jayewardene, which had gone from bad to worse during this period, could also have contributed its input into this significant decision made by Indian foreign office.

How did Colombo respond to the situation? In his book, *The Indo-Ceylon Problem: The Politics of Immigrant Labour,* WT Jayasinghe has turned a Nelson's eye to the momentous developments of 1981. In fact only one paragraph is devoted to the shocking incidents that took place. There is no mention about the organised violence, no mention about Abraham's visit to the plantations and no analysis of New Delhi's changed stance. Jayasinghe mentions that it was a bolt from the blue when in March 1982 the Indian high commission transmitted a third person note from the Indian government to the ministry of defence that the two agreements of 1964 and 1974 were no longer binding. Jayansinghe adds that India thus delivered its *coup de grace* to the two agreements.[13]

End to the Era of Indignity

The trade unions in the plantations were united in their demand that Sri Lankan citizenship should be conferred on the stateless people. What is more, they carried on their agitation both through parliamentary and extra-parliamentary struggles. Mention should be made in this connection to the successful nine-day plantation strike in April 1984 called by Ceylon Workers Congress and supported by all other trade unions. The first major victory was the unanimous decision taken by the all party conference to confer citizenship on 94,000 stateless people. However, there was inordinate delay in the implementation of the assurance and the trade unions again launched a three-month long prayer and meditation campaign from *Tai Pongal* to Tamil new years day in 1986. This agitation finally compelled the government to discard its long record of obduracy and to make the major concession, which fulfilled Indian aspirations.[14] It must also be mentioned that in the India-Sri Lanka Accord, 1987, it was provided that the return of the refugees from Tamil Nadu to Sri Lanka would be linked to the repatriation of Indian passport holders from Sri Lanka. Thondaman told the author that on this crucial issue affecting the people of Indian origin, his opinion was not sought either by New Delhi or by Colombo. However, it goes to the credit of Thondaman that he successfully used the argument that if no solution was found to the problem of the stateless people, India had every right to play its cards in the domestic politics of the island.

The enactment of Citizenship to Stateless Persons Act No 5 of 1986 and Grant of Citizenship to Stateless Persons (Special Provisions) Act 39 of 1988, theoretically ended statelessness among the Indian Tamils. Prime minister Ranasinghe Premadasa, while piloting the bill in parliament, explained the dilemma faced by the government of Sri Lanka. By solving the problem "once and for all" humanely and peacefully, Sri Lanka would be getting rid of a cancer, "a shadow that had been haunting us for several decades". Sri Lanka would be giving a "better deal to the so-called stateless people. They will feel more secure. They will feel for our country because they will now become citizens and not remain as stateless people". Premadasa also pointed out that so long as the problem of the people of Indian origin remained unsolved, "India may have reason to interfere in our internal affairs on the pretext that the persons of Indian origin have been affected."[15] The government of Sri Lanka estimated the number of stateless people to be around 94,000. The government spokesman mentioned that New Delhi had given an undertaking to grant citizenship to the balance of 84,793 applicants within six to eight months. Sri Lanka, on its part, would complete the granting of citizenship within eighteen months.

The future of Indian passport holders still remained a question mark. According to informed sources, their number was estimated to be 84,816 plus the natural increase and the natural increase of the natural increase. As mentioned earlier, they are the residue of the two agreements of 1964 and 1974. The repatriation of Indian citizens to India was suspended in 1984 after the outbreak of the ethnic violence in the island and consequent inflow of refugees into Tamil Nadu. In order to have a proper appreciation of the complexities of the problem, it is necessary to keep in mind certain basic realities. Many who had applied for Indian citizenship and got Indian passports were dead. Others did not want to be repatriated to India to start a new life. In fact, some had even sent applications to the Indian high commission seeking permission to withdraw their applications for citizenship. Some had declared themselves as Sri Lankan citizens in the 1981, 1991 and 2001 census. What is more, during recent years, there had been a movement of young people from the plantations to the urban areas in search of employment. There were no official records of these people. Many had also migrated to the north and the east following the communal violence in 1977 and 1981.

As time went on, a perceptible change started taking place among the major Sinhala political parties on the future of Indian passport holders. The (SLFP) and the UNP, especially their gifted leaders, Chandrika Kumaratunga and Ranil Wikramasinghe, wanted to confer citizenship on Indian passport holders, almost all of whom were born in the island and had taken roots in the country. It also goes to the credit of Indian diplomats that they were able to win over the Janata Vimukti Peramuna (JVP) on this issue. Gradually a consensus developed that citizenship should be conferred on all people of Indian origin living in the island. The citizenship provisions of the draft constitution of 2000, which was introduced in the parliament and could not be passed due to partisan politics, contained two provisions, which would have conferred Sri Lankan citizenship on all persons who were permanently resident in Sri Lanka from 30 October 1964. The second provision provided for Sri Lankan citizenship to the descendants of any person who were permanently resident in Sri Lanka on or after 30 October 1964.

The UNP led coalition government, led by Ranil Wikramasinghe, delinked the citizenship provisions from the draft constitution and introduced the enabling legislation for the conferment of Sri Lankan citizenship to the Indian passport holders and their natural increase. The legislation was passed unanimously because there was convergence of interests among major political parties on the issue. All of them were eager to do justice to a community, which had contributed so much for the economic development of the island. Thus the era of indignity finally came to an end.

Rehabilitation of Sri Lankan Repatriates

Immediately after the Sirmavo-Shastri Pact was signed, the Indian high commission in Colombo launched a publicity campaign among the Indian Tamils to attract them to India. Glossy booklets in English and Tamil were widely distributed in the plantations, which held out the promise of a decent secure life in India. The rehabilitation assistance included employment in the plantations, factories, sugar mills, spinning mills and transport corporations; settlement in land colonies; loans for purchase of land; business loans on attractive terms; housing loans; educational facilities for children and customs and travel concessions. But the hopes were soon to be shattered. Most of the grandiose schemes failed due to bureaucratic bungling and red tapism. For the repatriates, it was a bitter homecoming.

As mentioned earlier, though the process of repatriation was expected to commence in 1965, the Sri Lankan government introduced the enabling legislation only in 1967. Repatriation commenced in 1968 and moved slowly through the seventies. The whole process was callous, brutal and dehumanising. No principle was enunciated either for granting of citizenship or for being repatriated. Also, the settlement of gratuity and provident fund of the workers took inordinate delays, causing them considerable hardships. The Estimates Committee of Indian Parliament has pointed out that Indians awaiting repatriation were often held up in Sri Lanka merely due to this delay.[16]

Rehabilitation is planned on a family basis.[17] After the passport was obtained, the repatriates were required to apply to the Indian high commission in Kandy for a family card. The family card, with details of the family, the type of occupation of its members, amounts and grants of loans to which they are entitled; their place of employment in India etc. is the repatriate's golden key to rehabilitation. The entries in it seal their fate in India. The gullible migrants, totally at sea because of their ignorance of the ways of life in India, fall an easy prey to touts and come to grief sooner or later. The Indian high commission did not find it necessary to start any meaningful counselling for them regarding the facilities available in India.

Before evaluating the effectiveness of the schemes of rehabilitation, it is necessary to highlight certain facts about the repatriates. According to the Indian high commission in Sri Lanka, the occupational break-up of the repatriates are as follows: plantation workers – eighty two per cent; business hawkers – twelve per cent and other categories such as urban labourers, commercial and government employees and estate supervisory personnel – one per cent. Five per cent of the repatriates had assets worth about Rs. 10,000 and, therefore, were not eligible for any rehabilitation assistance. Though the family cards do not contain the caste background, unofficial studies reveal that the overwhelming majority of them belong to the scheduled castes and most backward classes. As far as educational attainments are concerned, thirty three per cent of them are illiterates;thirty nine per cent have studied up to primary level; fourteen per cent up to secondary level and three per cent up to higher secondary level. Because of their low level of educational attainments, most of them could not avail of the preferential quota sanctioned by the state and central governments in white-collar jobs. As far as assets in the form of cash and jewellery are concerned, seventeen per cent had no savings; eleven per cent below Rs. 500; fourteen per cent between Rs. 501 and Rs. 1000; thirteen per cent between Rs. 1001 and Rs. 2000; twenty three per cent between Rs. 2001 and Rs. 3000 and twenty two per cent above Rs. 3001.

The government of India provided rehabilitation assistance to the repatriates under the following heads: 1) Employment in tea, rubber and cinchona plantations and state farm corporations and land colonisation schemes : 5,062 families or 5.3 per cent have been absorbed in plantations in different parts of the state. In plantations employment is provided to two members of the family. 2) The repatriate families, interested in agricultural pursuits, are given three acres of dry land free of cost. Agricultural loan amounting to Rs. 6,850 per family is given for the reclamation of the land, sinking of irrigation wells, purchase of bullocks, implements etc. Two thousand one hundred and sixty one families or 2.3 per cent have been settled under this scheme.3) Employment in cooperative spinning mills. Only one member in the family in the age group of 18-35 is given employment. So far 3, 871 families or four per cent of the repatriates have been employed in various spinning mills in Tamil Nadu. The government of India sanctioned a straight loan of Rs. 20,000 per repatriate to be employed in the cooperative spinning mills to the state government for investing the amount in the share capital of the respective mills. 4) Business loans of Rs. 5,000 per family for self-employment. Seventy six thousand five hundred and sixty families or 78.8 per cent come under this category. The business loan was subsequently raised to Rs. 7,500, in addition to business premises loan of Rs. 2,500 in urban areas and Rs. 1,000 in rural areas. 5) Repatriate Bank schemes. 4,313 families or 4.5 per cent are employed in industries financed by the Repatriate Cooperative Finance and Development Bank. The Bank secures jobs for the repatriates by offering financial incentives to the employers. 6) Purchase of private agricultural land: Repatriate families, who want to pursue agricultural operations, are eligible for loan at the rate of Rs. 2,000 per acre up to three acres of land. 7) All repatriate families are entitled for housing loan up to Rs. 10,000 in urban areas and Rs. 6,000 in the rural areas. The housing loan is disbursed in four instalments.

The repatriates coming from Sri Lanka are permitted to bring along free of customs duty personal belongings and personal jewellery up to Rs. 16,000 and stock-in-trade up to Rs. 16,000. On arrival at Rameshwaram and after formalities of registration and scrutiny of family cards, the repatriates are sent to the two transit camps at Mandapam and Tiruchirapally. It is the height of irony that the very spot where the repatriates arrive at Mandapam was used by the government of Ceylon to quarantine labourers before they were sent to the island. With inadequate facilities of water supply, sanitation and electricity the repatriates huddle in dingy, claustrophobic rooms. There they stay for a week or few months, till they are sent to their place of vocation. On admission to the transit camp, cash allowance is paid to families bringing assets less than Rs. 5,000, at the rate ranging from Rs. 110 to Rs. 557.50 per month, depending on the size of the family, for a maximum period of three months. They are also given subsidised ration at the rate fifty seven paise per kilogram of rice and medical facilities free of cost.

The entire financial burden of rehabilitation is undertaken by the central government and the planning of rehabilitation is also done by the ministry of rehabilitation in New Delhi. The government of Tamil Nadu does the implementation of various schemes. Since most of the repatriates are of Tamil origin, the major physical burden of rehabilitation has fallen on Tamil Nadu. As on 31 January 1984, out of the 1,07,345 families, who have come to India, 83,690 or seventy eight per cent have been rehabilitated in Tamil Nadu alone. The balance has been rehabilitated in Kerala, Andhra Pradesh, Karnataka and Andaman and Nicobar islands. Even those who were assigned to these states got dissatisfied soon and flocked back to Tamil Nadu. Demonstrations by the repatriates settled in Andhra Pradesh were a regular phenomenon before the office of the Director of Rehabilitation in Chennai.

The business loan is the most popular form of rehabilitation assistance and is also the classic illustration of government's apathy towards the repatriates. As stated earlier, 78.8 per cent of the repatriates came under this category. For officials in the Indian high commission in Kandy, sanctioning a business loan was the easiest way to get rid of a repatriate. Being plantation workers, where they depended on the management from birth to death, the repatriates lacked the initiative, the drive and the willingness to take risk, without which a business operation cannot be thought of. But repatriates agreed to business loan because they had no other option available.

The business loan distributed in India has been invested in petty trades – which mostly consist of tea stalls, food stalls, grocery shops, cloth shops, vegetable shops, cycle shops, bullock carts and laundry. They are concentrated in the district of Nilgiris, in Valparai in Coimbatore district and in Kodaikanal in Madurai district. According to a survey conducted by the Centre for Research in New International Economic Order, only twelve per cent of those who received business loans "have utilised the amount in one trade or another. All others have failed miserably."

The objective of the Agricultural Land Colonisation Scheme, in which 2.3 per cent of the repatriates are engaged, was to make the repatriate an owner cultivator, but here again the aim was not fulfilled. The land colonisation schemes are located in the districts of Ramanathapuram, Madurai, Coimbatore, Thirunelveli, Salem and Dharmapuri districts, where the average rainfall is 850 mm. On an average, almost a quarter to one third of the land could not be made cultivable even after three or four years of dogged efforts. The crop produced could sustain the family only for five to six months; for the remaining period, the repatriates had to look for jobs elsewhere.

Of the various schemes of rehabilitation, the most successful is the category of employment in plantations. It is unfortunate that only 5.3 per cent of the repatriates could be absorbed into this category. The environment and working conditions are ideally suited for repatriates who were engaged in the same vocation in Sri Lanka. In addition to daily wages, the workers are also entitled for paid holidays, living quarters, medical facilities and free education for children. If the government of India had made sincere efforts to employ these people in plantations in different parts of India, the repatriates could have been successfully integrated into the Indian society.

About four per cent of the repatriates are employed in spinning mills and factories financed by the Repatriate Cooperative Finance and Development Bank. For many repatriates, the change over from the plantations to industries is an arduous task. Moreover, only one member of the family gets employment in the industry, whereas in the plantations in Sri Lanka all able bodied persons used to get employment. In terms of pay and allowances, those engaged in this category are better off than others. However, the management frequently complains that the repatriates are not up to the mark and in case of retrenchment or lock out, they are the first to be affected.

A large number of repatriates, after failing in small business and land colonisation, have flocked to Nilgiris and Kodaikanal in search of a vocation akin to what they had in Sri Lanka. As mentioned earlier, the repatriate families, who have been employed by the Tamil Nadu government owned tea estates, known as the TANTEA, are relatively well off having secure jobs, minimum wages, residential and medical facilities. But there are also hundreds of repatriate families, who were migrating to Kotagiri every year having reached the end of the tether in the plains. These people find employment in small-scale tea holdings owned by the Badaga community. A kind of semi-bonded labour system prevailed in some of the repatriate settlements, with attendant insecurity, human degradation and unimaginable humiliation. They were paid less than the prescribed minimum wages and their working hours extended from early morning till late evening. The repatriate colonies lacked basic amenities like water, electricity, schools, health centres and even approach roads. What is more, for a long time, there were under currents of social tension between the Badagas and the repatriate Tamils, occasionally leading to violence and consequent detention of repatriate leaders.

The inhuman conditions under which the bonded Sri Lankan repatriates eked out their living in the Kodaikanal hills came into sharp focus in June 1986 due to the untiring efforts of voluntary organisations, human rights activists, a sympathetic sub-collector and, above all, a vigilant Supreme Court. The Sri Lankan repatriates lived in isolated colonies in the forests of Kodaikanal. They were lured from the plains by the contractors on the promise of a decent life to peel the bark of the wattle trees, which grew all around. The contractors sold the wattle to Tan India, a company engaged in the production of wattle extract, an essential ingredient in tanning. The repatriates huddled in tiny, ill ventilated, thatched huts with hardly any warm clothing to protect them from the biting cold.

Medical care was non-existent. They had to work seven days a week, for five or six years continuously, with no regular wages. And, above all, they were ruled by fear. Escape was unthinkable, because they had no money, they had no friends and they did not know where to go. Their occasional protests and resistance were met with savage reprisals. Even their womenfolk were not spared and many young girls fell easy victims to sexual exploitation.

Passage of Time solves the Problem

The above survey clearly brings out that the rehabilitation schemes undertaken from 1968 to 1984 miserably failed and most of the repatriates were marginalized and pauperised. What is more, they also felt alienated. However, as time went on, number of factors contributed to the mitigation of their suffering, and what is more, to their successful assimilation and integration into the Tamil Nadu society. The elder generation among the repatriates, who were nostalgic about their lives in Sri Lanka, are dead and a new generation, born in India, have taken their place. They have become an integral part of the working class in Tamil Nadu. In terms of political allegiance, they support the Dravidian parties - the DMK and the AIADMK -, the left parties or the Congress. Repatriation stopped in 1984 and twenty-two years have passed since the last repatriate reached the shores of India. What is more, the conferment of citizenship to the Indian passport holders by the Sri Lankan government has solved the problem once and for all. Voluntary organisations from among the repatriates, like the *Malaiha Makkal Maru Vazhvu Manram*, founded by RR Sivalingam and Thiruchanduran, sensitised the general public in Tamil Nadu about the problems of repatriates and the necessity to give them a fair deal. The work initiated by Sivalingam and Thiruchanduran is being carried forward by a new team of activists led by Chandrasekharan.

One silver living should be highlighted. The younger generation among the repatriates are availing of the reservation facilities in the field of education, which is given to the scheduled castes and backward classes. There is definitely an upward mobility and the repatriates are taking up jobs like that of teachers, mechanics, nurses, shop keepers and white collar workers. Sri Lanka watchers in India feel that such a transformation has not taken place among the Indian Tamils living in Sri Lanka.

Author concludes this paper with an extract from the Report of the Satyodaya Study team, which came to South India in September-October 2000, to study the living conditions of the repatriates. To quote:

We met scores of repatriates both on the plantations and the roads. We found them unanimously happy about the freedom they experience in India. "At the beginning" they said to us again and again, "we had a lot of difficulties, as we did not know the country. Now, though the work is hard, we realize that hard work is our only gateway to the future". "Above all", they said, " here we have freedom. On the other hand, in Sri Lanka our life on the tea estate is an open prison ... Here we can build our own future."[18]

This essay is partly based on author's earlier writings on the subject.

References

1 Paul Caspersz, "The Other Tamils", *Frontier,* 10 September 1983, pp. 3-6

2 "Estate Labour", *Economic Review*, vol. 5, March 1980, pp. 3-18

3 Cited in *Justice, Peace and Love – A voice Crying from the Plantations of Sri Lanka* (A collection of letters by Pio Champa), Balangoda, 1981, p. 1 A.

4 Cited in Babu Lal Gupta, *Political and Civic Status of Indians in Ceylon,* Agra, 1963, p.8

5. W.T. Jayasinghe, *The Indo-Ceylon Talks : The Politics of Immigrant Labour*, Colombo, 2002, p. 3.

6 *Ibid.*, p. 48

7 S.V. Kodikara, *Indo-Ceylon Relations since Independence,* Colombo, 1965, p. 114

8 C.S. Jha, *From Bandung to Tashkent, Glimpses of India's Foreign Policy,* Madras, 1983, pp. 276-277

9 Letter from Lal Bahadur Shastri, prime minister of India to Sirimavo Bandaranaike, prime minister of Ceylon, 30 October, 1964 and letter from Indira Gandhi, prime minister of India to Sirimavo Bandaraniake, prime minister of Ceylon, 27 January 1974, *The Hindu,* 31 October 1964 and 28 January 1974.

10 President Jayawardene mentioned these figures in the 27th Convention of the Ceylon Indian Congress in 1982. Cited in Clarence Fernando, "No Early End to the Problems of Stateless People in Sight", *Commerce*, 22 May 1982, pp. 88-83.

11 Interview with Thomas Abraham, former high commissioner for India in Sri Lanka

12 Thomas Abraham, "The Repatriation Riddle", *The Hindu,* 16 April 1986

13 Jayasinghe, n. 5, p. 450.

14 For details of the parliamentary and non-parliamentary struggles see S. Nadesan, *A History of the Upcountry Tamil People,* Colombo, 1983.

16 *Sixteenth Report of the Estimates Committee, 1980-1981,* New Delhi, 1981, p. 4.

17 The facts and figures mentioned in the section on rehabilitation are taken from 1) V. Suryanarayan (ed), *Rehabilitation of Sri Lankan Repatriates: A Critical Appraisal,* Monograph 7, Centre for South and Southeast Asian studies, University of Madras, 1986 and M. Vamadevan, *Sri Lankan Repatriates in Tamil Nadu: Rehabilitation and Integration,* Chennai, 1989.

18 *The Sri Lankan Repatriates in South India (A Report of the Satyodaya Study Team to South India, 19 September 2000 – 6 October 2000)*, Kandy, 2001, pp. 10-11.

7

Facilitating the Return of Sri Lankan Refugees in India

S. H. Hasbullah

Introduction

It has been a remarkable achievement that there has been a spontaneous return of Internally Displaced Persons (IDPs) from the time of Cease–Fire Agreement (CFA) signed between the Sri Lanka government and the Liberation Tigers of Tamil Eelam (LTTE) in February 2002 in Sri Lanka. It was estimated that nearly one fourth of the IDPs returned home during the first year of the CFA. According to the present estimate, nearly half of the total IDPs, who wanted and were able, had returned home especially in the northern part of the country. Concerning the return of refugees, the flow was not significant to date. In the case of refugees and expatriates living in European countries and North America, a significant number of them were able to visit their homes in the war affected north and east. At the same time, Sri Lankan refugees living in India could not do the same through a normal channel due to various legal and bilateral problems. Thus, some have attempted to cross the Palk Straits (a narrow sea passage between India and Sri Lanka) illegally to reach Sri Lanka. There were a number of human tragedies associated with this illegal return of refugees. Though the trend in the illegal return of refugees has been continuing, no effective measures have been taken to prevent the flow of refugees illegally across the Palk Straits. The governments of both sides are helpless due to various practical as well as legal reasons in recognizing or facilitating repatriation of Sri Lankan refugees from India. Similarly, multilateral organization such as UNHCR faces problems in facilitating a formal return of refugees to Sri Lanka. Therefore, it is necessary to understand the problems associated with the return of refugees to Sri Lanka. At the same time, it is recognized the importance of mutual country cooperation between India and Sri Lanka in planning and in facilitating the return of refugees.

The paper addresses the following questions. Why has UNHCR not been able to facilitate the return of Sri Lankan refugees in India? Secondly, why have the refugees taking so much risk in crossing the border illegally? Whether the situation in Sri Lanka is conducive for a large-scale return of refugees from India? Is it possible to facilitate a phased out return of refugees who desperately want to return home?

The Issue of Return Home

The issue of return home in the context of refugees and IDPs is a subject, which had been given greater attention by those who seek durable solution to the problem of displacement. The issue of return could be looked at from negative and positive perspectives.

In a positive situation, return gives a new hope and opportunity for refugees to start a new life. For some people, the new situation could be better than the situation that they lived before. Refugees return home with new skills and experiences that could very well be used in building a new life. Return will give new opportunities for refugees to re-integrate with the rest of the people. Return may also erase old and backward attitudes and would stimulate a progressive thinking about the future. Return re-unit family and society. It integrated different communities. More importantly, their return also integrates isolated communities to into a greater global integration. The positive attitudes of expatriates towards their future return may encourage social, economic and cultural transactions between the host and home countries. Such positive trend is beneficial to the country of origin as well as to the host countries. If this hypothetical situation of positive impact of the refugee return is a reality, it will bring the nations closer and would encourage healthy interactions between nations.

At the same time, the return home especially without a proper plan and action could lead further suffering to the returnees. In fact, the undesirable circumstances in which the displaced people had to leave their homes have been constant remainders when they consider return home. Evidently, there are evidences that the returnees faced many hardships including repeated displacement even after they return home. However, the most preferred option identified by the United Nations as a durable solution to the displacement is return home.

The History of Conflict Induced Displacement in Sri Lanka

Within the last two decades, more than three million people have been displaced in Sri Lanka due to ethnic conflict and civil war alone[1]. This displacement, however, was confined to the people of the northern and eastern provinces and the people of the border areas of the provinces adjoining them. The displaced people belong to all three ethnic communities - the Tamils, the Sinhalese and the Muslims. Many are still waiting in welfare centres and refugee camps anticipating their return home.

Escalating ethnic tensions and prolonged civil war in the country have been often referred to as the reasons for recent displacement of people. The immediate cause driving affected people to abandon their habitats and seek refuge in other areas vary by region and by community. The patterns of displacement over the period reflect the differences in the causes and the magnitude of the displacement. Displacement has had tremendous socio-economic and cultural impacts on the people subjected to it. Emerging land issues as a result of large-scale displacement is one of most important problems of the day as well as the subject of this study. In order to understand the gravity of the land question arising from displacement, it is necessary to know the causes, trends and the destruction of displacement and displaced people.

Displacement due to ethnic tensions is by no means a very recent phenomenon. It occurred during the Sinhala-Muslim disturbances of 1915. It also occurred during the 1958 communal disturbances resulting in the displacement of Tamil people living in predominantly Sinhala areas and likewise caused the displacement of Sinhala people living in predominantly Tamil areas. Again, the 1983 riots against Tamils caused the displacement of more than 100,000 Tamil people (see Table 1).

From 1986 onwards, the causes and directions of displacement of people have changed. The major cause of the displacement was ethnic tensions and war. The war was mainly confined to the north and east. But ethnic tensions and other forms of threats against minorities existed in all areas of the country. War related displacement originated from mainly from the north and east. The movements of the displaced were within and outside of the north and east.

Table 1: Trends in Conflict Induced Displacement in Sri Lanka, 1983 - 2003

Year and Month	*Number Displaced*	*Year and Month*	*Number Displaced*
1983 July	100,000 (Estimate)	1992 January	590,000
1986 October	250,000	1992 March	595,000
1990 June	150,000	1992 April	580,000
1990 July	480,000	1993 April	607,000
1990 August	840,000	1994 May	598,000
1990 September	977,000	1995 January	505,000
1990 October	910,000	1995 April	515,000
1990 November	805,000	1996 January	787,000
1991 January	1030,000	1996 April	790,000
1991 February	700,000	1996 May	840,000
1991 March	700,000	1997 October	788,000
1991 May	540,000	2000 June	673,000
1991 June	525,000	2001 March	750,000
1991 August	780,000	2002 January	683,000
1991 October	780,000	2003 May	500,000

Source: Calculated from monthly records of IDPs from documents available at the Ministry of Rehabilitation, various Years.

The underlying cause of recent displacement is the ethnic question involving the Sinhalese, Tamil and the Muslims of Sri Lanka resulting in an armed conflict. The immediate causes may be identified as fear of Tamil people because of the advance of the government security forces, establishment of army camps leading to displacement, movement of people living near army camps to avoid being caught in the crossfire, need to escape from sea and air attacks by the security forces, forcible expulsion of Sinhalese, Tamils and Muslims by militants, ethnic tensions between Muslims and Tamils leading to the displacement of both communities, shortage of food and other essential items in the war zone areas.

The total number of displaced people has consistently been at a high level (Table 1). But there are fluctuations at the regional level, resulting from the shifting of the war into new areas causing displacement of people in that area combined with a slack in war activities in other areas. During the early stages of the conflict, Tamil people fled to the northern and eastern parts of Sri Lanka. The Muslims and Sinhalese who fled from predominantly Tamil areas of the northern and eastern provinces live in refugee camps or among their friends and relatives in Puttalam, Anuradhapura and Pollonnaruwa districts.

Sri Lankan Refugees

About a million of them fled the country and sought refuge in foreign countries. Of the total, nearly ninety per cent of Sri Lankan refugees live now in developed countries.[2] North America is one of the notable concentrations of Sri Lanka refugees in the world at present. The overwhelming majority of the Sri Lanka refugees are Tamil minority of the country who feel that they had been systematically discriminated by Sinhala majority government and by the ethnic war. It was estimated that between 1989 and 1998, about 60,000 Sri Lankans applied for asylum North America alone. But this number does not include other categories of expatriates in North America. There are several thousand Sri Lankan refugees are living in other parts (Europe, Australia, etc) of the developed countries of the world.

India is having an estimated 100,000 Sri Lankan refugees. UNHCR provide a statistics of Sri Lankan refugees where it indicates that in the year 2004 the estimated Sri Lankan refugees in India is about 71,000 (see Table 3). Those refugees are living 133 camps located in different part of Tamil Nadu (see Table 2). Others are living with friends and relatives and some used to be hosted in special places as some of documents indicates (——).

Table 2: Sri Lankan Refugees in India by District as on 31 December 1997

District	*Number of Camps*	*No of Families*	*No of Persons*
Kancheepuram	9	339	1292
Cuddalore	8	390	1462
Vellore	9	1061	4021
Tiruvannamalai	16	872	3408
Salem	9	658	2357
Dharmapuri	13	946	3626
Coimbatore	8	768	2951
Erode	4	1065	3993
Tiruchy	2	789	2956
Karur	2	584	2288
Perambalur	1	84	309
Pudukottai	3	950	3293
Villupuram	3	278	1131
Madurai	4	1279	4934
Dindugal	8	857	3303
Ramanathapuram	1	1866	6006
Sivaganga	7	933	3518
Virudhunagar	6	884	3399
Tirunelveli	8	792	2844
Tuticorin	3	364	1470
Kanniyakumari	4	255	980
Chennai	1	2	2
Tiruvallur	2	720	2741
Namakal	2	356	1244
Total	133	17092	63528

Source: Source is not given

The flow of refugees from Sri Lanka to India and especially to Tamil Nadu has been for a long time. In fact, the South Indian state of Tamil Nadu lies only twenty-two miles from Sri Lanka. Also more than fifty millions Tamils are living in Tamil Nadu. Tamil refugees began arriving in Tamil Nadu in the wake of the widespread violence against the Tamil community in July and

August 1983. In fact at that time, the majority of the (Tamil) refugees were from southern part of Sri Lanka where the Sinhala are the majority.

But army operations in north- east Sri Lanka from February 1985 resulted in people fleeing to Tamil Nadu in large numbers. By the beginning of the 1987 there were around 50,000 refugees in the Kottapattu, Trichy and Mandapam camps and some 100,000 living with friends, relatives or in rented accommodation according to available information.

Almost all refugees in camps in Tamil Nadu had returned to Sri Lanka by the time the Indian Peace Keeping Forces (IPKF) was withdrawn on 25 March 1990. According to Rodgers,[3] in Sri Lanka since 1987, there have been three major programmes design to promote the return of Sri Lankan Tamil refugees or to offer a safe alternative to flight abroad. The first of this assistance was the UNHCR special program of limited assistance to returnees in Sri Lanka, which returned 25,000 Tamil refugees from south India to port in northern Sri Lanka between December 1987 and April 1989. Second had begun September 1990 where UNHCR's programme of immediate relief assistance to returnees and displaced persons in Sri Lanka. The third one was the Indo-Sri Lankan government repatriation programme which begun in January 1992 and plans to voluntary return 30,000 Tamil refugees in south India to northern Sri Lanka.

But with escalation of hostilities from the middle of 1990 (from June 1990) which spreads to entire north and east. The spread and intensity of war between government forces and the LTTE has resulted in the displacement of thousands of people. The total number of internally displaced person has risen during this to more than one million and remained at high level for while (Table 1). Thus, the US Committee for Refugees' special report on Sri Lanka titled this report as "the Island of Refugees". The war started in 1990 has continued for a decade, till the time of the cease-fire agreement signed between these two warring factions. The displacement spilled over to other countries and to India in large number during the intense war during the above period. Those refugees who are now living in refugee camps were displaced during the above-mentioned period and have not returned to the country for the reasons of feeling insecure because of continuing war.

Return and Challenges Faced By Returnees

Since the signing of CFA, the emphasis of the peace talks has been on the return of displaced people - both internally displaced people (IDP) and those Sri Lankan who have fled to other countries. The number returned has been steady since February 2002 and it has reached to about 400,000 in early 2005 (see Tables). It was the IDPs who formed the largest number of returnees while the return of refugees from India and other countries was not significant during this period.

Jaffna district was the largest recipient of the returnees while Mannar, Mullaitivu; Kilinochchi districts of the northern province have also received a significant number of returnees during the last three years. The majority of IDPs who had returned had been displaced within the district while only less than five per cent of the returnees to north and east come from outside of the region. About half of the IDPs have yet to return home. In the mean time, the recent ethnic disturbances in Trincomalee district have added another 10,000 newly displaced families into the pool of total IDPs who are waiting to return home if the security situation improves and land issues are resolved.

It is expected that the movement of persons to and within the conflict-affected areas will continue although the trend may be slow in the near future for the following reasons. Many villages where returnees are expected to return are contaminated with landmines. Others are high security zones and entirely off–limits to civilians. A number of former habitations today are covered by jungle and not even the minimum of community infrastructure is available. At the same time, recent physical needs assessments by various development agencies indicate that much of the physical infrastructure such as roads, hospital, schools, etc. in the areas of returnees are in a state of near total destruction because of the war. Much of these necessary structures have to be rebuilt to facilitate the return of displaced people. But the funds are yet to be found for the rebuilding of war torn areas where returnees are expected to return. At the same time, a certain population of potential returnees (e.g., Muslim IDPs) has particularly strong concerns about the security situation they might face if they return home. From the available information, it is evident that conditions are not yet conducive to large-scale, organized resettlement of IDPs as well as refugees. In the mean time, the present stalemate in the peace talks may discourage displaced from returning home

Spontaneous Return of Refugees from India

The Cease-fire signed between Sri Lankan government and LTTE that lasted till today could not help the return of refugees from India. As Table 4 shows the majority of the Sri Lankan refugees in India are originally from the northern province. The former conflict zone, the north and the east, are divided by powers of armies and are being demarcated between these two warring factions. Though there has been an existence of cease-fire, tension has continued remain till today in those areas. Thus, it has been considered, as a large-scale return of refugees from India may not be possible. But the refuges has continued to arrive using illegal methods. As Table shows the spontaneous return of Sri Lankan refugees using illegal rout has continued to remain high during the period.

There are two thoughts of the timing and methods of the return of refugees from India. One type of thought is that until the situation is absolutely conducive for the return, Sri Lankan refugees in India will have to wait (———). The other is that the Sri Lankan refugees are with a lot of hardship and suffering as a result of continuing of their displacement. Thus their return needs to be planned and facilitated (——).

Table 3: The Trends in the Return of Refugees from India during the Cease-Fire Period

Year	*Spontaneous*	*UNHCR Facilitated*	*Total*
2002	1356	71	1427
2003	3612	1093	4605
2004	5681	1386	7067
Total	10549	2550	13099

Source: Calculated from Statistics of UNHCR, Colombo, 2004

Facilitating the Return of Refugees

Concerning aspect of facilitating the return of Sri Lankan refugees in India, there were a number of thoughts and suggestions presented state government and non-state agencies. There are two suggestions put forward by leading organizations in the welfare of those refuges. One is by Refugee International. Other is by offer.

Table 4: Return of Refugees from India by District after Cease-Fire Agreement

District	*2002*	*2003*	*2004*	*Total*
Mannar	203	1965	3762	5930
Jaffna	1068	1051	548	2667
Vavuniya	46	699	1601	2346
Trincomalee	59	221	459	739
Mullaitivu	8	316	339	663
Kilinochchi	28	233	321	582
Other N-E Districts	15	45	6	66
Other Districts	-	75	31	106
Total	1427	4605	7067	13099

Source: Calculated from Statistics of UNHCR, Colombo, 2004

Table 5: Return of IDPs and Refugees from the Time of Cease-Fire Agreement

Year	*IDPs*	*Refugee from India*	*From Other Countries*	*Total*
2002	269012	1427	-	270439
2003	76722	4605	493	81820
2004	28249	7067	85	35401
Total	373983	13099	578	387660

Source: Calculated from Statistics of UNHCR, Colombo, 2004

Refugee International has conducted a survey among the Sri Lankan refuges in India and had come out with some specific suggestions concerning the return of refugees. Refugee International placed the responsibility of facilitating the return to Indian and Sri Lankan governments and to UNHCR.

To the government of India, Refugee International suggests that the government of India must permit the UNHCR and other international aid agencies access to the camps to assist the refugees. It also suggests that the government must ease its restrictions on the movement of Sri Lankan refugees living in the camps.

Table 6: District of Origin of Sri Lankan Refugees in India

District	*Total Number of Refugees*	*%*
Mannar	20222	32
Vavuniya	17300	27
Jaffna	9282	14
Kilinochchi	6401	10
Trincomalee	5956	09
Mullaitivu	4084	06
From other Districts	943	01
Total	64188	100

Source: Calculated from Statistics of UNHCR, Colombo, 2004

To the Sri Lankan government, Refugee International indicates that as progress toward peace is made, visit the refugee camps, ascertain the residents' problems and concerns, and discuss with UNHCR and the government of India, with input from the refugees, the details of repatriation to Sri Lanka, so that plans can be made on when and how to bring back the refugees safely and with dignity to their homeland.

At the same time, the responsibilities of the UNHCR are according to the Refugee International's suggestions that UNHCR must continue to request permission from the government of India to visit the camps to facilitate the return of refugees willing to go back at this time; publish and have distributed in the camps a pamphlet outlining UNHCR policy toward returns to Sri Lanka to ensure there is no misunderstanding by the refugees; when conditions become more favourable for refugees returning to Sri Lanka, in collaboration with the governments of Sri Lanka and India, provide an alternative means of transportation so that refugees have the option of returning by boat with all their belongings. Finally, it says that in collaboration with the government of India; make plans for the permanent resettlement or relocation of those few refugees who do not wish to return to Sri Lanka.

The ofERR, an organization working among Sri Lankan refugees in India called for series of consultation meetings among the refugees after the signing of CFA between the government of

Sri Lanka and the LTTE. Finally, ofERR arrived at a declaration on the issue of the return of Sri Lanka refugees in India.. Some of the highlights of sections of that declaration are the following:

- A lasting peace is a prerequisite for the return.
- There must be specific provision for the return of refugees through the inclusion of written accords that guarantee the rights, safety and security of those returning and their social and material well-being.
- Returns can only take place on a voluntary basis, upholding international standards of safety and dignity, and underwritten by a bilateral agreement between the governments of India and Sri Lanka.
- Such returns should only take place when refugees can return to their homes or home areas. Transferring refugees from camps in India to camps in Ceylon will impede peace rather than promote it.
- IDPs should be resettled, prior to the return of refugees to make available the homes of refugees, currently occupied, and as a demonstrable indicator of an effective rehabilitation process.
- Risks to the safety and security of refugees, such as landmines and explosive remnants of war (ERW) must be fully cleared and removed, before refugees can return home.
- The agreement must contain a commitment to the speedy reintegration of refugees through the recognition of identity documents, acquired in exile, such as refugee identity certificates and those documents certifying births, marriages and deaths as well as educational and professional qualifications acquired outside Ceylon.
- The agreement must contain a clear commitment to restorative justice at both the material and social levels. Refugees and other Ceylonese who have lost property, relatives and livelihoods must be adequately compensated. Provision should also be made for a Truth and Reconciliation Commission (TRC) that promotes a meaningful healing process in all segments of Ceylonese society.

Conclusion

The subject of the return of Sri Lankan refugees in India is surrounded by series of complex issues. They need to be investigated well before taking decision on this matter. It is necessary to understand the socio-economic and psychological status of the refugees and properness for the return. This will have to be done among refugees in India. At the same time, it is also necessary to investigate ground situation of the original places where the refugees will be returning ultimately. During the last two decades, there have been a number of changes in the places of origin of the refugees. They all have to be taken into account when planning the return.

References

1. Tsunami in December 2004 also caused much disaster to the people of this as well. Total number of deaths in Sri Lanka by Tsunami Disaster amounts to 31, 229 and 4,100 people have disappeared. And 516,150 people were displaced and 250,000 houses were wiped out by Tsunami in few minutes. Eight districts in Sri Lanka have been badly affected by this disaster and total losses across all sectors amount to billions of rupees.
2. Tamil Refugee International Network, 1997
3. Malcom Rodgers, *Refugees and International Aid Sri lanka : A case Study Joint ILO-UNHCR Meeting on Ineternational Aid as a Means to Reduce the Need for Emigration,* Geneva:UNHCR, May 1992.

SECTION-IV
MARITIME COOPERATION BETWEEN INDIA AND SRI LANKA

8

Role of Maritime Forces in Disaster Management

R.S. Vasan

The Tsunami that struck many coasts in the Indian Ocean on 26 December 2004 has indeed been the most major event of the century in terms of a natural disaster striking so many countries simultaneously when it brought large scale loss of life, damage, destruction and despair. In the Indian context it is the first time that many Indians even heard of the term. Enough has been written and discussed about the origin of the Tsunami on that fateful day along with the scientific explanations with graphic details. From the point of view of maritime forces in India namely the Indian navy and the coast guard, it was a challenge to firstly try and save the drowning by their rescue efforts and then secondly provide relief measures to see that the people who survived the tragedy were provided life saving equipment, food and other relief material till the civil administration was able to take control and various measures both long term and short term.

While that was the event of the century, there were two subsequent watershed incidents in 2005. The first one was during the south west monsoons when torrential rains resulting in large-scale destruction and death hit Mumbai.

While this was the story on the west coast, some four months later, it was the turn of Tamil Nadu to suffer the same fate during the north east monsoons. Here again, there were a total of five depressions that caused heavy rains with attendant destruction and inflicted heavy damage and loss of lives. It appears that Chennai may have responded marginally better than its counter part on the west coast in tackling the relief measures. It is also a fact that both the cities in comparison fared much better than New Orleans, which could not come to grips with Katrina and its aftermath.

The events in the last one year commencing with the Tsunami has clearly brought out the need for us to be prepared and to take stock of the assets to ensure that our contingencies are in place and we are proactive in our approach in mitigating natural disasters.

This paper aims to look at these three events and analyse them to draw lessons for the future. What stood out during the Tsunami was the participation of our navy and the coast guard in a show of solidarity with our neighbours despite the tragedy even along our own eastern coast. The event brought out the inherent strengths of the country and indicated to the rest of the world that is poised to take a lead role in such contingencies in the region.

Let us look at the Tsunami first and see what lessons can be drawn from the event. After the earthquake, which registered richter 8.5, the sea just erupted with enormous force and created the Tsunami. The released energy that was transferred to the surrounding seas resulted in the waves that travelled at incredible speeds. After the neighbouring South Eastern countries, it was the turn of our strategic outpost Car Nicobar to be hit with devastating effect. The Indian air force station at Car Nicobar with its infrastructure and buildings were damaged along with the loss of lives too. There was considerable anxiety about the tribals[1] who have avoided contact with the civil administration. It has been indicated that the telephone call from the island to Delhi went to a wrong person and though the news was known, no one in living memory had seen or remembered what a Tsunami was. The Tsunami took just about three and a half hours to travel from the Andaman & Nicobar to reach the eastern coast of India.[2] The initial reporting by the media did not give any indications of the extent of the damage or the intensity of the waves that lashed the eastern shores. With every subsequent updates and live pictures being transmitted it was clear that the nation was going through a marine tragedy of immense proportions. From the interviews aired with the top naval officers at that time it was clear that there was no clear understanding of the dimensions of the catastrophe as it inundated fishing villages and caused havoc along the entire coast.

The pictures from our south eastern neighbour and southern neighbour were particularly disturbing as the scales of death and devastation grew with each report. The minimum force levels of helicopters of the coast guard and the navy were trying to do their best by trying to save those who were washed away. Available ships were sailed with despatch to the rescue of people. The passage of the Tsunami was as if it moved at ferocious speed stealthily with no visible indication on the surface and stalked its prey along the coasts. It built up its energy and broke up all along the coast. Even the residual energy on breaking up allowed it to travel many kilometres inland carrying with it people, boats, bridges, trees and even houses.

While the navy and the coast guard got busy along the coast, it was left to the civil administration and the NGOs to rush to the rescue inland. The criticism that not enough was done was heard in many places along the eastern coast. Yet, the speed at which the civil administration was able to gear up its civil and military machinery was still commendable as it was for the first time that the nation had witnessed the Tsunami in many decades of public memory. It is not the intention of this paper to analyse the strengths or weaknesses of the civil machinery. The analysis is aimed more at looking at the actions taken by the navy and the coast guard and to see how it can be improved up on.

The supreme commander of the armed forces had this to say while addressing the joint session of parliament last year on 25 February 2005. "I must place on record the Nation's appreciation of the rescue, relief and rehabilitation work undertaken by state and local governments, the armed forces and non-government organizations." He brought out the element of the surprise by stating that "Given the nature of the disaster and the fact that this part of the world had not been visited upon by a tsunami in the living memory of anyone in this region, there was an element of surprise."

He went on to add that[3] "The Indian Navy, Air Force, Coast Guard and Central Paramilitary forces played a heroic role in providing immediate relief not just to our people but also to the affected people in Sri Lanka, Maldives and Indonesia."

The way ahead was definitely chalked out in his assertion that "We must convert this tragedy into an opportunity by modernizing the maritime economy and protecting the coastal ecology". The president also indicated that the government would shortly create a National Disaster Management Authority. A Central legislation on disaster management would soon be introduced in parliament. He recommended that this authority should have a strong science and technology component built into its activities.

The president's address provides the backdrop for some deliberations on the roles of the two maritime services post Tsunami in the Indian context. The armed forces traditionally are always prepared with a well-oiled structure to be able to rush to the aid of the civil authorities in times of need such as the one witnessed now. The command structure, the infrastructure, the mobility, availability of trained manpower makes it easy to utilise the services of the armed forces under such trying conditions. In addition, aid to civil power is a secondary task assigned to the armed forces.

Before undertaking a review of the roles of the two maritime services, we could very briefly look at the way the operations were conducted post tsunami by the Indian navy and the Indian coast guard. Not having witnessed one, and not having the benefit of recorded history about the way the Tsunami affected the Indian sub continent, it took some time for the scales of the tragedy to register in the minds of the planners both military and civil. But, it is definitely to the credit of the agencies concerned that they rose as one and provided help in a manner that makes us proud as Indians. It is not that there were no hiccups, but looking at the scales of the tragedy and its widespread impact, the manner in which our maritime and armed forces reached out alongside their civilian counterparts definitely has brought in a lot of cheer and confidence in disaster mitigation.

Soon after the realisation of the extent of the tragedy, the navy and the coast guard swung into action on our shores with ships, helicopters, aircraft and marine forces pressed into service. As this paper is aimed at examining the tasks undertaken by the two maritime forces, details of similar exemplary work undertaken by the air force, the army and other agencies are not being discussed. Plenty of relief material, medical supplies and logistics were moved to even remote corners. While essentially, the entire exercise was aimed at providing immediate help, there was urgent need to save lives minutes after the tsunami stuck the shores in Tamil Nadu, Andhra, Kerala and Pondicherry. The operations were mounted in different parts of the sub continent and the affected Indian Ocean Region (IOR) countries. They were also codenamed depending on the area of operation to enable ease of reference and coordination. A brief description is given in the succeeding paragraphs. These are based on the briefing provided by the navy and the integrated defence head quarters (IDHQs) and also the portals that were updated during the Tsunami.

Operation Madad[4]

This was mainly for the rescue and relief operations undertaken within our country. As it was the Tamil Nadu coast that bore the brunt of the Tsunami major efforts were in fact concentrated along the Tamil Nadu coast. Ships, aircraft, helicopters and trained personnel were pressed into service alongside the civil agencies. The survey units and the naval/coast guard divers played a major role in clearing the approaches and ensuring that the channels leading to the ports were cleared for operation in a short time. The prompt aerial survey and recovery of survivors in the initial stages and dead bodies during the later stages by both the forces despite odds and limitations of the SAR helicopter are noteworthy.

Operation Sea Waves

While Madad was confined to the eastern coast and our own coast, operation sea waves was launched in the sensitive Andaman & Nicobar group of Islands. It is also the first time that the IDHQs was seen actively participating in the planning and conduct of the rescue efforts. The armed forces launched operation "Sea Waves" for relief, rescue and evacuation in the wake of Tsunami disaster, which was coordinated by Integrated Defence Staff (IDS). A total of twenty one IN ships, twelve helicopters and four fixed wing aircrafts of the Indian navy were engaged in relief operations in the Tsunami affected areas, of which five ships were deployed in Nicobar group of island, four in Nancowry Group, LCU in Car Nicobar and two in Little Andaman. five army columns were engaged in Tamil Nadu and five in Kerala. Six hundred and fifty six MT of relief materials were supplied inter island with flying efforts of 455 sorties.

The major damages were in the Nicobar group of islands. The air force base at Car Nicobar was the worst hit. The air force had much casualty and also had to face the daunting task of mounting rescue and relief operation by rehabilitating the runway and the support infra structure to receive supplies. The use of available surface assets of the navy and the coast guard to evacuate large number of survivors was indeed well accomplished.

External Criticism

The services and the nation unfortunately had also been criticized for not allowing foreign organisations that were keen to move to the islands. What they did not understand was that the eco sensitive delicate islands could not have accommodated the large number of people wanting to render help. The logistic chains were already stretched to their limits and one needed only minimum numbers that were required to provide the help. In fact, most of the help that was to be provided was already catered for by the local agencies. The long-term relief measures did not need the number of people who wanted to get to the islands to render help.

It was suggested that there was something to be hidden as far as military secrets were concerned. Nothing could be farther from the truth, as with the capabilities of the present day satellites, it is a cakewalk for any spying satellite to pass real time pictures with excellent resolution to the monitoring stations. For that matter, even the google earth today can take you to those remote corners of the earth with the software launched lost year. Even an elementary analyst today can discern the pattern of operations and make out a summary in no time. It is just that the West could not swallow the refusal of India to accept help. The West also noted grudgingly that India had come out of the shell and was in a position to help itself and others in such times of need.

The entire geography has undergone a transformation post tsunami. Many submerged portions of islands are now visible and many other portions of islands have disappeared bringing about change in depth contours and inclinations.

The islands also had to encounter a special situation wherein many ex servicemen (settlers for over four decades) were having second thoughts about their role and presence in the islands. It needs to be remembered that they were brought in the first place to prevent foreign settlers from setting foot on our territory. Any serious reverse migration of this community would definitely affect the strategic interests in the region. The vacuum created by the reverse migration would bring in foreign settlers from the neighbourhood, which is detrimental to the security interests of the nation.

Since jetties were usable only by small ships, MoD is continued relief supplies by naval ships and small local boats. They are also continued air dropping by IAF helicopters ex Car Nicobar and by naval helicopters ex Port Blair in two inaccessible areas. Medical teams were deployed. Two ships were deployed in Tamil Nadu / Pondicherry.

Ministry of Shipping[5]

A mention also needs to be made of the efforts of the mercantile marine as coordinated by the ministry of shipping. The Shipping Corporation of India rendered twenty seven berthing position (Harbours/Jetties) functional out of forty nine. Three Jetties; one each at Car Nicobar, Nancowry (Kamorta) and Nancowry (Champin) were fit for operations in a short time. An eleven commercial ships were deployed from main land ex- Chennai, Kolkata, Haldia and Vizag for carrying relief supplies. Out of sixty five inter island vessels of Andaman & Nicobar administration, forty vessels were operational, eighteen vessels were not operational due to annual repairs and seven vessels were damaged in Tsunami. Eighteen vessels were deployed between Port Blair and Mayabunder, Havelock, Baratang, Diglipur, Neil Island, Rangat, Hut Bay, Long island and Campbell Bay. Six private vessels were operated between Port Blair and Rangat, Havelock, Diglipur, Mayabunder and Neil Islands. Out of thirty numbers of lighthouses in Andaman & Nicobar islands only two functioned in South Andaman and East islands. It was estimated that an amount of Rs. 304 crores was required to restore the damages to the shipping sector in the islands.

Special teams were deputed along with necessary materials required for repairs of damage structures at Hut Bay Wharf, Campbell Bay and Mus. Two boats each at Kamotra, Nancowry and Champin were provided for inter-Island movement within Nancowry group of islands. The ministry of shipping had issued instructions for transporting the relief material to the Tsunami affected areas free of cost, to Relief Commissioner/District Magistrate of the affected States/UTs for all donated items. This facility of free transport was extended to NGOs, Trusts and other organisations including corporate sector to provide the relief material including material for rehabilitation and reconstruction.

Reaching out in the neighbourhood:

Not only were we required to look after our own coastline particularly along the Tamil Nadu coast, but also we reached out to the neighbouring countries answering readily their call for help. Twenty four ships, sixteen helicopters and five fixed wing aircrafts of the Indian navy were engaged in relief operations, deploying 4,500 naval personnel in our neighbourhood.

At the government level, India recollected the close and friendly ties existing with the countries affected and described the relief assistance extended as symbolic of the friendship, solidarity and fellow feeling that India has for Sri Lanka, Maldives and Indonesia. The operation undertaken in Sri Lanka was designated as Operation Rainbow.

Operation Rainbow

Operation Rainbow[6] was launched by Indian navy[7] to provide relief and rescue assistance to Sri Lanka. Four navy vessels, with integrated helicopters, were based in Trincomalee and Galle. These carried on board relief and rescue material as well as medical teams. The simultaneous deployment of our maritime forces in Sri Lanka soon after the incident was highly appreciated by all the leaders in Sri Lanka from the president downwards. Port of Galle was cleared by our survey ships and rendered safe for navigation. The quick response in sending medical supplies relief material and trained personnel has surprised many western observers who grudgingly now admit that the marine forces of the country are well prepared and can be trusted to take on such challenges in the region. Under operation "Rainbow" for Sri Lanka, 230 sorties were undertaken and 181 personnel evacuated. In addition:

- Two navy dorniers landed in Colombo, with 350 kgs. of medicines and medical teams, which proceeded inland, with temporary shelter material, diving teams and communications equipment.
- Navy medical teams apuram set up in Trinciomalee, Galle and Hambantota.

- Three additional vessels LCU 33, INS Ghorpad and INS Kirch reached on 30 December and hospital ship reached on 30 December 2004.

The appreciation by the former president of Sri Lanka, Kumaratunga sums it up all when it comes to the way that our gesture was received. She had this to say in her letter made public on 26 February 2005, "Not with standing the consequences of this unprecedented natural catastrophe in some states of India itself, relief supplies from India started arriving in Sri Lanka on the same day of the disaster.... The massive relief and recovery operation mounted by India which was watched with heartfelt appreciation by our people is emblematic of the enduring ties of friendship and cooperation between our two countries...."

At a strategic level, it is important to note that our regional potential for leadership in the region has been recognised. Kumaratunga had this to say which amply reflects the views of Sri Lanka if not the entire region. "... time of such humanitarian need in the region demonstrates not only your solidarity with and sensitivity to the problems faced by our neighbours but also India's capability and readiness to meet challenges (that) manifest in our region"

The foreign minister of Sri Lanka during a press conference at New Delhi in February 2005 stressed that the Indian navy was "a first grade force" that put India in the forefront of modern naval powers.

The naval and coast guard units were deployed on the same day and were crucial in initiating immediate relief measures. Most of the initial help obviously was to save victims whereever possible. The recovery of the dead bodies was equally important as the relatives had to be sure of their unfortunate losses in terms of life and property. The most important application of the navy was to clear the debris in harbours and approaches to enable relief supplies and medical help to reach. The restoration of basic amenities was very important and as such, drinking water, medical supplies, clothing, and food definitely were the first items to be rushed. The coordination with the district authorities for speedy implementation was another pre requisite to ensure that there were no bureaucratic hurdles.

Operation Gambhir

Indonesia was the worst hit amongst the countries in the Indian Ocean region. The navy did not lose any time in dispatching its assets for providing immediate succour. The conversion of two survey ships as hospital ships with beds and an operation theatre tested many wartime concepts requiring mass evacuation and medical help simultaneously. With many naval and coast guard assets, the forces were able to transport large quantities of relief material for the affected areas in under operation "Gambhir" for Indonesia, the navy provided relief materials besides running a medical camp. The ships, dornier aircrafts and personnel of the Indian coast guard also supported the navy in its efforts.

Operation Castor

Maldives luckily by its geography and topography was not as badly hit. Yet, there was a need for external help to be provided without wasting time. The navy and the coast guard again rose to the occasion and were amongst the first to reach the country with medical stores, relief material and man power. Under operation "Castor" for Maldives fifty sorties were undertaken and fifteen peoples were evacuated from outlying islands.

External Criticism

The nation had to ward off criticism from the West for refusing aid with the willingness to handle the situation ourselves. In the end, India has demonstrated that not only does India has an inherent ability, willingness and leadership to manage disasters on home soil, but also has the reach and ability to extend helping hand to our neighbours.

While the Tsunami is behind us, and the services have learnt their own lessons for the future, a re-examination of the roles of the two maritime services in this context would be quite in order.

Examination of the Roles of the two Maritime Services

The navy has traditionally been the marine component to be used as an instrument of national will for power projection and for defending our shores in times of war. However, the defence services have always been trained to show its benign face and be able to provide aid to civil power in times of crisis. The Indian navy has grown from strength to strength and has now the imprints of a blue water navy. In the century of the seas, that has also been termed the Asian century, India has been projected to rank alongside the top four economies of the world. Such growth is essentially dependent on the safety of the seas to promote sea borne trade, which on date is ninety seven per cent by volume. The growth patterns and the energy requirements are such that the security of our sea-lanes, ports and related infrastructure assumes paramount importance. Essentially, therefore, the navy consciously need to prepare to take on these responsibilities and thus is so structured as to be able to take on these maritime challenges. Though the principal task would still to be prepared for war, the Tsunami has brought out that the navy simultaneously would need to have its plans in place to work alongside other forces using its strengths. The announcement last year that the navy was looking at larger landing ships which could serve the enhanced roles both during war and peace is indicative of the new thinking of the additional responsibility that the navy and the nation are willing to add to their charter.

Observations: Search and Rescue (SAR)

Search and Rescue was the exclusive role of the navy till the passing of the responsibilities to the coast guard. Thus, the navy had a mechanism for providing the SAR cover in the IOR. However, with the formal transfer of this role, the navy would be less preoccupied with that role except for its own requirements of combat SAR. It does not mean that the assets would not be used when required. In addition, there are areas that are still out of reach as far as the coast guard's air arm is concerned. These areas require the naval air arm to reach out to provide even first hand reports in such distant areas. As per the current orders, the coast guard would be the nodal agency and has set up the required mechanism to respond to alerts and to coordinate the SAR efforts in the designated areas of Indian Ocean, which is actually nearly three times the EEZ area.

If one were to examine the efforts of the Indian navy during the Tsunami in the light of this arrangement, it may appear that there is some duplication of efforts. But in reality, it is not so. It is just that the scales of the calamity were so large that all the available assets of the Indian navy and the coast guard had to be pooled to provide immediate help. It is also true that not all the war vessels are capable of providing dedicated support to such missions. We did see a missile Destroyer, Rajput transporting over 300 on the weather decks from Hut bay. Then, we saw the survey ships converted as forty eight bedded hospital ships with operation theatres and dedicated medical teams. But these are indeed special arrangements necessitated by the very special circumstances. But, having done it once it would be easy to adopt the procedures in the Standard Operating Procedures (SOPs) for future application.

Specific reference to the SAR Helicopter and vertical envelopment

Take a specific example of the helicopter designated as the SAR helicopter in the navy and the coast guard. The main stay of both the services is still the Chetak helicopter (The Navy does use the Seakings also in the SAR role). While it has served the interests well in limited scenarios; its utility for such large-scale evacuations and SAR is questionable. The ability of this helicopter to just rescue one at a time is a handicap in an emergency of this nature. The coast guard is understood to have cleared the ALH to be deployed for rescue missions as it has a better payload. The issue of mobilizing a large number of life saving devices (even simple life buoys, life rafts and life belts that could be dispensed from the helicopter/aircraft when large numbers are involved) is another important issue to be addressed.

The ranging and scaling of life saving devices would need to be reviewed. The district administration would need to stock up such items to be lifted by the services in such an eventuality. A part of the stock would need to be also stocked at the airfields and ports to cater for their immediate availability and use. It is noteworthy that there were press reports of the naval plans to procure huge Landing Platform Docks (LPD) from US to augment our sealift /vertical lift capability.[8]

Turf Wars?

Some observers were curious to know if there were turf wars between the navy and the coast guard regarding the roles. The sole aim of the services would be to join hands and get on with the gigantic task at hand. Following the MZI Act of 1976 and the creation of the coast guard, this service has been made the nodal agency for both SAR and also for formulating the National Oil Spill Disaster and Contingency plans (NOSDCP). By such designation, the shape and size of the vessels as well as the special type of equipment that goes on board would radically differ from that of the navy, which is meant to primarily defend the seas. The fact that the coast guard was specially created to take the load off the navy in a cost effective way should not be lost sight off. The coast guard vessels are optimised for their role comprising EEZ patrol, SAR, anti poaching, anti smuggling, protection off shore assets and oil spill contingencies.

Strategic Imperatives

In addition to the inferences on this count earlier as above, at the strategic level there are some very important observations that need to be taken note of. The reaching out of the marine forces to our neighbouring countries has enhanced the image of the navy as a credible benign force with capability, potential and intent absolutely in tact and in the right place. The enormous good will that has been generated would need to be transformed to provide India with a leadership role in the region. It would not be easy to achieve such status in the present global politico, military context. Yet, the doors are wide open for us to make an entry into the big league. Already, there are enough forums where both the Indian navy and the coast guard are interacting with the regional navies and coast guards. With the established credentials of the two maritime services, there are opportunities galore for creating space for the top slot in the regional arena. Some analysts have averred that perhaps there is still a degree of reluctance in accepting our leadership role; thus India's initiatives for being at the center of the regional warning system were not supported by Indonesia and Malaysia. The notable support came from Sri Lanka. But this may have more to do with geography than unwillingness to let the mantle of leadership role fall on India. It should be only a matter of time before our true potential is realised in the region.

Regional Thrusts

In the meanwhile, it would be necessary to continue with our thrusts in regional cooperation in many other fields. There are many bilateral exercises and agreements that are helping the maritime forces to come together. The coast guards today are cooperating to combat piracy, to enhance SAR, pollution control etc, this would need to be expanded to include regional contingencies. Thus, regular exercises to face such contingencies would go a long way in bringing about a convergence of views in the region for the long term good in the region.

Conclusion

In conclusion, the navy and the coast guard are entrusted with responsibilities, which *are not necessarily mutually exclusive*. While both the services have their tasks cut out, there are moments such as this one when the nation has to act as one to transcend those barriers and provide collective and timely response. The maritime activity could definitely be divided into many areas for ease of planning, monitoring and for even creation of special agencies. But the oceans by the inherent overlapping character forces us to bring all the resources to bear together to face both the natural or man-made calamities. The nation needs to invest in not just the warning mechanisms but also a flexible force structure that is capable of responding to the challenges at sea.

There are many lessons for us in the Tsunami, and more recently in the heavy rains on both the coasts that put the ability of the government and the security forces to test. It would be essential to rehearse the contingencies on a regular basis to see that the state, central and other agencies involved are able to act in consonance in times of need. Similarly, there is a need to work at the regional level to see that India is ready to play its leading role in the even of natural disasters any where in its neighbourhood.

Both the navy and the coast guard need to utilise the opportunity to extend their reach and the sphere of influence in the region to facilitate the nation to achieve its rightful place as a maritime leader into the next century. Similarly, there has to be greater involvement within the country in an institutionalised manner with the state and other agencies to see that the disaster mitigation during the incessant rains and other natural calamities are always catered for.

References

1 http://www.ndmindia.nic.in/Tsunami2004/mtribal.htm

2 Indomer-Alkyon Coastal Hydraulics Flash media player displaying the Tsunami movement.

3 Press Reports PTI, 26 February 20054, http://www.ndmindia.nic.in/Tsunami2004/mdefence.htm

5 http://www.ndmindia.nic.in/Tsunami2004/mship.htm
6 http://www.ndmindia.nic.in/Tsunami2004/mearep.htm
7 http://indiannavy.nic.in/
8 PTI Press Release, 19 October 2005, http://pib.nic.in/release/release.asp?relid=13733&kwd=indian+navy

9

India and Sri Lanka: Assessing Maritime Security Relationship

Vijay Sakhuja

An audit of India's relations with its immediate southern neighbour Sri Lanka reveals a mixed bag of successes and failures. This is primarily due to its dominant position both in geographical and economic context. Besides, it has on occasions, ineptly handled its relatively smaller neighbour who has often accused India as being a big bully and overbearing. However, in recent times, the Indian polity has been conscious of the mistrust and lack of confidence from Colombo towards New Delhi and has now taken firm initiatives to address the respective bilateral concerns. It has made some noteworthy efforts also at improving the security environment in the subcontinent. Consequently, today New Delhi enjoys a relatively good degree of trust and confidence with Sri Lanka.

The two sides appear to have shelved the bitter past of the deployment of the Indian Peace Keeping Force (IPKF) 1987-1990. Today the bilateral relations are dynamic, growing with confidence and there appears to be some kind of understanding between the two sides on the security environment in the Palk Bay particularly with regards to the LTTE. The most important facet of the growing joint activity is that both Colombo and New Delhi have now entered into a phase of building an extraordinary relationship to ward off destabilizing actors and contribute to regional stability.

This paper attempts to highlight the maritime dimensions of security relationship between India and Sri Lanka. It highlights the proposed Indo – Sri Lankan Defence Cooperation Agreement and examines the bilateral relationship in the context of the LTTE. The paper also discusses the role of extra regional powers in the Sri Lankan security.

India-Sri Lankan Bilateral Defence Cooperation Agreement (DCA)

India has always had a stake in Sri Lanka's security. Beginning in 1971, Indian naval ships operated off Sri Lanka to blockade any supply of arms and ammunitions/stores for the militant group Janatha Vimukti Perumuna (JVP). This was in response to a Sri Lankan request that India provide naval vessels to carry out patrolling in waters in south Sri Lanka and prevent gun running /incursions by the militant groups. India also provided six helicopters of the Indian air force for relief, rescue and humanitarian duties.[1]

The Indian navy participated in *Operation Pawan* in pursuance of a request made by the Sri Lankan government to counter the LTTE.[2] The Indian navy was required to undertake maritime operations in the waters around Sri Lanka and particularly Palk Bay, north of Sri Lanka. Palk Bay was frequently used by the LTTE for carrying out strikes against the Sri Lankan naval forces and to keep the arms supply lines open at sea. The LTTE had several small vessels to transport arms, ammunition, stores, and logistics to sustain them. These vessels would originate from several South East Asian countries and transit through the Bay of Bengal .The Indian navy was tasked to:

- Provide tactical support operations through joint patrolling of Sri Lankan waters in conjunction with the Sri Lankan navy to prevent military activity such as movement of arms and personnel in Sri Lankan waters.
- Conduct joint operations with the army and the air force.
- Conduct military operations to support the Sri Lankan political agenda.
- Provide humanitarian relief.
- Help in detents and refugee transfers. [3]

The IPKF finally withdrew from Sri Lanka in 1990. After a hiatus of nearly over a decade, in 2003, the Sri Lankan government has again sought to strengthen its defence relations with India.

Colombo was keen to sign the defence cooperation agreement aimed at better training for Sri Lankan defence personnel at Indian training establishments, procurement of modern arms and ammunition particularly naval ships and helicopters, and joint naval exercises/ patrolling. All these are essentially targeted against the LTTE. At the political front, in Sri Lanka, the once suspicious and critical political parties like the JVP were also urging New Delhi to help find a solution to the problematical ethnic conflict. For India too, it could not allow the Sri Lanka imbroglio to continue festering, as it would have devastating consequences for India's geopolitical and strategic interests.

Finally, on 19 October 2004, a five-member delegation from India's ministry of defence held discussions in Colombo with their counterparts from Sri Lanka. The Sri Lankan team was headed by defence secretary Cyril Herath and comprised of the service chiefs, senior officials of the ministry of foreign affairs and Nigel Hatch, the president's counsel for the proposed agreement between India and Sri Lanka concerning cooperation in defence. The two sides agreed to enhance the existing bilateral military cooperation in the field of military training, joint military exercises, exchange of military intelligence and information, maritime surveillance to prevent illegal activities affecting both countries. This agreement is over and above the existing hotlines between the two navies and the Indian coast guard.

The LTTE has been critical of the defence cooperation agreement and have noted that it will "undermine" the fragile ceasefire between Sri Lanka and the LTTE. According to Anton Balasingham, LTTE's chief peace negotiator "such an agreement is irrelevant during the time of a peace process, suspended though, but altogether not given up and therefore would tilt the military equilibrium, the underlying principle of the ceasefire agreement." It appears that the LTTE has conveyed their views on the defence agreement to India, arguing that it would affect the balance of forces. The Tamil National Alliance (TNA), a party seen as a surrogate of LTTE rebels has urged India not to go ahead with the defence cooperation pact, as it would be harmful to the ongoing peace process.[4] The LTTE has also been critical of the Sri Lankan and the Indian government's initiatives to sign an agreement for the extension and reconstruction of the Palaly airport. They have argued that in the past too Tamil areas were forcefully taken away to extend the airport.

Although the DCA had yet to be brought into force, the two sides have begun joint exercises. In December 2004, the Indian coast guard and the Sri Lanka navy held a joint maritime exercise code-named 'Operation Ek Sath' (it means 'together') that involved anti-piracy, search and rescue and anti-pollution exercise. Offshore Patrol Vessels (OPVs), Fast Attack Crafts (FACs), maritime surveillance aircraft and helicopter from both sides participated in these manoeuvres.[5] The exercises gained more significance with the visit of Vice Admiral A. K. Singh, the director general Indian coast guard to Colombo during the exercises. The joint exercises preceded refitting of SLNS Sayura. [6] In December 2005, the first ever joint naval exercise between the navies of the two countries was held. It involved ships and aircraft from both sides and a variety of tactical manoeuvres including professional fleet management and transfer of personnel between ships.[7] There have also been several transfers of military equipment such as radars to detect low-level aircraft which marks the resumption of non-lethal military aid after five years. This was essentially in response to the LTTE acquiring prowess in air operations based on two micro-light aircraft and two airstrips in areas under its control. However, the DCA has run into jeopardy due to Indian domestic political conditions.

The growing capabilities of the LTTE have brought the two maritime forces together and are being supported by several initiatives such as the proposed DCA. New Delhi has taken important steps to provide political and military support to the Sri Lankan government. There have been several high level military visits and the Indian navy chief, Admiral Arun Prakash has visited Sri Lanka to discuss the rising threat of the LTTE sea tigers and stopping the LTTE arms procurements as also scuttling the arms supply chain to naxalites in Machilipatnam and Guntur district of Andhra Pradesh in India.

Maritime Security Challenges from LTTE

From a very humble beginning, the LTTE maritime capability has improved and today it can boast of a sophisticated network. Its maritime assets and organization are quite capable and can well compete with the maritime facilities of a small island state including the navy. The present day LTTE commercial maritime infrastructure includes a fleet of merchant ships, a large number of fishing trawlers, high-speed motor launches, and a professionally trained crew to steer these vessels.

An attritional long drawn asymmetrical conflict demands huge and sustained resources. The LTTE has engaged in sea piracy, gunrunning and drug trafficking that had fuelled funds for procurement of arms and fuelling operations. It had established and sustained contacts in several Southeast Asian countries and as far as Japan and North Korea. The LTTE has front companies in these countries that take care of procurement and shipment.[8]

As far as sea piracy is concerned, the LTTE has resorted to hijack of vessels and changed its name and physical characteristics and creating a phantom shipping fleet that has effectively evaded monitoring and detection. According to Rohan Gunaratna, a terrorism expert,

"Some Southeast Asian intelligence agencies believe that the LTTE has hijacked foreign vessels, but the affected governments have failed to present conclusive evidence implicating the LTTE. Since the LTTE has demonstrated quite regularly its mastery of phantom shipping - changing the ship's name and appearance - it is likely that it is also engaged in maritime crime even outside Sri Lankan waters."[9]

For instance, *M V Sik Yang*, a 2,818-ton, Malaysian-flag cargo ship, was reported missing. The ship sailed from Tuticorin, India on 25 May 1999 with a cargo of bagged salt and was due on 31 May 1999 at the Malaysian port of Malacca. The ship however disappeared and the fate of the ship's crew of fifteen is still unknown. The vessel was apparently hijacked by the LTTE and may be engaged as a phantom vessel. A subsequent report on 30 June 1999 confirmed that the vessel had been hijacked by the LTTE. [10]

In yet another case, a ship with a cargo of 32,000 mortar shells from Zimbabwe Defence Industries (ZDI) left the Mozambican port of Beira on 23 May 1997 supposedly en-route to Colombo. The consignment was belonged to the Sri Lankan government. The ship did not reach its destination. ZDI assumed that the Sri Lankan government had sent a ship to collect the munitions, but the company alleged that the consignment was loaded onto a ship called the *Limassol,* which was one of the LTTE freighters and the cargo transferred to the LTTE.

In some cases, the LTTE has not been so successful. A case in point is the ship that anchored off Cochin port in south India in 1993. The vessel was carrying a consignment of AK-47 rifles from a Russian company for the ministry of defence (MOD) of the government of India[11]. The Captain had informed the port authorities of the cargo and the consignee. The MOD denied having ordered any such consignment. Enquiries revealed that a person, who had visited the company's headquarters in Moscow posing as a senior official of the MOD with forged identity papers, had ordered the consignment. He had the payment for the consignment made by a bank remittance from New York. Nobody claimed the consignment and it was confiscated. The Indian authorities strongly suspected LTTE had ordered the consignment and its plans to effect a mid-sea transfer from the ship to one of its own smaller vessels and it had failed.

In the past the LTTE has hijacked several vessels. Some of the reported cases relate to the hijacking of *Irish Mona* (August 1995), *Princess Wave* (August 1996), *Athena* (May 1997), *Misen* (July 1997), *Morong Bong* (July 1997), *Cordiality* (Sept 1997) and *Princess Kash* (August 1998). [12]

Gun Running

In its long drawn struggle to fight against the Sri Lankan military and later the IPKF, the LTTE obtained arm supplies from the international market. With its operational bases in southern India closed and it could no longer rely on supply routes from Tamil Nadu shores and hence began to rely on the longer logistic supply chains in distant shores. In terms of its regional access and source points in the Bay of Bengal – Southeast Asia region particularly Cambodia has been the main source of weapons for the LTTE. Apart from Cambodia, Thailand and Myanmar too have been important source of materials for LTTE operations. The LTTE had established a very sophisticated network of gun running. These activities are conducted using its fleet of ships. The gunrunning operations originate from Cambodian ports of Sihanoukville and Koh Kong, moving along the coast to Thai ports at the northern end of the Gulf of Thailand such as Sattahip and Rayong and thence by land past Bangkok and south to the ports on Thailand's Andaman Sea coast, most notably Ranong and Phuket.[13] The gun trade route passes through the Bay of Bengal and Andaman sea. These are loaded onboard small fishing trawlers and these vessels then transfer the consignment to larger vessels at sea for onward passage to Sri Lanka.

During *Operation Pawan*, the LTTE gun route was much different and followed a circuitous direction. For instance, *MV Illiana* (Black Crow) made several voyages transporting arms and ammunition from Thailand/Singapore/Cambodia transiting along their coast in the Andaman Sea. There is also an alternate route through which consignments are shipped directly across the Gulf of Thailand to the southern provinces of Chumporn and Songkhla and then moved by land across the Kra Isthmus to the Andaman Sea coast[14]. The LTTE is also reported to hire the services of Arakanese smugglers operating across the Bay of Bengal between Ranong in Thailand and Cox's Bazaar and Chittagong in southern Bangladesh[15]. Once known as the Arakan army, this is essentially a maritime mafia operation that is known to have shipped weapons as well as narcotics for various regional insurgent groups including the LTTE and insurgent factions operating from Myanmar and the Indian northeast. [16] It necessitated the Sri Lankan foreign minister had to undertake a dedicated tour of Laos, Cambodia, Vietnam and Thailand to seek their governments cooperation to stop illegal arms smuggling by LTTE, further confirms the existence of gun runners in the Malacca Strait - Andaman Sea region. However, the LTTE is deeply involved in drug trafficking. For this purpose, a significant number of its merchant ships are manned by its cadres/ personnel.[17] The entire LTTE activity in Myanmar has been legitimised with the connivance of some leaders of the military junta thus it offers an important base for LTTE drug trafficking network. As per an internal Indonesian military report, some Acehnese in the remote areas of the province are resorting to small-scale 'ganja' cultivation. Aceh rebels are known to engage in gunrunning and drug smuggling to further finance their insurgency.

The LTTE's arms and ammunitions supplies are generally carried onboard larger vessels that operate on the high sea. In order to discharge their cargo, the vessels close the shore and wait for the arrival of the smaller boats/ launches. These smaller vessels are escorted by gunboats and explosive laden craft manned by armed Sea Tigers. Thereafter, the cargo is transported to shore. In the event of detection by the Sri lankan navy, these vessels ram into the naval vessels. There have been several such incidents in the past. Sea areas off Mullaitheevu are well known for such activity. The areas contiguous to Mullaitheevu are known to be the strongholds of the LTTE and they are also the maritime approaches to the island. Besides, Mullaitheevu, the Veruhal - Vaakharai coast has also been a safe 'harbour' for LTTE to transport its cadres, provisions, military hardware and supplies by boat from the northern coast of Mullaitheevu.

In December 2005, Sri Lankan president Mahinda Rajapaksa had summoned his military commanders amidst rising fears of a return to war. There were reports that a LTTE ship with a large quantity of weapons and ammunition was operating off Mullaittivu and the Sri Lankan navy and air force had commenced tight surveillance to intercept the vessel. Assistance had also been sought from the Indian authorities to support the operations.

But worst was waiting to happen. The fragile truce, effective from 23 February 2002, between the Sri Lankan government and the LTTE was finally shattered after the Tamil Tiger rebels blew up a Sri Lankan navy Dvora class gunboat outside Trincomalee harbour on 5 January 2006. The suicide attack was the work of an LTTE owned explosives-packed fishing boat that rammed into the naval vessel resulting in thirteen sailors missing and presumed dead. Earlier, three sailors aboard a smaller naval patrol craft were killed in a sea battle with rebels off the northwestern town of Mannar. The attack off Trincomalee was similar to the April 1995 incident in which the LTTE had infiltrated the tightly guarded naval base in Trincomalee and destroyed two craft that were anchored there.

The Rise of a LTTE Navy and Air Force

In the past, there have been several such incidents involving the Sri Lankan navy and the LTTE gunboats. Both sides have lost vessels. In particular the Sri Lankan navy has lost about half of its force to the high-speed gunboats of the LTTE. In the ensuing conflict dynamics, the achievements of the LTTE has resulted in the LTTE to seek a formal recognition of Sea Tigers on par with the Sri Lankan navy.

The proposal to that effect (a scheme of three proposals) was made by Colonel Soosai, Commander, Sea Tigers force, to the Scandinavian-staffed Sri Lanka (Ceasefire) Monitoring Mission (SLMM) to prevent clashes at sea that have claimed more than fifty lives so far. The other two proposals include a prohibited zone for the Sri Lankan navy and an embargo against the use of force against any LTTE vessel, military or civilian, in the absence of a monitor from the SLMM. The LTTE had complained that the

Sri Lankan navy, as part of its "Operation Waruna Kirana", was launching offensive attacks aimed at blocking its sea-lanes.

Like the navy, the LTTE is also known to possess a small air force. Though not so developed and sophisticated as the navy, the LTTE has a few aircraft in its inventory. Analysts believe that it has been using the Czech origin aircraft ZLIN Z-143 from an airstrip of about 1250 meters in the LTTE controlled territory. [18] Interestingly, the airstrip is well defended with close range anti aircraft guns, surface to air missiles, radar and some electronic infrastructure to facilitate air operations. In response to this new capability acquired by the LTTE , the SLMM Chief Mr Hagrup Haukland noted: "This ....is a serious matter, which impinges on Sri Lanka 's security. India is concerned too," Secondly, on the point of control and sovereignty he added that: "The skies over Sri Lanka were under the sovereign control of the government of Sri Lanka . Any flying in Sri Lankan skies would have to have the express sanction of the Sri Lankan government. As for the use of international air space, that was also controlled by international agreements. Flying by an unrecognized group like the LTTE would therefore be against international law,"

The LTTE has been under the watchful eyes of the Sri Lankan air force too. Air force commander Air Vice Marshall Donald Perera has expressed his intention to neutralizing the LTTE's air power comprising of an airstrip at Iranamadu, in the rebel controlled area and the two light aircraft in their possession. A second airstrip is being built by the LTTE in a location within the area under their control in the Mullaitivu district.

Stakes in Sri Lankan Energy Security through Lanka IOC

In 2002, the Indian and the Sri Lankan governments signed a MoU that paved the way for the Indian Oil Corporation (IOC) to emerge as Lanka IOC, a wholly owned subsidiary. It acquired 100 filling stations and a one-third stake in the oil storage facilities for $75 million to become a complete player in the island's downstream petroleum segment. [19] Interestingly, Sri Lankan petroleum market is much smaller than that of the Tamil Nadu. The island's total demand is 3.5 million tonne per annum (tpa) while the country's refining capacity is 2.2 million tpa. The deficit is provided through imports. Lanka IOC now has a market share of about thirty per cent in the petrol, twenty three per cent in the diesel and thirty eight per cent in the lubricant markets and aims to own about fifty per cent market share by 2006. At the same time, it aims to make Trincomalee a bunkering hub by 2005 at a cost of about $4 million.

The China bay tank farm comprising of ninety nine tanks spread over 850 acres of land at Trincomalee has been taken on a thirty five-year lease. The takeover cost the IOC US $ 100,000 as the lease payment for the first year. Currently, seventeen of the tanks are operational and each tank has a capacity of 12,250 kilolitres. The tank farm renovation cost Lanka IOC about $10 million and included construction of two floating roof tanks of 6,000 kilolitres capacity, twelve new bay tank lorry filling sheds, new pump house, new fire hydrant system and safety system. The throughput of Trincomalee has now gone up from 5,000kl per month to 22,000kl. Besides, the farm has the road network, and is also connected by rail and sea.

Given the sensitive nature of Indian investment, Colombo is conscious of the vulnerability of this strategic infrastructure. Lakshman Kadirgamar, the late Sri Lankan foreign minister, had noted that, "I am seeking to sensitise India to the looming danger (from the LTTE) particularly to the port of Trincomalee. The port of Trincomalee is today ringed by the LTTE". [20] Reportedly, the LTTE has eleven strongholds around the southern rim of the port. The oil farm is well within the reach of the LTTE artillery.

As noted above, Sea Tigers, the naval wing of the LTTE, also has a good naval capability that includes high-speed boats fitted with outboard engines as powerful as 750 hp. The LTTE has developed a sophisticated strategy of attacking maritime targets like Sri Lankan navy ships and other commercial vessels. Sri Lanka has lost at least a dozen naval vessels, both in harbour and at sea, as a result of LTTE attacks. The LTTE has engaged in wolf pack tactics, used high-speed boats filled with explosives that rammed into naval vessels. Sea Tigers have emerged as one of the most ruthless and dangerous maritime capable terrorist groups in the world. The LTTE was reported to have developed human suicide torpedo. It has expertise in using underwater explosives such as mines. Off the shelf communication equipment and water sport/diving equipment are part of its inventory. In the absence of technological superiority over the Sri Lankan navy, it has adopted asymmetric strategies and options to challenge naval forces and inflict unacceptable costs.

Extra Regional Players

Situated at the southern tip of India, Sri Lanka, though small in size and population, has long remained influenced in cultural, social and political areas by its powerful neighbour India. In the past, in order to erode the strong Indian influence, Colombo has been trying to befriend several regional and extra regional countries and encourage involvement in the promotion of Sri Lanka's development, diversification of arms purchases and trade. Colombo approached Beijing and encouraged China's involvement in Sri Lanka's development, diversification of arms purchases and trade. In this connection Mahinda Werake, a Sri Lankan academic has noted, "From the point of view of the small states of South Asia a stronger presence of China as a countervailing force is a desirable phenomenon in view of the growing and unquestionable supremacy of India in the region". [21] A similar response was echoed by a Chinese scholar Lin Lian Guang of Peking University, "The sole dominant power in South Asia has vitiated the strategic environment in South Asia".[22]

The Chinese have long viewed India as a predominant regional power and have on occasions voiced their concern to the Sri Lankan leadership. During the visit in 1989 by Harry Jayawardene, the special envoy of president Jayawardene, the Chinese foreign minister Wu Xueqian extended China's support to Sri Lanka's efforts to safeguard its sovereignty and oppose foreign interference in its internal affairs. Chinese vice foreign minister further reiterated Chinese support to Sri Lanka in 1984 in Colombo when he stated, 'Big should not bully the small'. PLA navy ships visiting the Indian Ocean states of Pakistan, Sri Lanka and Bangladesh on goodwill visits followed up these statements in 1985. The Chinese response to the ethnic problem in Sri Lanka was that of advising Colombo to seek a political solution to the problem. In 1987, Ranil Wikramasinghe visited PRC to mobilise Chinese support, but China preferred a political solution of the problem. President Jayawardene summed up China's role as: "They were good friends and gave us military equipment, guns etc at reasonable terms. But what could they do? I could not ask them to start a war in the North to keep the Indians busy. Even if I had, I doubt if they would have done it." The Chinese initiative towards Sri Lanka have also to be viewed in the context of China's appreciation of Sri Lanka's geographic location in terms of its energy sea lanes as also a strategic base for scuttling any Indian efforts to strangulate the umbilical cord of the Chinese economy in the Indian Ocean. Sri Lanka also offers yet another platform for China to prevent any dominance by India in regional politics. Military aid and arms sales are only part of the stark realities of the large Chinese design as also the indication of an enhanced naval interest in the Indian Ocean.

As far as the US is concerned, it has been interested in building military relations with Sri Lanka. This is primarily due to Sri Lanka's strategic location astride the sea-lane from Hormuz to Malacca. Also, of strategic significance is Trincomalee, a deep-water port on Sri Lanka's eastern coast that was developed as a major naval base by the British, who retained access after independence in 1948, up to 1956.

Since 1994, US has been providing military help in terms of hardware and US Special Forces have been training the Sri Lankan army to fight the LTTE. Even before the agreement was signed, US warships had begun to dock in Colombo harbour to refuel. *USS Hopper* was the first American navy vessel to dock in Colombo in eight years. The tilt towards US was logical since Colombo could not draw much from New Delhi in its war against the LTTE. Referring to the Sri Lankan army's loss of the key Elephant Pass base in 2000, a local newspaper had noted that, if countries in the region are unable to help Sri Lanka with military support, then Colombo is free to enter into agreements with any country that would help. Sri Lankan government has signed an agreement known as the Acquisition and Cross Servicing Agreement (ACSA) that is the first such pact entered into with a major Western power since the country's independence in 1948. The US military is quite active in the island and US SEALS are training the army and navy. The police teams are being sent to the United States for anti-terrorism courses. The US is also supplying a US coast guard cutter to the Sri Lankan navy.

Conclusion

Sri Lanka has long remained influenced in cultural, social and political sphere by its powerful neighbour India. Notwithstanding the past bitter experiences of the IPKF deployment, New Delhi has been encouraging Colombo to find a political solution to the ethnic problem. Important fallout of the ethnic conflict in Sri Lanka has been the boost to the modernisation of the Sri Lanka's armed forces. From a mere ceremonial military, the Sri Lankan armed forces are engaged in fighting the LTTE and have emerged as a professional force.

Today India is an important component of the security calculus of Sri Lankan. India has provided naval hardware, naval expertise, have established hot lines and a constant consultative mechanism for sharing intelligence. With the passage of time, India-Sri Lanka maritime relations have matured and recent trends are indicative of the growing bonds of trust and confidence.

References

1 Lieutenant Commander B. M. Dimri, "Naval Diplomacy and UNCLOS III", *Strategic Analysis*, April 1994, p.67.

2 *Ibid.*

3 *Ibid.*

4 The TNA has seats in the Sri Lankan parliament.

5. Sri Lankan naval participation included OPVs Sayura and Jayasagar, and two Dvora fast attack craft and Indian coast guard was represented by CGS Sarang and CGS Dugabhai Deshmukh, maritime surviellance aircraft and an Indian built Chetak helicopter

6 Agreement on the refit of the vessel was signed during President Chandrika Kumaratunga's visit to New Delhi in November 2004.

7 'Sri Lanka, India in First Ever Joint Naval Exercise', 14 December 2005 , athttp://news.indiainfo.com/2005/12/14/1412sri-lanka-india-naval-exercise.html.

Two Indian navy ships, INS Sukanya and INS Kirpan, together with an Indian navy helicopter and a Donnier aircraft participated with three Sri Lankan navy ships, a gun boat and a fast attack craft.

8 R Sridhar, "Maritime Terrorism Capabilities of the Sea Tigers of Sri Lanka", paper presented at the International Workshop on Maritime Counter Terrorism, 29-30 November 2004 held at Observer Research Foundation New Delhi, India.

9 Rohan Gunaratna, 'The Asymmetric Threat From Maritime Terrorism', *Jane's Navy International*, 1 October 2001.

10 Reference Number: 1999-54, 1999 Anti- Shipping Activity Messages (ASAM), http://www.fas.org/irp/world/para/docs/ASAM-1999.htm

11 B. Rraman, maritime Terrorism: An Indian Perspective" Paper no.1154, 10 October 2004, http://www.saag.org/papers12/paper1154.html

12 Gunaratna, n.9.

13 *Ibid.*

14 *Ibid.*

15 *Ibid.*

16 *Ibid.* Also see Anthony Davis, "Tamil Tigers Continue Procurement", *Jane's Intelligence Review,* 1May 2002.

17 Rohan Gunaratna, "Illicit Transfer of conventional weapons: The Role of State and Non-State actors in South Asia", in Jayanth Dhanapala, *(ed)Small Arms Control Old Weapons, New Issues,* Vermont; Ashgate Publishing Ltd, 1999, p. 266.

18 Commodore RS Vasan, "The Real Implications of Possession of Air Capability by LTTE" Paper no. 1401, http://www.saag.com.

19 Venkatachari Jagannathan, 'LankaIOC Storming Sri Lanka', available at http://www.domain-b.com/companies/companies_i/indian_oil_corporation/20041020_storming.html

20 Amit Baruah, "Trincomalee Oil Farms Vulnerable to Aattacks by LTTE, says Kadirgamar" , *The Hindu*, 15 August 2003.

21 *Ibid*, p.212.

22 *Ibid.*

10

Maritime Issues between India and Sri Lanka

A. Subramanyam Raju

India and Sri Lanka signed bilateral agreements on the Boundary in Historic Waters in June 1974 and on the maritime boundary in the Gulf of Mannar and the Bay of Bengal in March 1976. They also signed a Supplementary agreement in November 1976 on the extension of the maritime boundary between the two countries in the Gulf of Mannar from position 13m to the trijunction point between India, Sri Lanka and the Maldives (point T). However, both countries have differences on some maritime issues.

India recognized Sri Lanka's sovereignty over Kachchativu island, and, in return, Sri Lanka recognized India's sovereignty over Wadge Bank in 1976. Sri Lanka began objecting to Indian fishermen moving in the region adjacent to Kachchativu island, which adversely affected the livelihood of many Indian fishermen. The mining and fishing rights of both countries around Kachchativu island became contentious issues.

An attempt has been made, in the paper, to examine issues such as the Kachchativu issue; fishermen's problems; the land bridge between India and Sri Lanka; Sethusamudram Ship Canal project and its implications; and threat from the Sea Tigers.

Kachchativu Island

Kachchativu is one of the issues that continue to disturb good-neighbourly relations between the two countries. Kachchativu island is one mile long, 300 yards broad, and has an area of 285.2 acres. The British had used this island since 1920 as a naval gunnery practice range. It is a barren, uninhabited place and without drinking water. It was believed that a fisherman from Ramanathapuram built the Catholic church here dedicated to St. Anthony. The church was considered as the guardian of fishermen. The fishermen and pilgrims of both the countries used to visit the church in March every year for a religious festival, in the belief that St. Anthony would protect them from turbulent seas and inclement weather. People of both countries from northern Sri Lanka and Tamil Nadu used to share their culture and ideas. Historically, the fishermen communities of both countries have similarities. They speak Tamil and continued to have relations for centuries. There was free movement of people before independence and it continued till 1974. After the 1974 and 1976 agreements and the eruption of civil war in Sri Lanka in 1983, the situation changed entirely and the relationship between the peoples of the two countries underwent a transformation.

Though the island is barren and uninhabited, its surroundings have an abundance of prawns. The island is not strategically important for India. But for the Indian fishermen it is a very important place for their livelihood. After independence, Sri Lanka claimed rights over the island. Later in 1974, India and Sri Lanka signed an agreement, which ensured the sovereign right of Sri Lanka over the disputed island of Kachchativu.[1]

According to the 1974 agreement, the Indian fishermen and pilgrims would continue to enjoy their traditional rights. However, the Sri Lankan government did not subscribe to the Indian government's view. It argued that the agreement did not give any fishing rights, but only the rights to dry their fishing nets, to rest, and the right of the pilgrims to visit the island for religious purposes. The agreement was drafted in such a way that it can lead to ambiguity.

Later, India and Sri Lanka had another agreement on the boundary in the Bay of Bengal and the Gulf of Mannar in 1976. Unlike the earlier agreement, this one did not deal with any disputed island. Therefore, the problems of ownership of the island of Kachchativu and controversies surrounding Indian fishermen's fishing rights in and around Kachchativu were resolved once and for all by the agreements of 1974 and 1976. The government of

India accepted this position. While demarcating the maritime boundary with Sri Lanka, India tried to have a trade-off between Kachchativu and the Palk Straits. This resulted in the sacrificing of the fishermen's fishing rights in both the areas.

However, Indian fishermen are being not allowed to go near the island by the Sri Lankan navy. The Sri Lankan government argues that the island was used for illegal activities and hence it has been preventing the entry of foreign elements on Kachchativu. The Indian government never raised its voice against the Sri Lankan move. The government in New Delhi could not take the problems of the fishermen of Tamil Nadu into consideration in its policy towards Sri Lanka. It adopted a sort of accommodative attitude towards the neighbour.

Problems of the Fishermen

Since fishermen are living below the poverty line, so they go in search of fish wherever they are available. In their pursuit, they hardly respect maritime boundaries. As is the case everywhere, so is with Indian and Sri Lankan fishermen. Indian fishermen are cross the maritime boundary and enter Sri Lankan waters. Similarly, Sri Lankan fishermen cross the boundary and enter Indian and Maldives waters for fishing. Since the distance between Rameswaram and Talaimannar is about twelve kilometers, it would not be possible to restrict the fishermen crossing neighbouring waters.

Prawns are available in abundance in the Palk Straits and particularly in Sri Lankan waters, so Indian fishermen cross over to their waters to catch prawns, in spite of the restrictions imposed by the Indian navy and attacks carried out by the Sri Lankan navy. They argue that they do not have any other alternative than this as their survival depends on fishing in Sri Lankan waters. Similarly, the Sri Lankan fishermen cross over to the Maldives waters, where tuna fish is in abundance. Entering into others' waters and carrying out fishing activity is illegal. However, under Art 146 of the UN Law of Sea, "measures will be taken to ensure effective protection of human life". Further, Art 73 mentions that littoral states can take measures "including boarding, inspection, arrest and judicial proceedings to ensure compliance with the laws and regulations".[2]

During the civil war, the Sri Lankan navy was not able to distinguish between fishing boats and boats involved in nefarious activities. The Sri Lankan navy, instead of identifying the boats engaged in illegal activities, treated all as threats to its security and used to fire at them resulting in killing of fishermen. They followed a policy of shooting first and questioning later. The navy argued that they suspected the sailors as being LTTE forces and they couldn't go close to them for identification because the LTTE cadres may attack the navy men. The number of incidents has decreased since 1998. This is because of the Indian navy's persuasion not to kill the people without identifying the fishermen.

On the Indian side, the authorities are also arresting Sri Lankan fishermen who enter Indian waters. Once the fishermen are caught and brought before the authorities, it is a long procedure to release them. Both the central and state governments are involved in the decision-making process: there are different ministries/departments, i.e. the ministry of home affairs, ministry of external affairs, ministry of agriculture, and also state government departments. Punishment against foreigners indulging in illegal fishing in India is more severe than in Sri Lanka. Though India takes a long time to give verdicts on those who are arrested by the Indian navy, but they were never killed.

Foreign fishing vessels that are involved in illegal activities are asked to pay penalty, which is beyond the capacity of almost all the fishermen. In a few cases courts in India ordered payment of a fine of Rs. 1,00,000. Apart from the penalty, they may undergo on imprisonment for about six months. The Maritime Zone of India Act of 1981 (MZI) provides for imprisonment not exceeding three years, or with fine not exceeding Rs. 15,00,000, or with both if the foreign vessels are found in any area within the territorial waters of India, or punishable with fine not exceeding Rs. 10,00,000.[3] This is against UNCLOS-III Art 73, which forbids the imprisonment of fishermen who are found poaching.[4]

In an interview, Suryanarayana told the author that sixty to seventy per cent of the illegal fishing by Indian fishermen occurred in the area of Kachchativu island. However, the author was told by some of the coast guard personnel in Chennai in 2005,[5] that the Sri Lankan navy often handed over the fishermen, who strayed into Sri Lankan waters, to the Indian navy. They said that the Sri Lankan navy was cooperating and the fault lay on the Indian side. When the author asked why they could not prevent the illegal fishing, they replied that they were being instructed not to punish the fishermen who were entering neighbouring waters and they could only give suggestions to them. They suggested that instead of poaching in Sri Lankan waters, the government should encourage the fishermen to fish in and around the Andaman & Nicobar islands, where fish is in abundance. When Indian government had settled the maritime borders and recognized the Sri Lankan sovereignty over the Kachchativu island, it should have equally concentrated on welfare of the fishermen who used to fish in the Indo-Sri Lankan waters. Though the Tamil Nadu government has initiated a few welfare programmes to help the fishermen, but according to the fishermen none of the schemes are reaching them. The central and state governments did not bother to take steps in finding the alternative livelihood to protect the fishermen. This problem will continue to remain as long as a political will is lacking.

It is noteworthy to mention here that NGOs are playing a significant role in promoting the welfare of the fishing community in India and Sri Lanka. For instance, Alliance for Release of Innocent Fishermen (ARIF), Thrivendrum, is sincerely working for the release of fishermen from India and Sri Lanka. The author met people who are working for release of the fishermen of both countries. In an interview, the author was informed that they provide information to the affected families about the whereabouts of their kin. They also meet and talk to the authorities of both countries to release the fishermen. The affected fishermen in Tuticorin told the author that only ARIF was concerned about their welfare, and they were being informed by ARIF about their kin's whereabouts.

Similarly, in Sri Lanka, there are a number of organizations that are involved in securing the release of arrested Indian fishermen. NGOs, trade unions, fishermen's organizations, some of them in Sri Lanka, are working for their release. In Sri Lanka, these organizations are more effective; in India, the NGOs are not that influential and effective in securing the release of Sri Lankan fishermen. Still, they are playing a significant role. The staff of ARIF told the author that the government often gets help from them in dealing with fishermen's issues.

Threat from the Sea Tigers

The LTTE has its own navy, considered to be a match for the Sri Lankan navy. It controls some of the areas in the northern part of Sri Lanka. It has emerged as the most powerful organization there and spread its activities in the northern and eastern provinces and expanded in other parts of the country by carrying out attacks on military establishments, government officials, political leaders, and the Sinhalese people. It seeks to extend its supremacy over the vital sea-lanes. Tamil Nadu was considered a base for their activities. A few Indian Tamils are believed to be sympathizers of the LTTE. However, when the Sri Lankan naval authorities arrested, prosecuted, and sometimes even shoot the fishermen from Tamil Nadu, the LTTE has never shown any sympathy towards them, according to the some of the fishermen in Pamban. The LTTE has also become a threat to the Indian fishermen as they confronted them during fishing. Sometimes, they fired at fishermen resulting in their killing. Fishermen's groups from Sri Lanka are also involved in attacks against Indian fishermen and are the "front organizations" of the LTTE[6]. Such incidents against Indian fishermen have increased in recent times. In the interviews conducted by the author in different places in Ramnathapuram district, fishermen narrated their woes saying that they were being more severely punished by the LTTE rather than by the Sri Lankan navy. The LTTE was responsible for attacking, destroying, damaging, or hijacking ships owned by the Indians[7] .

There is another dimension to the problem. The LTTE is demanding that the Sri Lankan government grant them the status of a de facto navy. For them, access to the sea is very important to link with its overseas network.[8] In its proposal for an Interim Self-Governing Authority (ISGA), the LTTE mentioned that it "shall have control over the marine and offshore resources of the adjacent seas and the power to regulate access thereto". This will include the Palk Straits, where both countries share the boundary line. Some Indian observers believe that if this proposal were acceptable, it would become a serious problem for India as two-thirds of the Sri Lanka sea would be under the control of the LTTE. For instance, Indian Oil Corporation had been permitted by the Sri Lankan government to use oil tanks for storage and trade. If the LTTE's plans succeed, it may pose a threat to Indian investors.

Land Bridge between India and Sri Lanka

Sri Lanka proposed a land bridge between Rameswaram in Tamil Nadu and Talaimannar in Sri Lanka. Both the governments (India and Sri Lanka) signed an agreement to construct a bridge in July 2002. Through this, road, rail and bridge links would be developed, which would offer huge economic benefits to both sides of the Palk Straits.[9] This can be one of the steps promoting cooperation between the two countries. Through this bridge, movement of people and cargo would be increased, which would result in increasing economic opportunities for both the countries. It would reduce travel and time and cost for the movement of goods and services. This bridge would establish a link between the northern Sri Lanka and Southern India and provide various facilities to the people. Also the education and health sectors would be improved. More and more private ventures in both the countries would come up. It would also reduce the travel cost for the tourists of southern India and Sri Lanka. Through tourism, areas like northern Sri Lanka and southern region of India would be developed.

This bridge will facilitate improving trade between the two countries and enhance the capacity of Trincomalee port in addition to that of Colombo port. The Bureau of Investigation of Sri Lanka prepared a detailed study for the proposed bridge and estimated the construction cost at Sri Lankan rupees eighty eight billion ($926 million). It was reported that the depth of water does not exceed seven meters at any point. The study proposed a six-lane combination of bridges, causeways, and rail track.

Since the distance between Mannar and Dhanushkodi is about twenty two kilometers, it is difficult to construct a single bridge.[10] There should be structures, which have a combination of bridges, trestles, and causeways.[11]

The bridge could become a connecting link between the national highways in south India and those in Sri Lanka. It would facilitate a continuous road and ferry link from Madurai to Trincomalee for cargo and passengers. Through this, Madurai and major cities of southern India can be connected through road and rail linkages.[12] The bridge would offer linkage to industries and agro-industries in south India and Sri Lanka.

However, the Tamil Nadu government opposed the construction of a land bridge between Tamil Nadu and Sri Lanka. Chief minister of Tamil Nadu Jayalalitha argued that the matter must be viewed not only from the economic point of view but also from the angle of the security of Tamil Nadu and India.[13] She felt that the LTTE brought the "gun culture and worse still, the horror of suicide bombing" into the peaceful state of Tamil Nadu.[14] She argued that though peace talks were being held between the LTTE and the Sri Lankan government, "the LTTE had always found some pretext to revert to its patented brand of ugly terrorism after a quiet phase of peace negotiations".[15] Hence, she felt that the proposed bridge would be premature and unwise.

The Tamil Nadu government's apprehensions about the security of Tamil Nadu may be unfounded. It is not difficult to prevent the activities of the LTTE and their crossing into Indian territory. It may not be difficult for the Indian security agencies preventing the LTTE guerrillas and sympathizers crossing the Sri Lankan border and entering India through a land bridge compared to crossing on sea. Through bridge, trade can improve between India and Sri Lanka and the link between Bangalore–Chennai–Trincomalee–Colombo would be possible and improve relations between India and Sri Lanka in general and particularly between South India–Sri Lanka." [16]

Though both the countries had agreed at government level to construct a bridge between them but it has yet to materialize.

Sethusamudram Canal Project

The proposal was not a recent one and many proposals were considered since 1860 onwards. The United Progressive Alliance (UPA) government approved a Rs. 2,427 crore for Sethusamudram Ship Canal Project (SSCP) in June 2005. On 2 July 2005, prime minister Manmohan Singh laid its foundation in Madurai and this project would be completed within three and half years. The project's objective is to link Palk Bay with the Gulf of Mannar on India's east coast by building a shipping canal through Rameswaram. The canal starts from Tuticorin, extends north-east in a straight line up to Mansfield patch south of Pamban island, then cuts through the east of the Kodandaramaswamy temple and then turns north-east to join the Bay of Bengal channel.[17] The whole project would be within Indian waters. Since the Palk Bay is narrower and the depth is not beyond fifty meters at any point, all the ships from Chennai to the west coast presently sail via Colombo harbour (Map-1).

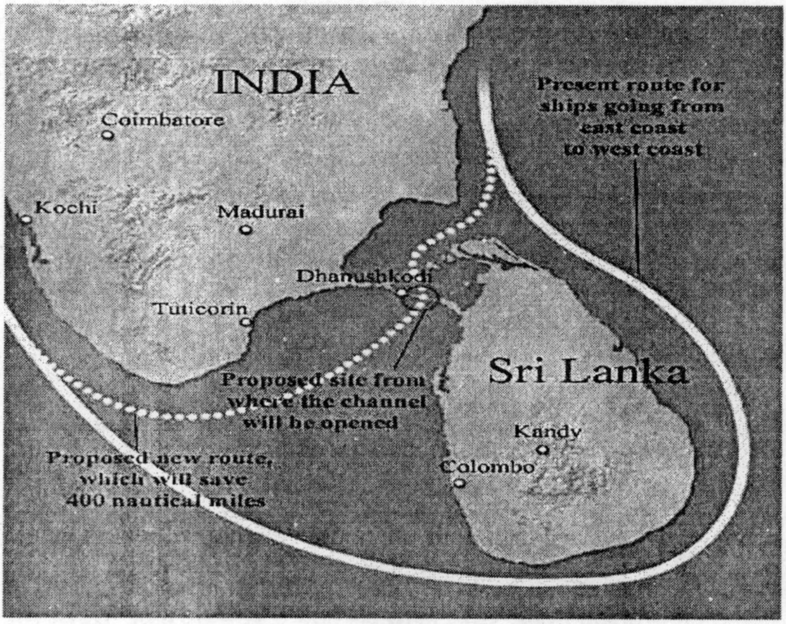

Map 1 Sethusamudram Canal Project

Source: Outlook, vol. 64, no. 41, 18 October 2004, p. 19.

Benefits

The canal will provide berthing facilities for international vessels at Tuticorin port. It will: promote economic development of the backward areas of Ramanathpuram and Tirunelveli districts of Tamil Nadu; preclude circumnavigation of ships around Sri Lanka, saving fuel costs and standing charges associated with extra period of voyage and improve operation of fishing vessels; linking of the Pamban, Archankovil, and Vaippar rivers will facilitate irrigation of about 2.26 lakh acres of dry land in Virudhunagar, Tuticorin, and Tirunelveli districts; promote coastal shipping; generate employment opportunities; and India can get foreign exchange from toll collections from foreign ships, which form fifty per cent of the traffic. Tuticorin will regain its old commercial glory. It would attract foreign investment in Tuticorin district. It can be used in transporting coal from Haldia, Paradip, and Vishakapatnam ports for the thermal power plant in Tuticorin.

Though India has 7,500 km of coastline, it does not have a continuous navigable sea-lane running within its territorial waters. Consequently, ships sailing from the east coast of India to Tuticorin have to go around Sri Lanka. This canal would reduce the distance between the east and the west coasts: between Tuticorin and Chennai from 769 to 335 nm; Tuticorin to Vishakapatnam from 1,028 to 652 nm; Tuticorin to Calcutta (now Kolkata) 1,371 to 1,031 nm; Kanyakumari to Kolkata from 1,377 to 1,098 nm; Kanyakumari to Vishakapatnam 1,014 to 719 nm; and Kanyakumari to Chennai 755 to 402 nm. N. K. Raghupathi, chairman, Tuticorin Port Trust, had said that the entire sea route through this canal was only between six and twenty one kilometers and it would not affect fish breeding.[18]

The SSCP will also serve as a strategic base, and reduce the response time of Indian navy and coast guard vessels. It will increase defense vessels patrolling in and around the peninsula.[19]

Disadvantages

The government of India maintains that once the SSCP is completed, ships would save thirty six hours voyage time. However, there is a view that only ships of 30' draft can be allowed to cross the SSCP because of its narrow depth. Hence, for safety, ships would have to reduce their speed to half while crossing the SSCP. Manitham, an NGO, argues that a ship will take at least twenty to twenty four hours to cross the SSCP. According to a retired marine engineer who worked in Tuticorin port, hardly two or three ships will cross daily.[20]

Fishermen, along with scientists, economists, environmentalists and human activists from Tamil Nadu, however, are opposing the Sethusamudram project. The livelihood of five lakh fishermen in 138 fishing stations along the five coastal districts will be severely affected. There is also concern over the impact on the environment. It involves extensive dredging of the Pamban channel where coral reef is in abundance, which will lead to the depletion of fish and the destruction of the marine ecology.[21] The Gulf of Mannar area (10,500 sq. km) is home to about 3,600 species of plants and animals.[22] The Global Environment Facility (GEF) of the UNDP said in its report that, "Of the 2,200 fish species in Indian waters, 450 species (twenty per cent) are found in the Gulf of Mannar, making it the single richest coastal area in the

Indian subcontinent in terms of fish diversity."[23] The National Environmental Engineering Research Institute (NEERI), Nagpur, examined the viability of the project. The NEERI report of May 2004 stated that the project was environmentally safe. It was silent on the impact of the project on the lives of fishermen. However, its report mentioned that "there is hard strata under the soft sediment and may require blasting if the strata encountered during dredging were to be hard rock, which may cause marine death".[24]

Sri Lanka has reservations on India's proposed project. For it, dredging of the sea might have an adverse impact on the environment and it could mean an intrusion into Sri Lankan territorial waters.[25] K. T. Rajasingham argued that there is a possibility of many islands in the west and northern coasts of Sri Lanka going under the sea. The canal may cause ports in Sri Lanka to lose more than half of its present earnings, as the project would reduce the significance of Colombo port as a hub. The Sri Lanka government appointed an inter-ministerial panel to look into the implications of the project. It feared that this project would cause heavy financial losses to Sri Lanka—ships would bypass Galle harbour and the proposed Hambantota harbour in the south, which was to open in November 2004, with Colombo harbour being the worst affected. According to Raghupathy, "Colombo will lose seventy per cent of its container traffic."[26]

The canal might also cause damage to coral reefs in the region. Once the construction of the canal is completed, it would break the continuous limestone formation. This would cause sudden tilting drifts, and gravitational pull on various other violent processes.[27] Rajasingham cautioned that eighty five islands off the north-west coast of Sri Lanka and a part of the Jaffna mainland would go under water if the Gulf of Mannar was dredged.[28] Also, a portion of the Jaffna peninsula could go under water,[29] once Miocene-era limestone reefs are extracted and its continuity forcefully terminated.[30]

It seems that the Indian government has taken only the economic benefits of the project into consideration, ignoring the ramifications, consequences and calamities neighbouring Sri Lanka would experience, once dredging of the sea is undertaken.[31]

As mentioned elsewhere, India and Sri Lanka are signatories to the UNCLOS-III. The Indian government should have obtained "no objection" from the government of Sri Lanka as per UNCLOS.

The Sri Lankan government perceived the threat to marine life in its territorial waters along the Pamban channel.[32] It also feels that the project would reduce the importance of Sri Lankan harbours.

The LTTE also opposed the project, as it would prevent their illegal trade. The Sea Tigers are using the present shallow Palk Straits. Small boats, which are being used by the Tigers, will have problems once the canal is built. The movements of the Tigers will be stopped or minimized. Through this project, the navy and coast guard can move around the Palk Straits to keep constant vigil on India's maritime assets.[33]

However, the Sri Lankan government was not taking the issue too seriously as it did not want to compromise the prevailing cordial relations with India, which is critical to counter threats from the LTTE. Sri Lanka may also have been glad to accept adverse impact on the LTTE, as the Indian security activities will have to be increased once the canal begins to function. Increased Indian surveillance has the potential of preventing the illegal smuggling activities of the LTTE. Therefore, the general feeling among the people in Sri Lanka, specially the Tamils, is that the canal project has Sri Lankan consent, expressed rather indirectly.

Both countries should have discussed and conducted studies on the project. Though the proposed project is located in its own territorial waters, India should not ignore the neighbouring country's concerns as well as the various groups in India which have expressed their reservations.

Conclusion

There is greater need to enhance mutual cooperation between India and Sri Lanka on maritime security. With cooperation, both countries can improve shipbuilding, weather forecasting, prevention of pollution, and combating maritime terrorism.

The Indian and Sri Lankan governments cannot ignore the problems of Tamil Nadu when they talk about their mutual relationship. India, on its part, cannot ignore the security concerns of Sri Lanka, and vice versa. India and Sri Lanka have to come to an understanding in addressing the problems faced by fishermen in their respective countries. It is very important for both governments to view the fishermen's problems on humanitarian grounds, while respecting the law. The policy makers in both countries can explore the possibilities of resolving the problem. It is a known fact that the fishermen from Tamil Nadu are violating the maritime laws. Both central and state governments have to take measures in discouraging its fishermen entering into Sri Lankan waters.

References

1 The 1974 agreement has two clauses, which protect a few activities of the Indian fishermen. Article 5 maintains that, "Subject to the foregoing, the Indian fishermen and pilgrims will enjoy access to visit Kachchativu as *hitherto* and will not be required by Sri Lanka to obtain travel documents or visas for these purposes." Article 6 of the agreement states that, "The vessels of Sri Lanka and India will enjoy each other's waters such rights as they have enjoyed therein."

2 National Fishworkers Forum, *Charter of Demands 2002*, Thiruvananthapuram: National Fishworkers Forum, 2002, p. 23.

3 [The] Maritime Zones of India (Regulations of Fishing by Foreign Vessels), Act, 1981 (Act No. 42 of 1981), Chapter IV, no. 10.

4 V. Vivekanandan, "Crossing Maritime Borders: The Problem and Solution in the Indo-Sri Lankan Context" in K. G. Kumar (ed) *Forging Unity: Coastal Communities and the Indian Ocean's Future*, Chennai: International Collective in Support of Fish Workers, 2003, p. 86.

5 Author participated in a seminar entitled "Maritime Security: Emerging Trends", Department of Defence and Strategic Studies, University of Madras, 18 December 2005.

6 "Navy Coast Guard to Step Up Vigil", *Hindu*, 8 March 2003, p. 6.

7 See Rohan Gunaratne, "Trends in Maritime Terrorism: The Sri Lankan Case," www.is.lk/is/spot/sp0316/clip8.html

8 V. S. Sambandan, "The LTTE's Blueprint", *Frontline*,vol. 20, no. 23, 21 November 2003, p. 14.

9 Ranil Wickemesinghe, "Making Our People Rich", *Hindu*, 25 August 2004, p. 10.

10 The longest bridge is the 1.6-km-long Storbel in Denmark. See Arjuna Mahendram and Rajive Casie Chitty, "Hanuman's Bridge: Facilitating Trade and Investment between Sri Lanka and Southern India", *South Asian Survey*, vol. 7, no. 1, January–June 2000, p. 26.

11 The following places have such structures: Lake Ponchartain, Louisiana, USA (38.4 km); Chesapeake Bay Bridge Tunnel,

Virginia, USA (28.3 km); King Fahd Causeway, Bahrain, KSA (25 km); Sunshine Skyway, Florida, USA (24.5 km). See *ibid.*

12 *Ibid*, p. 31.

13 "Drop India–Sri Lanka Bridge Project", *Hindu*, 25 Jul 2003, p. 6

14 *Ibid.*

15 *Ibid.*

16 Interview with V. Vivekanandan, Chief Executive, south Indian Federation Societies, Thiruvananthapuram.

17 www.Gisdevelopment.net/application/miscellaneous/misc016pf.html

18 see, www.buildnova.com-News

19 N. Ravi Kumar, "Strategic Significance for Security", *Hindu*, 2 July 2005, p. 11.

20 see, www.tamilinfoservice.com/manitham/environment/sscp/ir2.htm

21 Coral reefs are feeding and breeding grounds for various marine organisms. They act as carbon sinks by absorbing carbon dioxide and converting it into calcium carbonate. They protect the seashore from tidal erosion, providing people with living sea walls against tides, storm surges and hurricanes.

22 S. Anand, "India's Suez: Is it Ecocide?", *Outlook*, vol. 64, no. 41, 18 October 2004, p. 20.

23 *Ibid.*

24 *Ibid.*

25 P. K. Balachandran, "Lankans Filled with Misgivings about Fernande's Dream", http://k.t.rajasingam.tripod.com/canal.htm

26 Anand, n. 22.

27 Balachandran, n. 25.

28 *Ibid.*

29 S. U. Deraniyagala maintains that "The Jaffna Peninsula and the offshore islands present a monotonous flat landscape, with many of the physical features characteristic of limestone regions, such as caverns and sink-holes, brought about by the solution of the limestone along joints and fissures, as is the case with the northern coastal lowlands in general. There are large areas of blown sand, and this is especially marked on the eastern aspects of the peninsula and the islands".

According to geological survey, it became apparent that these limestone beds on which the peninsula sits, extend far beyond the island of Rameswaram, "The present bed of Palk Strait, which separates India from Lanka, consists of Miocene limestone, suggesting that the Jaffna limestone formation is a continuous one, extending from north-western Lanka up to southern India." See S. U. Deraniyagala, *The Prehistory of Sri Lanka*,cited in http://ktrcom.tripod.com/ktrajasingham/id27.html

30 K. T. Rajasingham, "A Canal...and an Island...!", *Asian Tribune*, 28 Aug 2002, www.asiantribune.com/show_article.php?id=25

31 *Ibid.*

32 Syed Ali Mujtaba, "India: Fishing for Trouble", *Himal*, vol. 16, n.10, October 2003, p. 10.

33 V. Suryanarayan, "Sri Lanka and India's Security", *Hindu*, 25 April 2003, p. 10.

SECTION-V
INDO-SRI LANKAN ECONOMIC RELATIONS

11

India and Sri Lanka: From Political Fissures To Economic Bridges

Manoj Soni

India and Sri Lanka – two star-crossed nations having historical, cultural and geographical affinity dating back to the Ramayana, yet ravaged by the very ties that bind them. The paper is divided into three parts. The first part of the paper identifies and addresses the broad areas of political divergence and conflict. In the second part it focuses on the possible areas of convergence and the third part explains why this convergence is important against the larger issue of South Asian resurgence.

India and Sri Lanka – Historical Memory or Historical Baggage?

India's proximity to Sri Lanka is not only geographical; it has cultural and ideological underpinnings. The largest ethnic group in Sri Lanka, i.e. the Sinhalese came from eastern India in the 5th century BC. They attribute their culture and religion to the Aryan north India. Meanwhile the Tamils of Sri Lanka, who were eighteen per cent and form the second largest group came from India too, around 3rd century BC and AD 1200. Tamils of Indian origin were *also* brought to Sri Lanka from India by colonial powers in early 19th century to work as labourers in plantations. The Sri Lankan

Tamils trace their origin to Dravidian south India. Thus both Sinhalese and Tamils consider India as their civilisational homeland.

While historical memory is important for any nation, in the case of Sri Lanka it has led to drawing ethnic boundaries, violence and bloodletting. Since the Sinhalese and Tamil dichotomy has an Aryan versus Dravidian underpinning, India has easily become the *bete noir* in Sri Lanka's internal troubles. The ties that bind have also become the ties that gag and Sri Lanka's Indian connection has been the cause of much suspicion and conflict between the two countries.

Geographical and Cultural Animosities

What does India owe Sri Lanka or – to rephrase it – why is Sri Lanka, a country that is fifty times smaller than India both geographically and demographically, important to India? Separated from India by a mere twenty two miles, Sri Lanka has a strategic location in the centre of Asia and the sea-lanes between the far east and the African and Arab world. Its security is important to India given the vulnerability of the Indian seacoast. At the same time, Sri Lanka feels overawed and threatened by India because of the latter's size and proximity. Threat perception in the past has led Sri Lanka to enter into a defence pact with the U.K. in 1947 and come under a British defence umbrella. During this time, India's vulnerable maritime assets led it to seek an Indo-British naval cooperation, which was viewed by Sri Lanka as expansionist. In 1956 there was a change in policy with the Sri Lankan Freedom Party (SLFP) coming into power. Though the 1947 pact was not abrogated, the SLFP policy was an accommodative 'pilot fish policy' whereby the small fish keeps close to the shark in order to avoid being eaten. However, in 1963 and 1971, much to India's concern Sri Lanka entered into a maritime agreement with China. This left India worried for its coastal and oceanic defence. Impending potential threats, however misplaced, have clouded the relationship between the two countries from the very dawn of independence.

Geographical discontents apart, the cultural affinity of Sri Lanka's Tamils to India has also been a soft ground to tread for the two countries. The 1964 Srimavo-Shashtri Pact and other agreements notwithstanding, there has been a lot of bitterness in this area. India's assistance of five frigates, military equipments, helicopters and Indian troop to suppress the armed revolt by an extremist Sinhala group called the Jatiya Vimukthi Peramuna (JVP) in April 1971, was viewed with suspicion. Majority of Sri Lankans felt that India's assistance came with ulterior motive. The exodus of Sri Lankan Tamils to India after the ethnic violence of 1983 forced India to mediate as Sri Lanka's internal problems had now spilled over to India and became a bilateral problem. Needless to say there was much resentment towards India in Sri Lanka. The country was projected as being sympathetic, even supportive to the Tamils and hence a threat to the strategic interest of Sri Lanka. Suspicion of India led to its isolation in the region even while Sri Lanka approached other countries for assistance. The result was the presence of powers inimical to India's security in the Indian sub-continent. India was doubly concerned about its security in the face of cold war alignments.

The Indo-Sri Lankan accord of 1987 has been called a watershed in Indo-Sri Lankan relations. This accord sought not only to address the Tamil issue but also the nagging security concerns of both the countries. However, while issues of convergence were being addressed events took a dramatic turn. The accord was followed by a Sihnalese nationalist rebellion, which had strong anti-Indian orientation. The young Sinhalese rebels described their objectives as 'liberating the motherland from India's hegemonic expansion.' The Indian Peace Keeping Force (IPKF) had to be dispatched. By the time it was withdrawn in March 1990 India had paid a heavy price in terms of military casualties and political bitterness. The subsequent SAARC summit in Colombo in 1991 was boycotted by an angry India.

Should India Look The Other Way?

The vicissitudes of Sri Lanka's ethnic conflicts have been such that India's attempt to control the conflict trajectories has failed. The question that arises is – should India look the other way? India's experience of mediation and then intrusion has not been a good one. However, for the sake of its own strategic interest India will continue to have a stake in Sri Lanka. While adopting a non-intrusive approach to the island's problem India should tackle the spill over of the problem firmly. One more reason why it cannot simply look away is Sri Lanka's moving closer to Pakistan and even turning to it for military assistance as in 1999 when LTTE rebels threatened to capture Jaffna. The need to balance a Pakistan cannot be ignored. Moreover, the pro-western, pro-American direction that Sri Lanka's policy took under president Jayawardane in the 1980s and the steps to establish diplomatic and military links with Israel has come as a potential challenge to India's doctrine of regional security that looks askance at external actors entering into the sub- continent.

The last decade of the twentieth century has seen India and Sri Lanka moving towards a much need convergence. India has taken justified steps in:

- The banning of LTTE in India.
- The deporting of Sri Lankan citizens found engaging in terrorist activities or secessionist movement.
- Identifying and banning non-state actors funding such activities.
- Enhancing defence cooperation, which would include training of security personnel by India and consultations between the defence chiefs of both the countries.

Even though the cold war calculations are no longer there, for its own strategic interests, India needs an undivided Sri Lanka consistent with democracy and pluralism. It is true that India has not joined the four other co-chairs of Sri Lankan peace – the US, the European Union, Japan and Norway, but India's policy of non-direct involvement cannot be called – *looking the other way*.

Building Economic Bridges

Moving beyond the compulsions of history and geography this paper now seeks to explore issues of economic convergence or why economic bridges need to be built. To begin with it questions the argument put forward by economists that a South-South cooperation does not lead to much gains, as would a North-South cooperation. Globalisation coming as it does with a list of gainers and losers, the global south has to work very hard to make it to the list of gainers. A North-South cooperation may yield results on the surface but without a South-South integration, these results cannot be sustainable. Another important fact is that along with globalisation the other dominant force that has been shaping the world economy is regionalisation. The current trend in forming regional trading blocs is evident from the fact that the WTO has a notification of 140 members participating in one or more Regional

Trade Agreements (RTAs). The global north has stood to benefit from such agreements and the East Asian countries are increasingly making their presence felt.

No doubt South Asia has integrated into the world economy with countries liberalising their economic policies. Sri Lanka adopted structural adjustment programmes as early 1977. India was among the last to adopt economic reforms in 1991. However, this integration does not bring magical gains per se. Until and unless there is integration at the regional level the bargaining capacity of South Asia will continue to be seriously dwarfed. At this juncture India and Sri Lanka need to examine their economic complementarities. Though both the countries are grappling with persistent poverty, high unemployment rates, negative trends in the patterns of income distribution, yet the fact remains that in South Asia, they are the most promising market oriented economies. Sri Lanka's major trading partner is India, its economic relations with Bangladesh, Pakistan, Nepal and Bhutan being marginal and insignificant. India on its part must view Sri Lanka as its name suggests *–land of plenty*.

The Indo –Sri Lankan Bilateral Free Trade Agreement (ISLBFTA) was worked out in 1998 and became operational in early 2000. Despite pessimism from several quarters, the first five years of the agreement show some encouraging figures. By 2004, bilateral trade amounted to 1.73 billion dollars. Moreover, India, which was the twenty first destination for Sri Lankan exports, has become the third largest destination with exports to India increasing from one per cent before the agreement to seven per cent of the total exports in 2004.

Fifty per cent of the Indian investment in the SAARC region today is in Sri Lanka and India is the fourth largest investor in the country after Singapore, U.K. and Australia. With the trade – investment nexus working out well for both the countries, the myth that an ISLBFTA type of agreement would benefit the larger country alone also stands exploded. In fact, both the countries are moving towards a Comprehensive Economic Partnership Agreement (CEPA). This shows that political fissures notwithstanding, if economic agreements are properly designed, economic bridges can be built. These in turn will help to mend political breeches. Such bridges would make a major contribution to the political and economic stability of Sri Lanka, which again is important for India's strategic interests. Then again, India and Sri Lanka need to work on issues of convergence not simply for the sake of Sri Lanka or India or both but for the larger sake of South Asian resurgence. The interlinkages simply cannot be ignored.

With bilateral free trade alliances in place, what South Asia needs is a dynamic regional trading agreement that will not be vulnerable to the fluctuating politics of South Asia and will withstand political shocks. No doubt there are limited complementarities in the region but South Asia has always had to deal with limited complementarities. Despite pursuing market-oriented policies and reducing barriers to trade and investment, the SAARC countries have not been able to work the magic of ASEAN. South Asian exports are more than seven times lower than East Asia and barely account for one per cent of the world total. The flow of private capital to South Asia is also ten times less than in East Asia and Latin America. The potential costs of being marginalized from the global economy must work as a wake up call for the SAARC countries. The SAFTA has been officially launched in January 2006 as the vehicle of free trade in South Asia. Of course, as of now the trade among countries in the region is low at about five per cent. However the existence of large cross-border illegal trade points to the immense potential of intra-regional trade. It will be important to rescue SAFTA from political bickering and discontents and allow it to work. While no one country can unilaterally level the ground for making SAARC an efficient body, India, because of its size and stature, has a clear responsibility there. It can take a lesson from Indonesia, which, despite being the biggest ASEAN member, has always maintained a low-key facilitator approach. The smaller members should also modify their attitude. The lack of integration in the region is worrisome. SAARC needs to transcend bilateral irritants and suspicion of each other. A multi-track approach to regional integration linking up governments, non-government organisations interested in the peace process, media, business and professional bodies is needed. Besides, a people to people contact in South Asia parallel to the official process should be encouraged. Immense effort has to be made indeed if South Asia is to be given a strong regional identity and rationality.

With the year 2005 ending on a violent note for Sri Lanka and January recording a death a day at the very minimum, the geographical map of killing and violence seems to have widened and intensified. Sri Lanka's internal peace and security is still an open-ended question. However, on India's part the evolving bilateral security linkages and economic bridges are helping to dilute what S. D. Muni has described as 'pangs of proximity' between the two countries. To conclude the author borrows a sentiment from Rohinton Mistry and say – *only twenty two miles but 'such a long journey'.*

12

Strategic Marketing Formulation for the Domestic Manufacturers Through the Operation of Regional Cooperation in the Context of Globalisation

K. Ishaq

Introduction

The rapid process of globalisation has had a significant impact on the world economy in the last decades. Increasing economic integration and interdependence between countries are some of the important changes taking place due to the rapid process of globalisation. This brings about the reorganization of products, interpenetration of industries and marketing across borders. All industries have undergone structural changes in terms of production methods, finance and investment, labour, technology, and marketing due to the accelerated process of globalisation. In the case of developing countries, the domestic production and its market, the pattern of supply and demand has changed during the second half of the century. In this context, all domestic manufacturers of various products in Sri Lanka and India have to face new challenges and the effect of globalisation through the operation of Transnational Corporations (TNCs) and Multinational Companies (MNCs) within the region.

The majority of domestic manufacturers cannot offer low-priced and quality product with innovation to customers compared with global competitors in the liberalized regional marketplace. This has a serious negative impact currently, keeping the industries far behind from the global and regional competitive position. The manufacturing industries in SAARC region have to rethink their strategies for the long- term survival. The Formulation of effective and suitable strategic marketing planning is imperative to overcome the competition.

The globalization process through the trade liberalization policy has a significant influence on the performance of various domestic manufacturers in all developing countries, including Sri Lanka and India.

It is essential to assess the influence of globalisation continuously. Decision makers must build their capacity and ability to react to and meet the challenges in the context of globalisation. Every single change will reach and affect any part of the world through modern communication and technology. Manufacturers in Sri Lanka and India are facing a number of challenges in the modern business world and they have to operate in a highly volatile marketing environment in this electronic era. Sophisticated technology plays an important role in the business environment's day-to-day operations in the world. Giant firms can win any market in the electronic world by applying dynamic means such as technology, well-developed human resources, huge investment, updated research and development. This would, however, weaken or defeat the business firms in developing countries, while those giant companies could even simply absorb them. This paper provides an insight into the concept of strategic marketing formulation especially in the SAARC region where India plays a major role in the region.

There has been a hot debate on the concept of globalisation since the late 1980s and early 1990s. Since the collapse of the Soviet Union, most scholars, politicians, business people and the media have been using the globalisation frequently.[1] A number of definitions are given by various theorists in order to understand the dimensions of globalisation. Kugut[2] defines globalisation as follows: "Globalisation means convergence among nations and companies towards common ways of doing things". Gill defines globalisation as the process of increasing economic integration and growing economic interdependence between the economies of countries.[3] Kiely defines globalisation as a world in which societies, cultures, politics and economies come closer together.[4] The movement of commodities, capital, finance, technology, ideas and information, are all used as part of a strategy of economic development in the New World order where the borders of countries have become blurred. Increasing economic integration and interdependence between countries are some of the important changes taking place due to the rapid process of globalisation.[5] This brings about the reorganization of products, interpenetration of industries, and marketing across borders.[6] A number of changes have taken place in investment, production methods and marketing in the world under globalisation.[7] TNCs and MNCs are playing an important role in the rapid globalisation process through their direct investment and technological power.[8] Most of the resource and liberated market in developing countries are controlled by the giant TNCs of developed countries.

TNCs have changed from being MNCs to becoming truly transnational corporations. TNCs have integrated its strategies on a worldwide scale rather than separate strategies on a country-by-country basis.[9] National government cannot, however, control the TNCs and only regulation agreed upon and enforced internationally could limit the power of these TNCs. A TNC is sometimes referred to as a "stateless corporation". According to the United Nations[10] there are now some 60,000 TNCs with around 500,000 foreign affiliates worldwide. The 100 largest TNCs control one-fifth of the global foreign assets and one-third of sales. The 500 largest industrial corporations in the world control 25% of the world's economic output. The top 300 TNCs (excluding financial institutions) own 25% of the world's productive assets. Global trends are clearly towards greater concentration of the control of markets and productive assets in the hands of a few giant companies.

According to Shafika,[11] the globalisation process has been accelerated by factors such as computerized technology and neo-liberal economic strategies. The International Monitory Fund (IMF) and World Bank play an important role in imposing globalisation and increasing control over the economy of the countries of the world, especially in developing countries.[12] New market rules, privatization, deregulation, cuts in government spending, high competition, an outward-orientated economy, trade liberalization, specialization in production and flexibility of factors, are the important features of a neo-liberal agenda in the globalisation process.[13] Governments are pressured to free their trade by reducing tax on imports under the policy of liberalization.[14]

World trade is controlled by the World Trade Organisation (WTO), which controls trade regulations to protect the interests and benefits of international Banks and TNCs.[15] The IMF and World Bank also changed their constitutions to the benefit of financial liberalization to accelerate the globalisation process.[16] The Uruguay Round agreement and Marrakesh agreement were the returning point of the world economy. These agreements have played a vital role in trade liberalization policies. All tariff reductions to free trade liberalization take place through these agreements. As a result of these changes TNCs are opening manufacturing companies in developing countries where cheaper labour and markets for products are available. TNCs transfer advanced technology, management techniques and work organization across the globe to control trade all over the world by means of the trade liberalization policies of governments.[17] In order to control the global market, TNCs are applying different production and marketing strategies, research and development (R&D) activities, human resource policy, operating styles, advanced technology and communication, sound financial capacity, sourcing policy, new innovated product development and investment policies.

Developing countries have to improve manufacturing methods to compete with global competitors in the context of globalisation. Most developing countries do not have sufficient skilled manpower, investment and technology to compete with global companies.[18] India and Sri Lanka are also unable in many ways to compete with the global companies. Tariff reduction has a direct negative impact on the overall performance of domestic manufacturers in Sri Lanka and India. Margin has reduced and the output of domestic sectors has decreased due to the increased imports of low-priced products and advanced technology in the domestic market. This has an impact on investment and increased competition in the domestic and regional market. The domestic industries could not reach economies of scale in production due to decreased market shares as global competitors eroded the domestic and regional market share. Fundamental changes are essential though in the operation of domestic manufacturers in India and Sri Lanka in order to compete in the globalised marketplace. Domestic manufacturers will have to improve efficiency, operate more cost-effectively and implement new manufacturing methods and strategic marketing.

Changes in global production patterns

Globalization has intensified not only in the financial and trade spheres but is also characterised by the emergence of a highly innovated worldwide production structure. Production processes are undergoing restructuring in order to meet the demands of a competitive global market. The nature of work and methods of production are an important part of an ongoing process of globalisation. Mass production methods gained ground over its craft-production technological rival throughout the nineteenth century. The disadvantages of mass production are rigidity and standardization. Mass production cannot cope with flexibility, cyclical recessions, increased competition or changing market tastes. This need brought a flexible production system that consisted of flexible production, work process, a flexible labour market, flexible education, communication, multiple skills and high-quality production with high added value on the international market.[19] This new method of production process invented by Toyota, called "Toyotaism". This method is referred to as "lean production". In addition to this lean production system, Toyota gradually introduced the just-in-time (JIT) production method. This means that Toyota stopped building motorcars in advance for unknown buyers and converted to a build-on-order system.[20]

The focused factory concept in lean production

Cost, quality and flexibility became collectively attainable goals in the manufacturing strategy in the 1990s. Today the focused factory (FF) concept is one of the most important principles used in large-scale factory reorganization. The manufacturing strategy for a plant consists of five major facets so that the products of that plant and processes are competitive. The areas are (a) Differentiation (technological sophistication and product features), (b) Flexibility (to modify products to suit customers and delivery volumes), (c) Manufacturing cost, (d) Timelines and (e) Quality (quality with regard to product performance, reliability and durability.[21]

The total quality management concept

Total quality management (TQM) indicates excellence of performance throughout the total system, including design, production, distribution, service, and the involvement of all categories of employees, customers and suppliers in the quality initiatives.[22] Toyota introduced the TQM system in order to achieve its goals through the flexible method.. All groups of the workforce and management at all level are involved in promoting the concepts and practice of TQM. The lean production and TQM have today become a most efficient manufacturing practice worldwide to increase their competitive advantages.

Computerized manufacturing technology

Computerized advanced manufacturing technology has been introduced in the manufacturing process in factories of global companies with huge amounts of investment. The following are some of these modern technologies: (a) Computer-aided manufacture (CAM), (b) Computer-aided design (CAD), and (c) Computer-aided planning (CAP). CAM techniques now include numerical control and computer numerical control machine tools and machinery center, industrial robotics and flexible manufacturing cells or flexible manufacturing systems. CAD techniques could vary from simple drafting aids to sophisticated computer system, which test alternative designs for stress and other characteristics when they become computer-aided engineering tools. A CAP technique includes software that links parts needed by suppliers and inventories such as manufacturing resources planning. CAP techniques also include computer-aided process planning, which routes parts through the factory in optimal ways.[23]

Communication technology

Communication technology plays a vital role in reinforcing global activities, which reduce the space, time, distance and social order in the exchange of commodities and service between countries. There is a close relation between the process of globalisation and modern communication.[24] Today, satellite communication systems can supposedly "shrink" distances because of its ability to cover large expanses of the earth's surface.[25] In recent times, the rapid development of the worldwide web (WWW) has accelerated the activities and functions of globalization all over the world. Mercantile colonialism seeks cheap labour, while electronic colonialism seeks mind. Global companies are setting up their factories not only where they can reduce manufacturing costs and where labour is cheap, they also locate their marketing staff in the most suitable and fruitful zone where efficient communication is available.[26] In this case, India is a good example where global companies are opening up their factories, communication headquarters and call centers as cheap labours and well-developed communication and computer software are available.

Developers should undertake a review of the effects of liberalization through globalization on the domestic industrial sectors and overall economy and draw lessons for future trade. Regional integration and cooperation are an important tool and strategy for trade and economic development in developing countries, especially in India and Sri Lanka under the Indo-Sri Lanka partnership programme.

Major changes at global level further underpin a direct impact on the performance of domestic manufacturers in India and Sri Lanka. These industries are not globally competitive, while many problems are keeping the industries from the major global market. Globalization has brought opportunities as well as several risks and insecurities for domestic manufacturers in India and Sri Lanka. The opportunities have to be availed and risks and insecurities are to be avoided through suitable and appropriate strategies. Now, from the above discussion, the necessity has arisen to domestic manufacturers in India and Sri Lanka to formulate their successful strategies to cope and react to global competitors in the domestic and regional globalized marketplace.

Strategic Marketing Formulation

The marketing management must pay more attention when formulating effective strategic marketing to react to global competitors in the domestic marketplace. The saturation of many local markets and fast technological changes, together with the liberalization of world trade, have led to increasing global competition. These major changes in the business environment have forced the domestic manufacturers in India and Sri Lanka to assess their opportunities and threats, strength and weakness from a different perspective compared to strictly local business. A domestic company could not survive in the domestic market without understanding the marketing strategies of the global companies. This is because a company could lose its domestic market to global competitors with lower costs, greater experience, better products and more value for customers. A deeper knowledge of global marketing is essential when a company compete with global competitors in the domestic market. Otherwise, they would lose their domestic markets because they will be pushed aside by stronger competitive global competitors. This section discuss what factors are to be considered to assess to formulate strategic marketing for domestic manufacturers to compete with the global companies in the domestic and regional marketplace.

Global strategic marketing

By 1980s, global trends had forced companies to consider a worldwide strategic approach and to adapt their organizational capabilities. Some seemed to be managing the transition successfully, while others were simply surviving and some encountered major difficulties.[27] Chae and Hill[28] argue that global strategic marketing planning is a subset of the global strategic planning process. Global strategic planning is a broader concept, encompassing marketing oriented decision, but financial, human resources, manufacturing and other functional strategies. The management of the domestic manufacturers must carefully assess and consider strength and weakness in order to formulate domestic and regional marketing strategies that maintain a match between corporate resources and marketplace development.

Assessing global competitors' strategies

Domestic manufacturers cannot achieve their objectives without understanding their consumers and competitors and what competitors are doing in the domestic and regional marketplace. An organization can review its position by analyzing its competitors' environment and considering the factors that influence the organization's capacity to find an effective competitive strategy.[29] TNCs and MNCs operating in the regional market and obtain economies of scale in production and are able also to invest in advertising and R&D in order to maintain their dominance. Management has to assess both types of competition-local and multinational- so as to identify the strategies of the competition.[30]

The company must focus on corporate policy, corporate strategy and management system and operations of the identified competitors. This will enable that company to identify the objectives, profitability, strengths and weaknesses of global competitors in the regional market.

In general, domestic manufacturers must watch carefully and continuously to learn the strategies and moves of the global companies in other countries. There is competition between global companies versus global companies in the domestic market as well as local companies versus global companies. Domestic manufacturers must design a proper system to undertake a competitor analysis, which includes human resources, financial and physical assets, market share and profitability of the global competitors.[31] Domestic manufacturers in India and Sri Lanka are facing different strategies from global companies. Therefore, the marketing management has to makes efforts to assess the strategies of the global companies.

Global information system

Each company must establish an information system to identify the opportunities and threats of global companies in the regional marketplace. A well-formulated intelligence system will enable management to determine the global competitiveness of the company and the role of major forces such as buyers, suppliers, new entrants, substitutes and global competitors. Global market research will provide sufficient information about global competitors to assist decision-making about marketing on a regional and global scale. Each company requires information that allows analysis across several global competitors in the domestic and regional market.

Internal analysis

According to Muhlbacher and others[32], once the competitors' analysis has been completed, the company must start an internal analysis in order to compare the data with the strengths and weaknesses of their own company. Corporate policy, corporate strategy, the management system and operations must be included as significant factors of the internal analysis. The starting point of the internal analysis is with the corporate policy. The domestic manufacturers must concentrate on and assess the corporate strategy, management system and operation before they formulate their strategies. Toyne and Walters[33] point out that the external environment analysis on its own is not sufficient to develop the company's competitive strategies in the globalized marketplace. Management has to assess the method of business, its resource organizational structure and climate, technical and managerial skills, in order to identify the capabilities and strengths of its resources to meet the complicated challenges in the global marketplace. Domestic manufacturers must analysis the corporate policy, strategy, management system and operations of the company with regard to its internal resource to increase its competitive abilities and advantages. The internal analysis enables domestic manufacturers to arrange its available internal resources to compete with the different strategies of global competitors.

Strategies of the global companies for Marketing Entry

Domestic manufacturers must observe and assess the entry strategies of the global companies under trade liberalization policy into the domestic and regional market to prosper in these enterprises and to promote marketing system. The giant companies are using different modes of entry strategies to capture the market or increase the market share in the globalized domestic marketplace in the developing countries. Marketing entry strategies of the global companies are:

- Indirect Export;
- Direct Export;
- Other direct exporting methods: Management contracts, Turnkey operation;
- Foreign product entry method: Licensing, Franchising, Assembly, Joint ventures, Local manufacturing and whole-owned subsidiaries, Contract manufacturing.

Domestic manufacturers in India and Sri Lanka must have the service of well-experienced managers possessing sufficient knowledge especially on global market entry with the ability to understand and to identify the strategies of the global companies in the regional market. The management must pay more and special attention to the entry strategy of the global companies in the domestic and regional marketplace in order to formulate their own strategies to react to the global competitors.

Global marketing strategy

After the completion of the analysis of the entry strategies, the next step is to analyse the global company's marketing strategies. The global marketing strategy is an important tool to implement and achieve the major goal of global strategic marketing. A company has to provide a suitable product to meet needs and respond to competitive challenges in the globalised market,like products design and branding strategies, packaging, labeling and warranty provisions. Customers do not buy product features but they expect more value what they buy.[34] In globalized marketplace, the product is the center of the marketing strategy of an organization. Domestic marketers have to face the challenge of formulating a coherent global product strategy in their domestic market. Manufacturers have to develop new products continually in order to secure their market from the global competitors in the domestic and regional market. They have to apply the computer-aided design and computer-aided manufacturing process to innovate their product to react to the global companies. They must have new product development committee to introduce new products in the market.[35]

Customer satisfaction is an important factor that impacts on the long-term success of a company. Marketers must consider the warranty and service policy of the global competitors who are operating in the domestic and regional market in order to increase the satisfaction of the customers. A well-designed distribution system is the key that creates customer value. Also the management must analyze the warehouse and inventory system, pricing strategy, which is a critical element and powerful weapon of the marketing mix of the global competitors, and promotion strategy that includes the advertising, personal selling strategy, sales promotional strategy, and public relations to enjoy the opportunities in the regional market in the context of globally competitive marketplace.

Some executives of local companies with limited international exposure fear that they will ill-equipped to face the established global competitors in domestic and regional market. However, managers do not have to go abroad to experience global competition. Sooner or later the world come to each manager. However, managers of local companies in this competitive market think in only three ways. One is to seek assistance from the government in the way of reinstated trade barriers or some other form of support. The second is to become a partner of a TNCs or MNCs, while the third is simply to sell out and leave the industry. There are many options for companies to face the stiffer foreign competition. Management must think and act quickly to react to competition in the domestic and regional market before they lose their market share. or even to increase their market share.

The domestic manufacturers in India and Sri Lanka could have a variety of marketing strategies. Some of these strategies might be risky, but the fact remains that most of them may be attracted by a trans -regional configuration. They should put the maximum efforts and design strategy into export markets and could cover the high volume segments of the regional market. It is possible to formulate their strategic marketing to respond to the condition of local demand and export with modified versions towards other regions where they could target low-volume niche markets. Local adaptation strategies are also necessary to compete with global players.

Regional Economic Integration

Since World War II, there has been a tremendous interest among nations in economic cooperation. This interest has been stimulated by the success of the European Community. There are major regional economic cooperations and agreements in the world. There are many degree of economic cooperation, ranging from agreement between two or more nations to reductions of barriers to trade, to the full-scale economic integration of two or more national economies.[36] There are four degree of economic cooperation and integration.

(a) **Free Trade Area:** A free trade area (FTA) is a group of countries that have agreed to abolish all internal barriers to trade among themselves. Countries that belong to a free trade area can and do maintain independent trade policies with third countries.

(b) **Customers Union:** A customs union represents the logical evolution of a FTA. In addition to trade, eliminating the internal barriers to trade, members of a customs union agree to the establishment of common external barriers.

(c) **Common Market:** A common market goes beyond the removal of internal barriers to trade and the establishment of common external barriers to the important next stage of eliminating the barriers to the flow of factors (labour and capital) within the market. A common market builds on the elimination of the internal tariff barriers and the establishment of common external barriers. It seeks to coordinate economic and social policies within the market to allow free flow of capital and labour from country to country. Thus, a common market creates an open market not only goods but also for service and capital.

(d) **Economic Union:** The full evolution of an economic Union would involve the creation of a unified Central Bank, the use of a single currency, and common policies on agriculture, social service and welfare, regional development, transport, taxation, competition and mergers, construction and building and so on.[37] A fully developed economic union requires extensive political unity, which makes it similar to a nation. The further integration of nations that were members of fully developed economic union would be the formation of a central government that would bring together independent political states into a single political framework.

SAARC and SAFTA

South Asian countries must soon resolve the existing conflicts among themselves. South Asia is the world's single largest market with a staggeringly vast empowered middle class. South Asian nations enjoyed political independence for over half a century but have not yet been able to reach many of the goals successfully achieved. A joint effort to strengthen individual programme of each member state designed to implement the accepted goals of the programme could prove to be an excellent starting point for the promotion of close cooperation between the members. In South Asia, fundamental areas concerning human development show even today a weak level of performance. GDP of a weal level is also the lowest in South Asia as compared with the developing world. The economy of the member countries in SAARC still remains weak with moderate GDP growth and per capita income is less compared with other countries as a whole. The institutes of SAARC must be strengthened to achieve these objectives in future.

SAARC has arrived at an essential point in its regional cooperation, when it signed the framework treaty on SAFTA in January 2004 at Islamabad and later in 2005 the agreement was ratified at Dhaka summit. It needs to adopt further measures for trade facilitation in order to ensure that the member countries achieve the full benefits of SAFTA in future

Indo-Sri Lanka Partnership

India and Sri Lanka are endowed with natural, technological, human resources and other production capacities, but the system and cooperation must be established among two countries to encourage the manufacturers and other key players who are contributing to the economic development of the countries. The resource and capacities are unevenly distributed across the countries. All these available resources are not utilized properly. It has under utilized. Both governments must establish effective inter country programmes to improve the technology, multi-skill labour force, structural changes in national demand, supply and prices. Joint programmes are very essential to improve the infrastructural facilities in both countries.

Firms and governments of both countries must take keen interest in evaluating the private or social economic returns of their innovative activities. In order to meet the challenges of entering the era of high technology, governments must support actively on industrial R & D in order for companies to improve their industrial technological capabilities. India and Sri Lanka must work together in many respects to improve their economy in the context of globalisation. There is a good relationship between them in various terms and interest for over the years. With the operation of the SAFTA, both countries should agree to adopt many necessary measurers to improve their economic development in the context of globalisation. India's investment in some areas such as scientific and information technology could be utilized to enjoy the regional market and it can share with Sri Lanka. Sri Lanka has also achieved notable success in the areas of human development. But the investment in human resources development is still urgent need of the both countries when compared with other developed countries.

Adequate institutional support and incentive system for investment, production, distribution, trade, information exchange, technology and skill development and transfer, payment are to be established by both the governments to promote the productivity and capacity of all manufacturers. Both governments must identify some specific industries from both countries to promote their export to other countries in the SAARC region. Manufacturers producing similar products could be mergered and work together in order to improve their capacity and formulate effective marketing strategies to react to the global companies in the regional market. Appropriate national and regional strategies for industrial cooperation and regional policy support systems and institutional mechanism to effect cooperative industrialization in the region is very important that will bring a number of benefits to both countries.

Under the Indo-Sri Lanka partnership programme, both countries must design a suitable framework for national and regional cooperative strategies to promote greater regional and extra-regional trade; joint ventures and collaborative institutional development need to be developed. Both governments must concentrate on some necessary programmes to improve their competitive advantage of the domestic manufacturers that are preferential market access within the region, exchange and flow of marketing information, technology and skill development, joint production and marketing for common exports, mobilization, pooling and flow of investment funds, capacity utilization and cost efficiency and payments, transfer, customs clearances etc.

Manufacturers in Sri Lanka can also be included as a partner in specific production programme. The regional projects can be started particularly for promoting intra-regional as well as international exports. Alternative regional industrial development plans in the framework of SAPTA and other regional mechanism must be established. Regional policies, strategies, institutional mechanism are imperative for implementing all those projects and plans. Implementations strategies and specific feasibility studies for step-by-step, product-by-product is very important. All these programmes have to design to ensure equitable distribution of benefits from the cooperation. Generating awareness regarding benefits from cooperation must be given to the domestic manufacturers in India and in Sri Lanka. Regional trade promotion through regional integration is to be established by both governments. Improving utilization of existing capacities in a regional framework, collaborative technological development, technology transfer, and provision of cost-effective infrastructural support are important aspects that enable the domestic small and medium size manufacturers to have efficient resource management in the region in future.

India and Sri Lanka must concentrate on harmonization of policies such as industrial development, foreign exchange and payments, preferential trade, export promotion and import substitution, fiscal and monetary incentives, foreign investment, promotion of joint ventures, skill development, employment, science and technology, transport, communication and storage. The effective customs union must be established under the cooperation. Both governments should take necessary and series of actions to eradicate the wastage of the resources, bureaucracy and red tapism, and corruption. Also severe concentration in strengthening the law and order is very essential in order to build a peaceful environment to work together toward the goals.

Some important institutions such as Regional Development Bank under the SAARC, Board of Technological Development and transfer, skill development and transfer center, Information Bank and exchange mechanism, public and private sector cooperation network (regional chambers, trade association and labour organization), joint acquisition and purchasing organization, regional chamber of commerce and industry should be brought under single system.

Governments of regional countries must have sufficient link and collaboration with each other as well as the manufacturers must work together to enjoy the support that extended by the governments to improve their capacities to formulate very effective strategic marketing to react to the global competitors in the domestic and regional market. Collaboration among the manufacturers, which ranging from micro level to large, is very important and inevitable to assess the strength and weakness of the global competitor who are operating in the regional market under the trade liberalization policy for over the decades.

Conclusion

The necessary theory and concepts are presented in this paper to explain the important aspects on which the government and domestic manufacturers must concentrate under a regional cooperation to rethink and formulate their strategic marketing to react to the global competitors in the domestic and regional markets. Domestic manufacturers are far behind from the global and regional market where the global giant companies have been eroding their market share for years. All manufactures and governments must work together in various levels under a systematic institutional framework to enhance their competitive advantages according to the changes in the global business environment. The knowledge based economic integration is very important to have a sustainable economic development and innovation in future. The domestic manufacturers have to assess the strength and weakness of the global competitors and have to compare with their internal assets they have. This process will enable them to formulate the effective strategic marketing with the support of the governments. There are so many alternative strategies that can be developed to face any challenges in the globalised competitive place but scanning and analyzing the situation continually is very essential. The process of globalisation is not stoppable but controllable. Also there are number of possibilities to have the plethora of benefits by applying appropriate strategies. Indo-Sri Lanka partnership programme is the ideal platform domestic manufactures and governments of both countries to work together to achieve the economic development that will lead to uplift the quality of the people in future.

References

1 S. Gill, "Globalization, democratization and the politics of indifference" in J.H. Mittelman (ed), *Globalization critical reflections: International political economy yearbook*, vol. 9, London: Rienner, 1996, p. 210.

2 B.Kugut, "What makes a company global?", *Harvard business review*, vol. 77, no.1, January-February 1999, p.165.

3 S.S.Gill, "India's economic security in the context of globalization", *Journal of development economics for Southern Africa*, vol.1, nos.4&5, September-December 1998, January-April 1999, p.70.

4 R.Kiely, "The crisis of global development", in R. Liely, & P. Marfleet (eds), *Globalization and the third world*, London: Routledge, 1998, p. 3.

5 Gill, n.3, pp.66-77.

6 J.H. Mittelman, "The dynamic of globalization", in Mittelman, n.1, p.2

7 R.W. Cox, "A perspective on globalization", in Mittelman, p. 22.

8 A. Hoogevelt, *Globalization and the postcolonial world: the new political economy of development*, London: Macmillan, 1997, p .69.

9 J.P. Jeannet & H.D. Hennessey, *Global marketing strategies*, Boston, Mass.: Houghton Mifflin, 1998, p.17.

10 United Nations, *The competitiveness challenges: transnational corporations and industrial restructuring in developing countries*, New York, 2000, p.18.

11 I. Shafika, *South Africa in the global economy: Understanding the challenges working towards alternatives*, Durban: Trade Union Research Project (TURP), 1997, p. 29.

12 Kiely, n.4, p. 26.

13 Shafika, n.11, p. 20.

14 Gill, n.1, p. 25.

15 S. Buthelezi, "Globalization, the South African state and its relations with other African states: South Africa in Africa in the new millennium", *Journal of development economies for Southern Africa*, vol. 1, nos.8-9, January-December 2000, p. 8.

16 Y. Tandon , "Globalization and Africa's option: Part II", *Journal of development economics for Southern Africa*, vol.1, nos.6 & 7, May-December1999, p. 109.

17 J. Braithwaite & P. Drahos, *Global business regulation*, New York: Cambridge, University Press, 2000, p. 208.

18 J. Humphrey, "Industrial reorganization in developing countries: from models to trajectories", *World development*, vol. 23, no.1, January 1999, p.150.

19 Hoogevelt , n.8, p. 93.

20 G.P. White, "Just-in-time manufacturing", in P.M. Swamidass (ed), *Innovations in competitive manufacturing,* New york: Amacon, 2002, p.174.

21 M. Swink, "Core manufacturing competencies", in Swamidass, *ibid,* p. 25.

22 R.N. Natarajan, "Total quality management", in Swamidas, *Ibid,* p. 69.

23 J. Mathews, *Tools of change: new technology and the democratization of work*, Sydney: Pluto Press, 1989, p.3; Hoogevelt, n. 8, p.102.

24 A. Mohammedali, "Communication and globalization process in the developing world", in A. Mohammedali (ed), *International communication and globalization: a critical introduction,* London: Sage Publications, 1997, p. 67.

25 C.S. Craig & S.P.Douglas, *International marketing research*, New York: Wiley, 2000, p. 8.

26 L. Stones, "Splitting up operations can be profitable", *Business Day,* 1October 1998, p.16.

27 C.A.Bartlett & S. Ghoshal, "Managing across boarders: new strategic requirements", *Sloan management review*, vol.28, no. 4, Summer 1987, p. 7.

28 M.Chae & J.S.Hill, "High versus low formality marketing planning in global industries: determinants and consequences", *Journal of strategic marketing,* vol. 5, no.1, March1997, p. 5.

29 H. Chee & R.Harris, *Global marketing strategy*, London: Pitman, 1998, p. 91.

30 *Ibid,* pp. 91-92.

31 Jeannet & Hennessey, n.9, pp.299-302.

32 H. Muhlbacher, L. Dahringer & H. Leihs, *International marketing: a global perspective*, London: Thomson, 1999, p. 333.

33 B. Toyne & P.G.P. Walters, *Global marketing management: a strategic perspective*, Boston, Mass.: Allyn & Bacon, 1993, pp. 99-100.

34 Chee & Harris, n.29, p. 370.

35 V. Terpstra & R. Sarathy, *International Marketing*, New York: Dryden, 2000, p.307.

36 W.J. Keegan, *Global marketing management*, New Delhi: Prentice-Hall, 2002, p. 50.

37 *Ibid,* p. 51.

13

Indo-Sri Lanka Free Trade Agreement:Can Trade Agreement Among Unequal Partners Work[1]?

Indra Nath Mukherji

1. Introduction

In recent years there has been an upsurge in Bilateral Free Trade Agreements (BFTA). As of now there are as many as thirty eight such agreements outside South Asia, the most recent ones being the Singapore-Japan and Singapore-New Zealand BFTAs. In addition, several regional groupings have developed bilateral trade linkages with non-members. To illustrate, the European Community (EC) has as many as twenty eight BFTA with individual member states. Similarly the European Free Trade Area (EFTA) has twelve bilateral trade agreements with member states.

In South Asia also there has been a surge in BFTA. India and Bhutan have BFTA since fifties. A BFTA between India and Sri Lanka became operational in March 2000. India is currently contemplating similar BFTA with Bangladesh and Maldives. Recently there have been initiatives to establish BFTA between Sri Lanka and Pakistan, Sri Lanka and Bangladesh, Nepal and Sri Lanka, and Nepal and Bangladesh. The recent shift in signing of BFTA has partly been due to the slow and tardy progress under South Asian Preferential Trading Arrangement (SAPTA) being negotiated under SAARC. Even though at long last SAFTA has been signed at the SAARC Summit at Dhaka in December 2005, according to which the agreement was to become effective from 1 January 2006, the customs notifications of Pakistan and Sri Lanka are yet to be issued at the time of writing.

In sharp contrast too the slow progress of SAFTA, Indo-Lanka Free Trade Agreement (ILFTA)has been on fast track. The commerce secretary of India and finance secretary of Sri Lanka exchanged letters that operationalise ILFTA between India and Sri Lanka signed in New Delhi on 28 December 1998 by the president of Sri Lanka and the prime minister of India with effect from 1March 2000.

The agreement provides for duty free as well as duty preference access for the goods manufactured in the two countries. Both the countries have listed products for immediate duty free entry into each other's territories. India has agreed to phase out its tariffs on a large number of items within a period of three years. Sri Lanka will likewise do so in eight years. Both the countries have drawn up negative lists in respect of which no duty concessions will apply. These lists include items on which protection to local industry has been considered essential. Both the countries intend to reduce the items in the negative list through periodic consultations.

The agreement sets out the rules of origin criteria for eligibility for preferential access. Products having domestic value addition of thirty five per cent will qualify for preferential market access. Sri Lanka's exports with a domestic value addition content of twenty five per cent will also qualify for entry to the Indian market if they have a minimum Indian content. In respect of a number of sensitive items preferential treatment is accorded with only partial lifting of quantitative restrictions. India will permit the import of Sri Lankan tea to the extent of fifteen million kg. per annum at a fixed tariff preference of fifty per cent. Under the initial terms of the agreement India would permit import of eight million pieces per annum from Sri Lanka at a fixed tariff preference of fifty per cent. Out of this, six million pieces fabric need to be sourced from India. A ceiling of 1.5 million pieces was prescribed for individual categories. In respect of textile items, India's offer is restricted to a maximum of twenty five per cent.

The agreement was renegotiated following commerce secretary level talks on 6 June 2002, Joint ministerial committee meeting on 7 June 2002 in New Delhi, followed by senior officials meeting in Colombo from 4-5 July 2002.

With respect to market access for tea, the Sri Lankan side responding to the request made by Indian side to export Indian teas for home consumption in Sri Lanka stated that it agreed to this request on payment of the prevailing MFN duty and subject to a number of quality parameters.

In respect of the request made by the Sri Lankan side for more entry ports for tea the Indian side responded positively and offered two more ports (in addition to existing Cochin and Kolkata) with immediate effect, namely, Mumbai on the West coast and Visakhapatnam on the East coast.

With respect to garments, India responded to Sri Lanka's request, deepening specific duty concessions on fifty one tariff lines at a six-digit Harmonized system level. India agreed to increase the specific duty tariff concession wherever applicable on requested tariff lines from fifty per cent to seventy five per cent. However, *ad valorem* duty concessions on these lines would continue at fifty per cent.

On Sri Lankan request, India agreed to increase the unrestricted quota of two million pieces in respect of which fabric of non-Indian origin is used when Sri Lanka fully utilizes this quota. On utilization unrestricted quota India agreed to give additional quota of two million pieces out of total of eight million pieces. Further, India agreed to increase the level of quota per category per annum from one and half million to two million pieces.

Responding to Sri Lanka's request to have more ports as entry points for garments, India agreed to provide Kolkata and JNPT (Mumbai) as additional ports.

On India's request for an increase in the Margin of Preference (MOP) to fifty per cent in respect of the imports of bulk cement from India from the present level of twenty per cent, the Sri Lankan side agreed to increase the MOP to thirty five per cent.[22] Agreed Minutes of the senior officials meeting under Indo-Sri Lanka Free Trade Agreement, Colombo, 4-5 July 2002.

The ILFTA between India and Sri Lanka is a landmark in the bilateral relations between the two countries. It is expected to bring about enhanced trade between the two countries as well as to expanded and diversified cooperation in a range of economic spheres, including investments. This is the first such agreement in the South Asian region which could serve as a model for similar bilateral agreements in the region. It has an institutional framework in the form of the Indo-Lanka Joint Commission, a dispute settlement mechanism, and so forth. Its significance further lies in that it can be implemented more expeditiously and also more flexibly, unlike the protracted nature of negotiations generally associated with multilateral arrangements.

The short, following features characterize Indo-Sri Lankan FTA:

2. Elimination of Tariffs

2.1 By India

1. **Zero duty** on items upon entering into force of the agreement – the list is to be finalized within sixty days of signing of the Agreement.(E): **1351 products**
2. Concessions on **Textile** items restricted to twenty five per cent on Chapters 51-56, 58-60, & 63. Four Chapters under the Textile sector retained in the negative list (Chapters 50,57,61 and 62) (TEX): 528 products
3. **Garments** (GAM) covering Chapters 61&62 while remaining in the negative list, will be given fifty per cent tariff concessions on a fixed basis, subject to an annual restriction of eight million pieces, of which six million shall be extended the concession only if made of Indian fabric. On utilization of the unrestricted quota, an additional quota of two million pieces out of eight million pieces is permitted. The quota level per category is increased from one and half million to two million pieces per category per year.
4. Fifty per cent tariff preference on five **tea** items, subject to a **quota** of fifteen million Kg. per year (TEA): **5 products.**
5. Fifty per cent margin of preference upon coming into force of this agreement on all items, except for those on the negative list. To be **phased** out to zero duty in three years.(IR): **2799 products**
6. A **Negative List** of items to be retained (D I): **429 products**

2.2 By Sri Lanka

1. **Zero duty** on about **319 items** upon entering into force of the Agreement (F I): 319 products

2. **Phasing** out of tariffs on items with fifty per cent margin of preference on 889 products upon coming into force of the agreement, with up to seventy at the end of the first year, up to ninety per cent at the end of the second year and 100% at the end of third year (F II): **889 products**.
3. For the remaining items, (except for those on the negative list), which is the **Residual List**, preference would be not less than thirty five per cent before the expiry of three years, seventy per cent before the expiry of six years and 100% before the expiry of eighth year.(SLR): **2724 products.**
4. A **Negative List** (D II): **1180 products.**

2.3 Plan of Study and Methodology

The plan of the study is to:

- Analyse the trend in India's trade with South Asian countries in general and with Sri Lanka in particular
- Analyze if the share of preferential bilateral trade – both imports and exports are increasing in relation to world trade following the exchange of concessions under different categories of concessions offered and received by India and Sri Lanka over the period 1999-2003,
- To analyze the top traded preferential products for both the countries under each category to identify the success stories if any,
- To analyze the impact of tariff reduction/removal on increased imports and whether the increased imports have caused trade diversification in terms of new products.

The main data source for this study is from Trade Analysis System on Personal Computer (PC-TAS) by International Trade Centre UNCTAD/WTO. At the time of writing, the latest version 1999-2003 was available. The commodity classification is Harmonized System Rev.1.For India the data is available for five years from 1999-2003. For Sri Lanka however, the data for 2000 and 2003 is missing. This series enabled the figures to be observed one year prior to liberalization, viz. 1999 and two to three years after liberalization. The impact of the agreement is observed in terms of the value shares of products under different categories in relation their world imports prior to and subsequent to bilateral trade liberalization. The study is done in terms of imports of the countries of one of the countries from the other in respect of products or categories of products for which concessions have been extended from the former to the latter.

Table 1 : India-Sri Lanka and South Asian Trade: Value in US $ Million

	1999-2000	*2000-2001*	*2001-2002*	*2002-2003*	*2003-2004*	*2004-2005*
India's Exports to Sri Lanka and South Asian Countries						
Export to the World :	36822	44560	43827	52719	63843	48389.85
Exports to Sri Lanka	499.27	640.14	630.89	920.98	1319.2	1355.23
(% Share of World)	1.36	1.44	1.44	1.75	2.07	2.80
Exports to South Asia	1427.83	1954.41	2050.38	2784.9	4293.55	4498.93
(% Share of World)	3.88	4.39	4.68	5.28	6.73	9.3
India's Imports from Sri Lanka and South Asian Countries :						
Imports from the World	49671	50536	51413	61412	78150	61937.79
Import from Sri Lanka	44.23	45.01	67.38	90.83	194.74	364.39
(% Share of World)	0.09	0.09	0.13	0.15	0.25	0.59
Import from South Asia	418.7	492.49	589.04	530.43	709.32	980.1
(% Share of World)	0.84	0.97	1.15	0.86	0.91	1.58
Trade Ratio (Export/Import)						
World :	0.74	0.88	0.85	0.86	0.82	0.78
Sri Lanka	11.29	14.22	9.36	10.14	6.77	3.72
Total South Asia	3.41	3.97	3.48	5.25	6.05	4.59

Table 2 : India's Imports from Sri Lanka and World Under Different Categories (Value in $ '000)

Concessions	*No. of Products*	*Partner/ Share*	*1999*	*2000*	*2001*	*2002*	*2003*	*1999-2003*
Negative List (NL)	**14**	World	56508	65095	90495	100207	158381	470686
		Sri Lanka	548	217	236	258	4525	5784
		Share (%)	0.97	0.33	0.26	0.26	2.86	1.23
Zero Duty (ZD)	**55**	World	1535995	1933475	1785472	2064873	2463872	9783687
		Sri Lanka	4477	10748	12617	6218	12264	46324
		Share (%)	0.29	0.56	0.71	0.3	0.5	0.47
Tea	**5**	World	5908	9774	14198	25771	13891	69542
		Sri Lanka	2014	1779	2469	981	682	7925
		Share (%)	34.09	18.2	17.39	3.81	4.91	11.4
Textile (TEX)	**35**	World	350340	332591	525954	389562	550895	2149342
		Sri Lanka	826	940	1229	1243	2816	7054
		Share (%)	0.24	0.28	0.23	0.32	0.51	0.33

(Contd.)

(Contd. Table 2)

Concessions	*No. of Products*	*Partner/ Share*	*1999*	*2000*	*2001*	*2002*	*2003*	*1999-2003*
Garment (GAR)	**5**	World	1934	2283	2221	9674	1522	17634
		Sri Lanka	299	0	61	36	172	568
		Share (%)	15.46	0	2.75	0.37	11.3	3.22
Residual (RES)	**205**	World	5360426	5636152	6369449	7572914	10626296	35565237
		Sri Lanka	31045	26332	45431	73796	160466	337070
		Share (%)	0.58	0.47	0.71	0.97	1.51	0.95
Total (NL+ZD+Tea+ TEX+GAR+RES)	**319**	World	7311111	7979370	8787789	10163001	13814857	48056128
		Sri Lanka	39209	40016	62043	82532	180925	404725
		Share (%)	0.54	0.50	0.71	0.81	1.31	0.84
Total (ZD+Tea+TEX+ GAR+RES)	**305**	World	7254603	7914275	8697294	10062794	13656476	47585442
		Sri Lanka	38661	39799	61807	82274	176400	398941
		Share (%)	0.53	0.50	0.71	0.82	1.29	0.84
Total Imports (All Categories)	**332**	World	49710774	51374343	51905070	61113981	77196379	291300547
		Sri Lanka	42835	43696	66127	88053	187485	428196
		Share (%)	0.09	0.09	0.13	0.14	0.24	0.15

3. India's Trade With Sri Lanka and South Asia

In this section we highlight the trend in India's trade with South Asian countries in general and with Sri Lanka in particular.

It will be seen in Table 1 that Indo-Sri Lankan trade has been increasing at a more rapid pace that India's world trade or trade with any other South Asian country. This is reflected in growing share of Sri Lanka in India's world exports and imports. It is also interesting to note that India's imports from Sri Lanka has been growing at a faster pace than its exports to that country. This has resulted in a significant decline in trade imbalance with Sri Lanka as may be seen in the remarkable decline in export/import ratio from as high as 14.22 in 2000-01 to 3.72 in 2004-05. This paper addresses as to how such a phenomenal change came about in Indo-Sri Lanka trade.

3.1 Extent of Trade Liberalization by Different Categories: India's Offer

Table 2 gives the value as well as value share of products offered concessions by India to Sri Lanka in respect of different categories. It will be seen that in 1999 India imported $ 4.5 billion of such products from Sri Lanka.

3.1.1 Zero Duty Products

After the offer of duty free concessions, India's imports increased to $ 46 billion in 2003. As a share of world imports, it increased from 0.29 per cent in 1999 to 0.47 per cent in 2003. Thus there remains considerable opportunity for India to further increase its imports share from Sri Lanka in respect of such products. Figure 1 shows the trend.

Figure 1 : India's Imports from Sri Lanka Under Zero Duty (%)

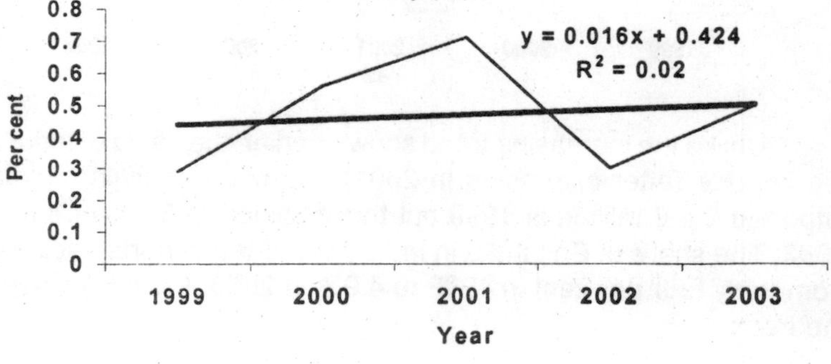

3.1.2 Residual Products

Figure 2 : India's Imports from Sri Lanka Under Residual (%)

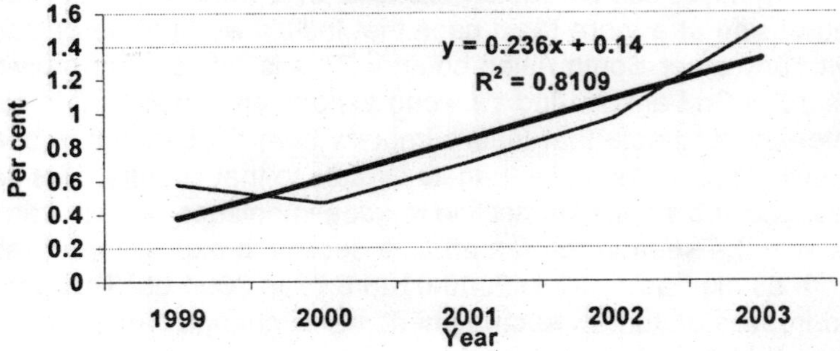

India's imports of residual products as a group increased from $ 31 million in 1999 to $ 160 million in 2003. Its share in world imports has also been increasing steadily from 0.58 % in 1999 to 1.5% in 2003. This increasing trend is shown in Figure 2.

3.1.3 Tea

Figure 3 : India's Imports from Sri Lanka Under Tea (%)

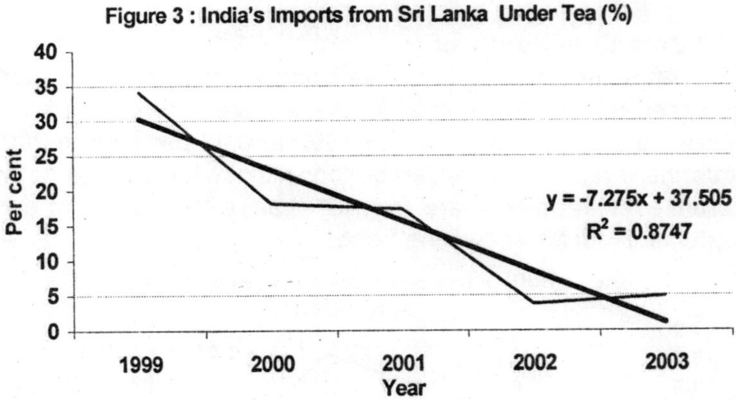

Unlike the increasing trend shown earlier, the value of India's tea imports (after increasing in 2001) has been declining. India imported $ 2.0 million in 1999 but this declined to $ 68 million in 2003. The share of Sri Lanka in India's world tea imports declined from thirty four per cent in 1999 to 4.9% in 2003. Figure 3 shows the trend.

3.1.4 Textiles

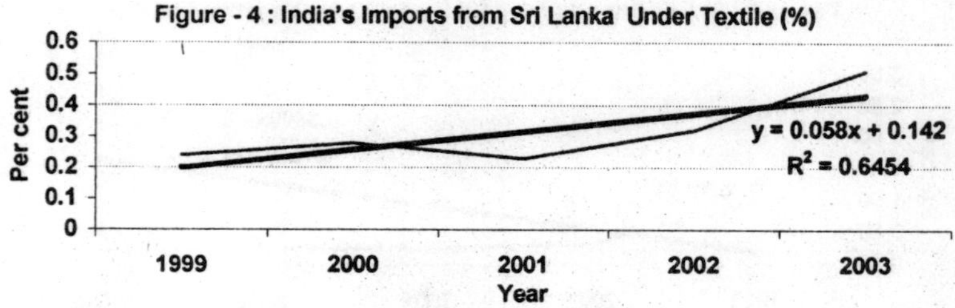

India's import of textiles from Sri lanka increased from $ 0.82 million in 1999 to $ 2.3 million in 2003. During this period its share in world imports increased from 0.24 % to 0.51%. This trend is presented in Figure 4.

3.1.5 Garments

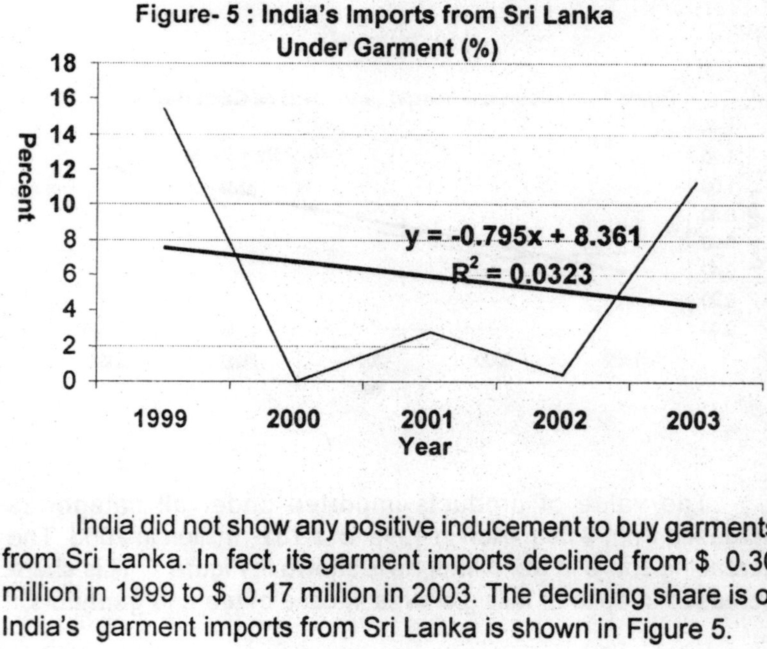

India did not show any positive inducement to buy garments from Sri Lanka. In fact, its garment imports declined from $ 0.30 million in 1999 to $ 0.17 million in 2003. The declining share is of India's garment imports from Sri Lanka is shown in Figure 5.

3.1.6 Negative List

Figure 6 : India's Imports from Sri Lanka Under Negative List (%)

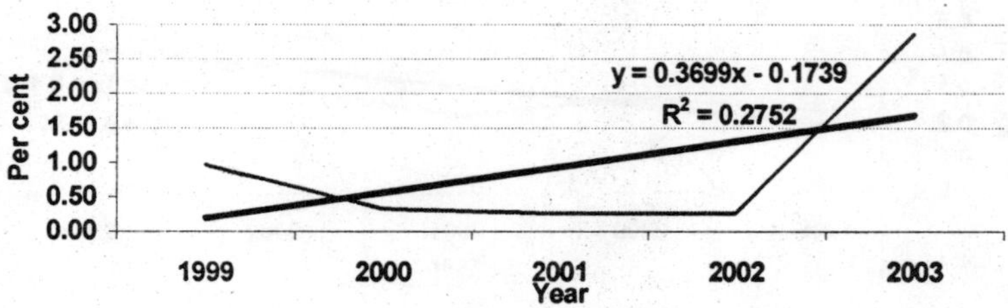

The products under negative list have not been offered tariff preferences and hence are not expected any positive impact on Indian imports from Sri Lanka. However the data reveals that India's imports under this list increased from $ 0.54 million in 1999 to $ 4,5 million in 2003. This trend is shown in Figure 6.

3.1.7 All Categories

Figure- 7 : India's Imports from Sri Lanka Under All Categories (%)

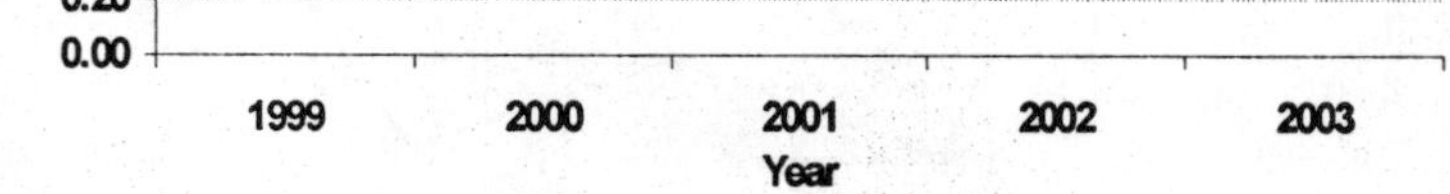

The value of products imported under all categories increased from $ 39 million in 1999 to $ 181 million in 2003. The increasing share in world imports is shown in Figure 7. This share increased in spite of falling shares in case of tea and garments.

Table A.2: Sri Lanka's Imports from India and World Under Different Categories(Value in $ '000)

Lists	*No. of Products*	*Partner /Share*	*1999*	*2001*	*2002*	*1999-2003*
Negative List (NL)	**277**	World	1458417	1219098	1712199	4389714
		India	213004	258771	396244	868019
		Share (%)	14.61	21.23	23.14	19.77
Zero Duty (ZD)	**26**	World	9483	8371	8760	26614
		India	3497	3091	3828	10416
		Share (%)	36.88	36.93	43.70	39.14
Phased (Pha)	**257**	World	349712	346975	472895	1169582
		India	59205	64524	115710	239439
		Share (%)	16.93	18.60	24.47	20.47
Total (NL+ZD+Pha)	**560**	World	1817612	1574444	2193854	5585910
		India	275706	326386	515782	1117874
		Share (%)	15.17	20.73	23.51	20.01
Total (ZD+Pha)	**283**	World	359195	355346	481655	1196196
		India	62702	67615	119538	249855
		Share (%)	17.46	19.03	24.82	20.89
Total Imports (All Caterories)	**1231**	World*	5322981	5393186	6024760	16740927
		India	494961	588143	817775	1900879
		Share (%)	9.30	10.91	13.57	11.35

3.2 Extent of Trade Liberalization by Different Categories: Sri Lanka's Offer

Now we turn to examine whether Sri Lanka has been able to increase its share of Indian imports in relation to world imports for products offered concessions by it. In this case we have data for 1999, 2001 and 2002. The trend for all categories is shown in Table 3.

3.2.1 Duty Free Products

Figure-8 : Sri Lanka's Imports from India Under Zero Duty

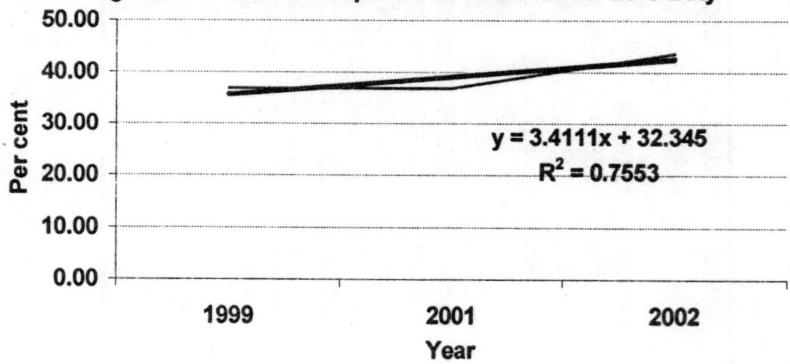

With respect to duty free products we notice that Sri Lanka's imports from India increased from $3.49 million in 1999 to $3.83 million in 2002. This reflected an increasing share from 36.88% in 1999 to 43.70% in 2003. Figure 8 illustrates this trend.

3.2.2 Phased Products

Figure- 9 : Sri Lanka's Imports from India Under Phased

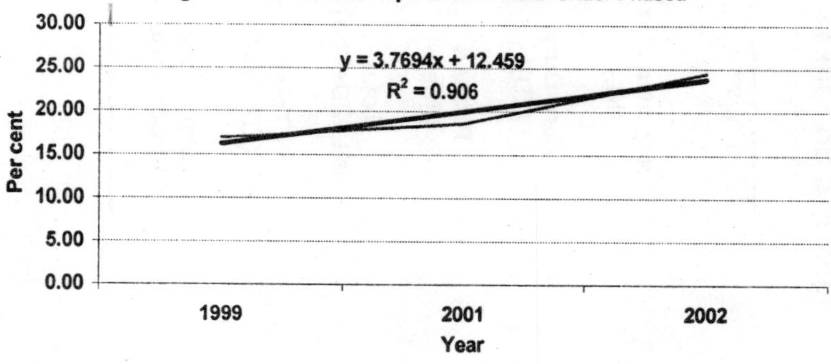

Sri Lanka's imports of phased products increased from \$59.20 million in 1999 to \$115.71 million in 2002. This reflected an increasing share from 16.93% in 1999 to 43.70% in 2003 as may be seen in Figure 9.

3.2.3 Negative List

Figure - 10 : Sri Lanka's Imports from India Under Negative List

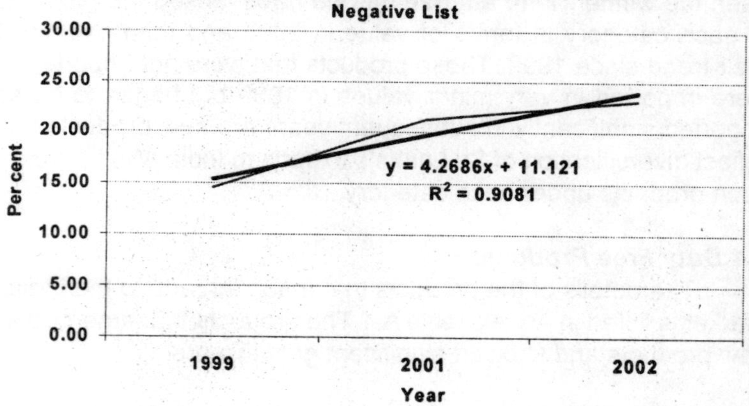

It is interesting to note that even in case of products under negative list Sri Lanka's imports from India increased significantly from \$313 million in 1999 to \$ 396 million in 2002. This reflected an increasing share in relation to world imports from 14.61% in 1999 to 23.145 in 2002. Figure 10 illustrates this trend.

3.2.4 All Categories

Chart - 11: Sri Lanka's Imports from India

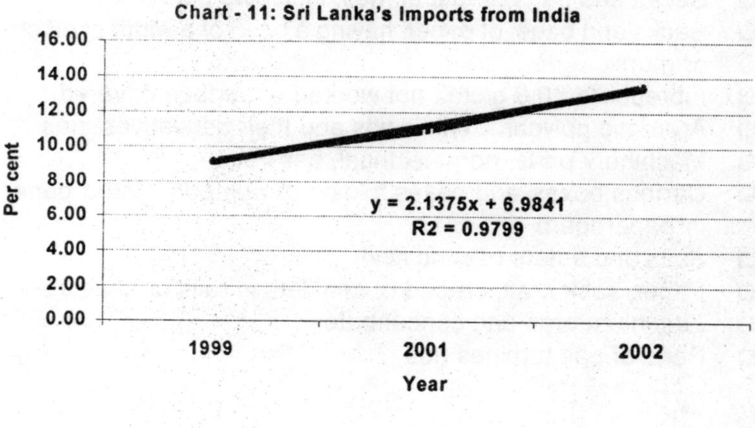

Sri Lanka's imports of all categories (excluding residual products) from India increased from $275 million in 1999 to $516 million reflecting an increasing share from 15.17% to 23.51% during the same period. This is illustrated in Figure 11.

4. Product Analysis: India's Offer

In this section we ask the question: 'which products have been the winners?' To analyze this we have ranked the products in each category in terms of value in 2003 and then examined their trend since 1999. Those products that were not imported or were imported in very minor values in 1999 but began to be so imported significantly in subsequent years are new products that reflect diversification of Sri Lanka's exports to India. We list below such products under each category.

4.1 Duty Free Products

The details of the products that made inroads to the Indian market is listed in Annex Table A.1.The products that emerged as new products and showed significant growth were

- Lead monoxide (litharge, massicot)
- Lead oxides nes
- Fibreboard >0.8 g/cm2 nes
- Mach f makg gimpd yarn/tulle/lace/embroidery/trimmgs/braid/net/tuftg
- Fibreboard nes (0.35 g/cm2 & less)
- Digital processing units not sold as complete systems
- Fibreboard >0.5 g/cm2 <0.8 g/cm2 nes
- Sacks and bags, of paper, nes; including cones
- Sacks and bags, of paper, having a base of a width of 40 cm or more
- Fibreboard >0.8 g/cm2 not worked or surface covered
- Aromatic polycarboxylic acids and their derivatives, nes
- Machinery parts, non-electrical, nes
- Cartons,boxes and cases,folding,of non-corrugated paper or paperboard
- Salts and esters of citric acid
- Paper, sack kraft, creped or crinkled, in rolls or sheets
- Zirconium ores and concentrates
- Parts of gas turbines nes

4.2 Residual Products

Among the residual products the following showed significant growth. Many of these were being imported for the first time since 1999. The details of such products have been presented in Annex Table A.2.

- Copper cathodes and sections of cathodes unwrought
- Refined copper products, unwrought, nes
- Pepper of the genus Piper,ex cubeb pepper,neither crushd nor ground
- Ferrous waste and scrap, iron or steel, nes
- Monumental/buildg stone,cut/sawn flat/even,marble/travertine/alabaster
- Wire bars, copper, unwrought
- Insulated (including enamelled or anodised) winding wire, nes
- Cloves (whole fruit, cloves and stems)
- Parts & accessories of automatic data processg machines&units thereof
- Colour television receivers
- Bars, rods and profiles of refined copper
- Glycerol crude, waters and lyes
- Plants &pts of plants(incl sed&fruit) usd in pharm,perf,insect etc nes
- Bars, rods and profiles, copper alloy nes
- Nutmeg
- Diamonds non-industrial nes excluding mounted or set diamonds
- Electric conductors, for a voltage >80V but not exceeding 1,000 V, nes
- Palm oil, crude
- Fluorescent lamps, hot cathode
- Aluminum unwrought, alloyed

4.3Tea

The offer of concessions by India does not seem to have lead to any appreciable increase in Indian imports of tea from Sri Lanka as may be seen in Annex Table A.3. There was an appreciable increase in imports of black tea since 1999 up to 2001 but this declined in subsequent years.

4.4 Textiles

In textiles some of the products, many of them new found entry to the Indian market since 1999 as has been presented in Annex Table A.4. Some these products are presented below.

- Denim fabrics of cotton,>/=85%, more than 200 g/m2
- Woven fabrics of cotton,>/=85%, not more than 200 g/m2, dyed, nes
- Waddg of oth textile materials&articles thereof,o/t sanitary articles
- Labels, badges and similar woven articles of textile materials
- Hand-made lace, in the piece, in strips or in motifs
- Textured yarn of synthetic filaments, nes, not put up
- Nonwovens, man-made filaments weighing 70-150g/m2
- Woven fabrics of cotton,>/=85%, not more than 200 g/m2, bleached, nes
- Twill weave cotton fabrics,>/=85%, not more than 200 g/m2, dyed
- Labels,badges and similar articles,not woven,of textile materials,nes
- Nonwovens, man-made filaments weighing <25g/m2
- Plain weave cotton fabric,>/=85%, not more than 100 g/m2, dyed
- Knittd or crochetd tex fab,w</=30 cm,>/=5% of elastomeric/rubber,nes
- Plain weave cotton fab,<85% mixd w m-m fib,not more than 200 g/m2,dyd
- Pile knitted or crocheted fabrics, of other textile materials, nes

4.5 Garments

The details of products that found entry to Indian market is presented in Annex Table A.5. Some products that found modest entry to the Indian market is presented below.

- Men/boys trousers and shorts, of other textile materials, not knitted
- Men/boys jackets and blazers, of cotton, not knitted
- Knitted or crocheted fabrics, of other materials, nes

5. Product Analysis: Sri Lanka's Offer

5.1Duty Free Products

The details of India's exports to the Sri Lankan market for duty free products are presented in Annex Table A.6. While some products no doubt increased their entry to the Sri Lankan market, the increase was not as marked as in case of Sri Lankan entry to the Indian market. Some products that performed well are presented below.

- Heterocyclic compds with nitrogen hetero-atom(s) only, nes
- O-,M-,P-phenylenediamine,diaminotoluenes&thr derivatives;salts thereof
- Dichlorodifluoromethane
- Heterocycl compds containg a benzothiazole ring-system not further used

5.2Phased Duty Products

The offer of concessions by Sri Lanka also opened up opportunities for Indian manufacturers to enter further the Sri Lankan market. However many of these products were earlier being marketed in Sri Lanka and hence were not new products as may be seen in Annex Table A.7. Some products that found deeper entry to Sri Lankan market are listed below.

- Electric generating sets
- Carbon (carbon blacks and other forms of carbon, nes)
- Tubes,pipe & hollow profiles,iron or nas,welded,of circ cross sect,nes
- Semi-fin prod,i/nas,rect/sq cross-sect cntg by wgt<.25% c,wdth<2X thk

6. Investment Linkages

While the exchange of tariff preference no doubt induced the accelerated flow of bilateral trade between the two countries, the more rapid increase in Sri Lankan exports to India had also much to do with the emergence of Sri Lanka as a production and profit center for Indian companies seeking access to regional and global markets. Over fifty per cent of Indian joint ventures and wholly owned subsidiaries in the South Asian region are located in Sri Lanka. The inflow of direct investment from Indian companies began in the wake of Sri Lanka's economic liberalization programme during the 1980s. By the end of June 2000 the number of Indian projects stood at 120 with an estimated investment of SLRs 12.5 billion. The principal sectors are steel, cement, rubber products, and service sector projects. During past three years, leading Indian companies such as Gujrat Ambuja, Asian Paints and Larsen and Toubro have committed substantial investments. The signing of ILFTA gave further impetus for Indian companies to set up their ventures in Sri Lanka with a view to buy back for the duty free Indian market, particularly in southern India. Such investment flows contributed in no small measure in promoting Sri Lankan products for the Indian market.

7. Conclusion

In view of our account of ILFTA as outlined above, it will not be an overstatement to maintain that the agreement has proved to be a success when viewed from the perspective of both the countries. It does serve as a model worth emulating in this region. Its win win situation has now prompted the political leadership of both the countries to proceed further towards a Comprehensive Economic Partnership Agreement (CEPA) that would include services, travel, tourism and investment.

What makes the ILFTA remarkable is to demonstrate that when an economic partnership agreement among two countries of vastly unequal size factors in a differentiated approach to each country's requirements, then the larger country need not cast its shadow on the smaller one-on the contrary the former can open up a window of opportunity for the smaller partner to enter its vast domestic market.

8.1Annex Table A.1: India's Imports of Products Offered Concessions Under Zero Duty ($ '000)

HS 6 Digit	Product Description	1999		2000		2001		2002		2003		1999-2003	
		SL	World	SL	World	SL	World	SL	World	SL	World	SL	World
470790	Waste&scrap of paper or paperboard,nes (includg unsorted waste&scrap)	3114	109268	2207	120336	2193	139389	1708	163610	3802	207117	13024	739720
282410	Lead monoxide (litharge, massicot)	0	1277	0	2892	0	2888	67	4305	2541	9121	2608	20483
282490	Lead oxides nes	0	151	0	299	0	353	0	931	783	1505	783	3239
441119	Fibreboard >0.8 g/cm2 nes	0	3895	0	2240	0	3392	558	4544	741	5049	1299	19120
470710	Waste and scrap of unbleached kraft or corrugated paper and paperboard	221	4799	194	4951	753	3437	82	2692	470	2873	1720	18752
481910	Cartons, boxes and cases, of corrugated paper or paperboard	459	3841	610	4376	374	5586	660	6461	415	4689	2518	24953
844790	Mach f makg gimpd yarn/tulle/lace/embroidery/trim mgs/braid/net/tuftg	0	28434	6	42819	81	40559	0	72500	390	67780	477	252092
441199	Fibreboard nes (0.35 g/cm2 & less)	0	2187	0	2302	2	2068	13	1857	340	2381	355	10795
847150	Digital processing units not sold as complete systems	0	9971	1	58390	1	43723	0	77716	278	136639	280	326439
441129	Fibreboard >0.5 g/cm2 <0.8 g/cm2 nes	0	1096	0	1734	0	2367	300	1418	257	1884	557	8499

(Contd.)

(Contd.)

HS 6 Digit	Product Description	1999		2000		2001		2002		2003		1999-2003	
		SL	World	SL	World	SL	World	SL	World	SL	World	SL	World
481940	Sacks and bags, of paper, nes; including cones	37	1519	18	932	161	1513	327	1482	254	1802	797	7248
481930	Sacks and bags, of paper, having a base of a width of 40 cm or more	44	544	93	621	257	633	295	604	228	647	917	3049
441111	Fibreboard >0.8 g/cm2 not worked or surface covered	0	586	0	1111	0	1568	45	1212	208	2042	253	6519
291739	Aromatic polycarboxylic acids and their derivatives, nes	0	9587	0	7247	0	14426	18	17388	201	29637	219	78285
848590	Machinery parts, non-electrical, nes	0	20777	27	34915	16	57818	58	60870	182	76275	283	250655
481920	Cartons,boxes and cases,folding,of non-corrugated paper or paperboard	1	2206	22	1810	1	2388	10	1834	120	1198	154	9436
291815	Salts and esters of citric acid	0	226	0	428	0	495	94	966	95	999	189	3114
480820	Paper, sack kraft, creped or crinkled, in rolls or sheets	0	10	14	93	11	275	35	944	95	1157	155	2479
261510	Zirconium ores and concentrates	0	2129	0	2569	0	4030	0	6492	93	7294	93	22514
841199	Parts of gas turbines nes	0	54067	0	46162	0	79052	0	83831	83	80688	83	343800
Top 20		3876	256570	3192	336227	3850	405960	4270	511657	11576	640777	26764	2151191
Total :		4477	1535995	10748	1933475	12617	1785472	6218	2064873	12264	2463872	46324	9783687
Share (Top 20/Total*100)		86.58	16.70	29.70	17.39	30.51	22.74	68.67	24.78	94.39	26.01	57.78	21.99

8.2 Annex Table A.2: India's Imports of Products Offered Concessions Under Residual ($ '000)

HS 6 Digit	Product Description	1999		2000		2001		2002		2003		1999-2003	
		SL	World	SL	World	SL	World	SL	World	SL	World	SL	World
740311	Copper cathodes and sections of cathodes unwrought	0	40732	0	8455	0	2107	133	8478	56239	71828	56372	131600
740319	Refined copper products, unwrought, nes	0	1176	0	1115	1913	4355	4871	5501	8207	13771	14991	25918
090411	Pepper of the genus Piper,ex cubeb pepper,neither crushd nor ground	7098	11587	6212	13377	3401	11948	11735	25465	7581	21519	36027	83896
720449	Ferrous waste and scrap, iron or steel, nes	4245	248527	4992	232571	2389	329330	2576	241672	7139	343678	21341	1395778
680221	Monumental/buildg stone,cut/sawn flat/even,marble/travertine/alabaster	0	501	106	1994	895	6236	604	10119	5959	17314	7564	36164
740312	Wire bars, copper, unwrought	0	34119	0	6947	842	4198	1776	5042	5819	9404	8437	59710
854419	Insulated (including enamelled or anodised) winding wire, nes	0	10097	0	10851	0	10386	0	16050	5596	20074	5596	67458
090700	Cloves (whole fruit, cloves and stems)	2379	3034	2552	6356	21454	34944	13748	24849	5060	29547	45193	98730
847330	Parts&accessories of automatic data processg machines&units thereof	1	428311	693	703722	738	645555	1970	646422	4609	807418	8011	3231428
852812	Colour television receivers	0	5640	0	3493	0	4785	0	7229	3330	37378	3330	58525
740710	Bars, rods and profiles of refined copper	0	22445	0	14490	641	16895	139	6963	2203	15704	2983	76497
152000	Glycerol crude, waters and lyes	2735	5303	2223	2839	1222	1876	1092	2321	2056	2947	9328	15286
121190	Plants &pts of plants(incl sed&fruit) usd in pharm,perf,insect etc nes	345	4086	559	5233	322	5405	1337	7935	1841	10655	4404	33314

(Contd.)

(Contd.AnnexA.2)

HS 6 Digit	Product Description	1999		2000		2001		2002		2003		1999-2003	
		SL	World	SL	World	SL	World	SL	World	SL	World	SL	World
740729	Bars, rods and profiles, copper alloy nes	0	4695	0	2766	0	2766	0	2405	1815	4386	1815	17018
090810	Nutmeg	1065	1367	1016	1147	859	961	2021	2340	1713	1844	6674	7659
710239	Diamonds non-industrial nes excluding mounted or set diamonds	245	420113	0	369573	0	320016	0	520421	1623	1021095	1868	2651218
854459	Electric conductors, for a voltage >80V but not exceeding 1,000 V, nes	0	10956	0	13438	0	17636	4	29245	1312	29797	1316	101072
151110	Palm oil, crude	0	36817	0	276507	0	516187	322	1064603	1300	1234130	1622	3128244
853931	Fluorescent lamps, hot cathode	0	8949	0	15384	5	11039	62	5944	1262	8191	1329	49507
760120	Aluminium unwrought, alloyed	0	15011	0	16236	0	18144	1053	22647	1242	25767	2295	97805
Top 20		18113	1313466	18353	1706494	34681	1964769	43443	2655651	125906	3726447	240496	11366827
Total:		**31045**	**5360426**	**26332**	**5636152**	**45431**	**6369449**	**73796**	**7572914**	**160466**	**10626296**	**337070**	**35565237**
Share (Top 20/Total*100)		58.34	24.50	69.70	30.28	76.34	30.85	58.87	35.07	78.46	35.07	71.35	31.96

Source: Estimated from PC-TAS CDROM Database 2004.

8.3 Annex Table A.3: India's Imports of Products Offered Concessions Under Tea (USD '000)

HS 6 Digit	Product Description	1999		2000		2001		2002		2003		1999-2003	
		SL	World	SL	World	SL	World	SL	World	SL	World	SL	World
090240	Black tea (fermented) & partly fermented tea in packages exceedg 3 kg	1291	4264	1182	7272	311	9888	639	19032	333	11414	3756	51870
090230	Black tea (fermented)&partly fermentd tea in packages not exceedg 3 kg	655	1357	275	2007	2104	3832	193	6087	313	1574	3540	14857
090220	Green tea (not fermented) in packages exceeding 3 kg	0	182	48	84	13	289	50	214	36	271	147	1040
090210	Green tea (not fermented) in packages not exceeding 3 kg	68	89	75	79	0	0	0	64	0	289	143	521
210120	Tea or mate extracts,essences & concentrates & preparations thereof	0	16	199	332	41	189	99	374	0	343	339	1254
	Total :	**2014**	**5908**	**1779**	**9774**	**2469**	**14198**	**981**	**25771**	**682**	**13891**	**7925**	**69542**

Source: **Estimated from PC-TAS CDROM Database 2004.**

8.4 Annex Table A.4: India's Imports of Products Offered Concessions Under Textiles ($ '000)

HS 6 Digit	Product Description	1999		2000		2001		2002		2003		1999-2003	
		SL	World	SL	World	SL	World	SL	World	SL	World	SL	World
520942	Denim fabrics of cotton,>/=85%, more than 200 g/m2	0	565	0	446	0	1393	0	4472	696	19660	696	26536
520839	Woven fabrics of cotton,>/=85%, not more than 200 g/m2, dyed, nes	88	5130	0	3864	1	6530	141	12951	487	27820	717	56295
560129	Waddg of oth textile materials&articles thereof,o/t sanitary articles	3	551	79	439	240	628	123	1114	268	1698	713	4430
580710	Labels, badges and similar woven articles of textile materials	25	7205	45	8546	239	9366	167	12246	182	14536	658	51899
580430	Hand-made lace, in the piece, in strips or in motifs	0	30	0	74	4	243	32	3365	170	5743	206	9455
540239	Textured yarn of synthetic filaments, nes, not put up	0	9147	0	7809	0	5741	0	6605	147	15546	147	44848
560313	Nonwovens, man-made filaments weighing 70-150g/m2	0	593	0	822	0	1149	13	1124	114	2401	127	6089
520829	Woven fabrics of cotton,>/=85%, nt more than 200 g/m2, bleached, nes	36	2573	0	1804	0	4619	166	9646	108	17995	310	36637
520833	Twill weave cotton fabrics,>/=85%, not more than 200 g/m2, dyed	2	148	0	117	0	369	54	688	99	14512	155	15834
580790	Labels,badges and similar articles,not woven,of textile materials,nes	6	2001	7	2144	46	2036	133	2894	97	3514	289	12589
560311	Nonwovens, man-made filaments weighing <25g/m2	53	3421	17	2092	10	2465	44	2423	78	5444	202	15845
520831	Plain weave cotton fabric,>/=85%, not more than 100 g/m2, dyed	0	160	0	503	0	261	1	1264	74	5774	75	7962
600210	Knittd or crochetd tex fab,w</=30 cm,>/=5% of elastomeric/rubber,nes	0	333	0	193	0	532	0	1175	65	7270	65	9503
521031	Plain weave cotton fab,<85% mixd w m-m fib,not more than 200 g/m2,dyd	0	145	0	482	0	2463	0	2103	58	3489	58	8682

(Contd.)

(Contd.Annex Table 4)

HS 6 Digit	Product Description	1999		2000		2001		2002		2003		1999-2003	
		SL	World	SL	World	SL	World	SL	World	SL	World	SL	World
520942	Denim fabrics of cotton,>/=85%, more than 200 g/m2	0	565	0	446	0	1393	0	4472	696	19660	696	26536
600199	Pile knitted or crocheted fabrics, of other textile materials, nes	16	990	0	1089	0	1099	29	1330	55	2938	100	7446
600191	Pile knitted or crocheted fabrics, of cotton, nes	68	101	0	117	0	298	18	397	27	156	113	1069
600110	"Long pile" knitted or crocheted textile fabrics	51	729	0	1319	0	1982	0	1912	19	2259	70	8201
600292	Knitted or crocheted fabrics, of cotton, nes	40	476	0	278	70	578	15	610	19	987	144	2929
600299	Knitted or crocheted fabrics, of other materials, nes	3	1104	0	1816	61	1761	25	7505	19	393	108	12579
580639	Narrow woven fabrics of other textile materials, nes	0	923	104	1468	18	1636	5	3782	12	6591	139	14400
	Top 20	391	36325	252	35422	689	45149	966	77606	2794	158726	5092	353228
	Total:	**826**	**350340**	**940**	**332591**	**1229**	**525954**	**1243**	**389562**	**2816**	**550895**	**7054**	**2149342**
	Share (Top 20/Total*100)	47.34	10.37	26.81	10.65	56.06	8.58	77.72	19.92	99.22	28.81	72.19	16.43

Source: Estimated from PC-TAS CDROM Database 2004.

8.5 Annex Table A.5: *India's Imports of Products Offered Concessions Under Garments ($ '000)*

HS 6 Digit	*Product Description*	*1999*		*2000*		*2001*		*2002*		*2003*		*1999-2003*	
		SL	*World*	*SL*	*World*	*SL*	*World*	*SL*	*World*	*SL*	*World*	*SL*	*World*
620349	Mens/boys trousers and shorts, of other textile materials, not knitted	9	161	n.a	103	0	141	9	162	100	447	118	1014
620332	Mens/boys jackets and blazers, of cotton, not knitted	0	3	n.a	31	0	40	0	35	53	99	53	208
600299	Knitted or crocheted fabrics, of other materials, nes	3	1104	n.a	1816	61	1761	25	7505	19	393	108	12579
621210	Brassieres and parts thereof, of textile materials	287	666	n.a	333	0	279	2	1972	0	583	289	3833
	Total:	**299**	**1934**	n.a	**2283**	**61**	**2221**	**36**	**9674**	**172**	**1522**	**568**	**17634**

Source: Estimated from PC-TAS CDROM Database 2004.

8.6 Annex Table A.6: Sri Lanka's Imports from India and the World Products Offered Concessions Under Zero Duty ($ '000)

HS 6 Digit	Product Description	1999		2000		2001		2002		2003		1999-2003	
		India	World	India	World	India	World	India	World	India	World	India	World
294190	Antibiotics nes, in bulk	1129	1408	n.a	n.a	956	1278	1275	1385	n.a	n.a	3360	4071
294110	Penicillins and their derivatives, in bulk; salts thereof	910	1197	n.a	n.a	201	678	608	891	n.a	n.a	1719	2766
293390	Heterocyclic compds with nitrogen hetero-atom(s) only, nes	0	1473	n.a	n.a	72	1259	248	835	n.a	n.a	320	3567
292151	O-,M-,P-phenylenediamine,diaminotoluenes&thr derivatives;salts thereof	124	325	n.a	n.a	157	404	185	420	n.a	n.a	466	1149
290342	Dichlorodifluoromethane	226	370	n.a	n.a	211	323	177	303	n.a	n.a	614	996
293420	Heterocycl compds containg a benzothiazole ring-system nt furthr fusd	87	709	n.a	n.a	118	820	175	1102	n.a	n.a	380	2631
291540	Mono-,di-or trichloroacetic acids, their salts and esters	95	96	n.a	n.a	338	342	141	153	n.a	n.a	574	591
291734	Orthophthalic acid esters, nes	39	61	n.a	n.a	70	194	96	328	n.a	n.a	205	583
294150	Erythromycin and its derivatives, in bulk; salts thereof	59	111	n.a	n.a	50	50	87	87	n.a	n.a	196	248
290490	Derivs of hydrocarbons cntg mixtures of sulpho,nitro or nitroso groups	3	336	n.a	n.a	0	8	83	95	n.a	n.a	86	439
293359	Hetercycl compds cntg pyrimidin rng/piperazine rng,nes;nucleic acid&sa	0	64	n.a	n.a	0	125	74	220	n.a	n.a	74	409
292511	Saccharin and its salts	0	46	n.a	n.a	23	57	69	120	n.a	n.a	92	223

(Contd.)

(Contd.Annex Table 6)

HS 6 Digit	Product Description	1999		2000		2001		2002		2003		1999-2003	
		India	World	India	World	India	World	India	World	India	World	India	World
291890	Carboxylic acids w additional oxygen functions,nes&their derivatives	6	341	n.a	n.a	4	381	68	584	n.a	n.a	78	1306
291550	Propionic acid, its salts and esters	73	190	n.a	n.a	71	186	67	135	n.a	n.a	211	511
290911	Diethyl ether	54	59	n.a	n.a	27	34	66	75	n.a	n.a	147	168
290349	Multi-halogenated derivs of acyclic hydrocarbons nes	8	73	n.a	n.a	39	98	64	190	n.a	n.a	111	361
291735	Phthalic anhydride	33	176	n.a	n.a	34	145	64	178	n.a	n.a	131	499
290810	Derivs of phenols or phenol-alc cntg only halogen subst & their salts	45	103	n.a	n.a	64	83	63	98	n.a	n.a	172	284
292519	Imides and their derivatives, nes; salts thereof	21	66	n.a	n.a	29	45	63	104	n.a	n.a	113	215
292390	Quarternary ammonium salts and hydroxides, nes	3	29	n.a	n.a	6	16	50	69	n.a	n.a	59	114
Top 20		**2915**	**7233**	**n.a**	**n.a**	**2470**	**6526**	**3723**	**7372**	**n.a**	**n.a**	**9108**	**21131**
Total:		**3497**	**9483**	n.a	n.a	**3091**	**8371**	**3828**	**8760**	n.a	n.a	**10416**	**26614**
Share (Top 20/Total*100)		**83.36**	**76.27**	n.a	n.a	**79.91**	**77.96**	**97.26**	**84.16**	n.a	n.a	**87.44**	**79.40**

Source: Estimated from PC-TAS CDROM Database 2004.

8.7 Annex Table A.7: Sir Lanka's Imports from India and the World Products Offered Concessions Under Phased Duty ($ '000)

HS 6 Digit	Product Description	1999		2000		2001		2002		2003		1999-2003	
		India	World	India	World	India	World	India	World	India	World	India	World
850239	Electric generating sets	346	1021	n.a	n.a	418	1690	34144	34879	n.a	n.a	34908	37590
280300	Carbon (carbon blacks and other forms of carbon, nes)	3270	6684	n.a	n.a	8171	10629	7609	11712	n.a	n.a	19050	29025
730630	Tubes,pipe & hollow profiles,iron or nas,welded,of circ cross sect,nes	2220	6215	n.a	n.a	4497	6820	6101	7763	n.a	n.a	12818	20798
720711	Semi-fin prod,i/nas,rect/sq cross-sect cntg by wgt<.25% c,wdth<2X thk	713	10754	n.a	n.a	853	11833	5224	20954	n.a	n.a	6790	43541
721391	Hot rolled bar/rod, irregular coils, <14mm diam	7766	10413	n.a	n.a	4441	7743	4527	10806	n.a	n.a	16734	28962
720719	Semi-fin prod, iron or non-alloy steel, cntg by wght <.25% carbon, nes	1705	15839	n.a	n.a	8611	10305	3506	4660	n.a	n.a	13822	30804
740811	Wire of refind copper of which the max cross sectional dimension > 6mm	0	6990	n.a	n.a	10	7192	3016	12298	n.a	n.a	3026	26480
720918	Cold rolled iron/steel, coils >600mm x <0.5mm	1077	1242	n.a	n.a	796	905	2066	2174	n.a	n.a	3939	4321
720927	Cold roll iron/steel, not coil>600mm x 0.5-1mm	1063	3342	n.a	n.a	1849	3224	1821	2116	n.a	n.a	4733	8682
730459	Tube,pipe&hollow profile,as,(o/t stainless) smls,circ cross sect,nes	612	952	n.a	n.a	636	882	1591	1816	n.a	n.a	2839	3650
730660	Tubes,pipe & hollow profiles,i/s,welded,of non circ cross sect,nes	406	944	n.a	n.a	688	1067	1556	1765	n.a	n.a	2650	3776
731100	Containers for compressed or liquefied gas of iron or steel	39	4095	n.a	n.a	372	3703	1296	3925	n.a	n.a	1707	11723

(Contd.)

(Contd.Annex Table 7)

HS 6 Digit	Product Description	1999		2000		2001		2002		2003		1999-2003	
		India	World	India	World	India	World	India	World	India	World	India	World
840999	Parts for diesel and semi-diesel engines	858	6632	n.a	n.a	846	5736	1282	6408	n.a	n.a	2986	18776
720852	Hot roll iron/steel, not coil >600mm x 4.75-10mm	590	1326	n.a	n.a	1062	1791	1227	2564	n.a	n.a	2879	5681
720917	Cold rolled iron/steel, coils >600mm x 0.5-1mm	714	1605	n.a	n.a	339	529	1187	1275	n.a	n.a	2240	3409
840820	Engines, diesel, for the vehicles of Chapter 87	4195	5505	n.a	n.a	796	1869	1163	2493	n.a	n.a	6154	9867
722100	Bars & rods, stainless steel, hot rolled in irregularly wound coils	591	3402	n.a	n.a	896	2872	1131	3895	n.a	n.a	2618	10169
722860	Bars & rods, as, o/t stainless, nes	673	1075	n.a	n.a	786	898	973	1059	n.a	n.a	2432	3032
720928	Cold roll iron/steel, not coil>600mm x <0.5mm	329	474	n.a	n.a	777	1107	878	1086	n.a	n.a	1984	2667
730690	Tubes, pipe & hollow profiles, iron or steel, welded, nes	203	2702	n.a	n.a	202	2009	865	1522	n.a	n.a	1270	6233
	Top 20	**27370**	**91212**	**0**	**0**	**37046**	**82804**	**81163**	**135170**	**0**	**0**	**145579**	**309186**
	TOTAL:	**59205**	**349712**	**n.a**	n.a	**64524**	**346975**	**115710**	**472895**	**n.a**	n.a	**239439**	**1169582**
	Share (Top 20/Total*100)	**46.23**	**26.08**	**n.a**	**n.a**	**57.41**	**23.86**	**70.14**	**28.58**	**n.a**	**n.a**	**60.80**	**26.44**

References

1 This paper draws on a more comprehensive study by I.N.Mukherji , Tilani Jayawerdhana and Saman Kelegama titled *Indo Lanka Free Trade Agreement: An Assessment of Potential and Impact* under auspices of South Asia Network of Research Institutes (SANEI) done in collaboration with the Institute for Policy Studies, Colombo. This study may be accessed in http://www.saneinetwork.net/pdf/SANEI_II/work_in_progress_Indo_Sri Lanka.pdf. Unlike the earlier study however, which used national source and used Indian financial year as basis for comparison, this data is based on Trade Analysis System on Personal Computer (PC-TAS) by International Trade Centre UNCTAD/WTO. This enables us to extend the data by another two years on calendar year basis and to assess whether the trends observed earlier continue to exist.

2 Agreed Minutes of the Senior Officials Meeting under Indo-Sri Lanka Free Trade Agreement, Colombo, 4-5 July 2002.

14

Free Trade Agreement between India and Sri Lanka: The Way Forward

M.Ganeshamoorthy

Introduction

The Indo-Sri Lanka Free Trade Agreement (ILFTA) which was signed in December 1998 in New Delhi has been considered as a forward step towards mutually beneficial bilateral trade between India and Sri Lanka expanding their domestic markets, through economic integration. This is also seen as a vital prerequisite for the acceleration of the process of economic development in both countries. The agreement was established under the provisions of the General Agreement on Tariffs and Trade 1994, and was expected to create the smooth progress of the economic cooperation through the expansion of free trade between the two signatories. The two countries agreed to pay due regard to the concept of reciprocity and to create a competitive environment conducive for free trade.

Significant progress has been achieved in bilateral trade under the agreement during the last five years and recently the two governments have agreed to transform the ILFTA to a Comprehensive Economic Partnership Agreement (CEPA). This shall lead to the expansion of the scope of the agreement to include not only free trade in goods but also services, strengthening of cooperation in investment and to address other specific issues. Nevertheless, measures need to be taken to remove the impediments prior to the two countries embark upon deeper economic integration. This paper endeavors to identify some of the issues that need to be addressed in the process of integration.

The Rationale

Theoretically, multilateral trade liberalization has been considered to be superior to any other forms of trade liberalization i.e., regional trade liberalization or bilateral trade liberalization. Bhagwati[1] for example argued that regionalism will be "stumbling blocks" rather than "building blocks" in the pursuit of global trade liberalization.

Nevertheless, there has been a resurgence of enthusiasm in the establishment of Regional Trade Agreements (RTA) all over the globe in the 1990s. The WTO was notified of the establishment of 153 RTAs between 1984 and 1998. Weerakoon and Wijayasiri[2] single out the protracted nature of negotiations under the Uruguay Round to be the most convincing reason for the resurgence of RTAs in the 1990s. Even after the successful conclusion of the Uruguay Round in 1993, the enthusiasm towards regionalism did not diminish. Countries are now moving towards more comprehensive forms of economic integration and to safeguard the interests at the individual country level and regional levels.

Following this global trend South Asian countries have established a Preferential Trading Agreement (SAPTA) and agreed to move towards a Free Trade Area (SAFTA) in the region. Although SAPTA has initiated with a good intention of creating more intra regional trade it's progress was, however limited due to practical reasons - both economic and political and the movement towards SAFTA was also very slow. The slowing pace of regional integration has led to the emergence of bilateral trade initiatives in the region. The ILFTA has been the first of such initiatives in the region.

Sri Lanka in particular has embarked on bilateralism partly due to the bleak prospects for Sri Lankan exports under the SAPTA. Indeed, SAPTA did not bring many benefits for Sri Lankan exports. Nearly 4700 tariff lines out of total 6000 under the Harmonized System (HS) of coding have been covered by SAPTA concessions. Of the 1750 concessions available to Sri Lanka under SAPTA, only 126 are of the export interests the country.[3] Sri Lanka's major export sector –the agriculture sector received merely 143 concessions while 539 concessions have been given to chemical products, a main import of the country.

Table 1. Trade Restrictions in India and Sri Lanka

Criteria	*India*	*Sri Lanka*
Exchange Rate	Unitary	Unitary
Exchange Rate Determination	Managed Float	Free Float
Payment Restrictions		
Current Account	No	No
Capital Account	Yes	Yes
State Monopolies in External Trade	Yes	Yes
Import Licenses	Yes	Yes [but very few]
Simplification of Tariffs	Yes	Yes
Average Tariff –1995%	48	24
Maximum Tariff Rate –1997	40	35
Existence of High Level of NTBs	Yes	No

Source: Dushni Weerakoon and Wijayasiri Janaka *Regional Economic Cooperation in South Asia: A Sri Lankan Perspective,* International Economic Series No.6, Institute of Policy Studies, Colombo, 2001.

Table 1 compares trade restrictions in Sri Lanka and India. Sri Lanka's liberalization started well before India and not surprisingly the country has the most open economy in the region. India has also been liberalized its economy in 1990s. The progress of other countries in this direction is slow and that provided a ground for bilateralism. The initiative towards bilateral agenda intended to "allow two or more countries to embark on 'fast track' liberalization and allow other members to join the process at a slower pace."[4]

Salient Features of the ILFTA

The ILFTA has been an initiative intended to provide a framework for bilateral trade liberalization in which trade restrictions to be removed over a stipulated time period. Under this agreement, India has removed tariffs on 1351 products and Sri Lanka granted duty free access to 319 Indian products. Both countries maintained a negative list with the intention of safeguarding sensitive domestic sectors. India's negative list consisted of 429 items whereas that of Sri Lanka consisted 1180 items. India agreed to phase out existing tariffs on other items over a three year period: Duty reduction of fifty per cent in the first year and seventy five per cent in the second year and 100% in the final year. Technically, therefore, Sri Lanka should have duty free access to all items excluding the negative list at the end of the three years.

From the Sri Lankan side, it was agreed to offer fifty per cent margin of preference on further 889 items. The preferential reduction increased to seventy, ninety, and 100 per cent over a three year period and the balance items excluding the negative list were expected to phase out in eight years in a gradual manner: thirty five per cent of prevailing duty level in three years, seventy per cent at the end of sixth year, and 100 per cent removal of duties at the end of eight years.

At the end of eight years of operation of the ILFTA India shall have duty free access to all items except those items in the negative list.

Table 2. Applicability of FTA to Indo-Sri Lanka Traded Commodities

	Sri Lanka's Concessions		*India's Concessions*	
	Numbers	*Per centage*	*Numbers*	*Per centage*
Negative	623	21.4	50	13.1
0%	3	0.1	68	17.9
50%	598	20.6	218	57.4
25%	-	-	44	11.6
Other	1683	57.9	-	-
Total	2907	100.0	380	100.0

Source: Dushni Weerakoon and Wijayasiri Janaka *Regional Economic Cooperation in South Asia: A Sri Lankan Perspective,* International Economic Series No.6, Institute of Policy Studies, Colombo, 2001.

Table 2 reveals the relevance of concessions exchanged between the two countries. Out of 1180 items in Sri Lanka's negative list, nearly 623 items were subject to imports from India. Of the total of 429 items of the Indian negative list, Sri Lankan exports consist of fifty items. Hence, at the first look, the negative lists appear to be favourable to Sri Lankan exports.

Looking at the list of items qualify for zero tariff, it is apparent that out of 319 items in the zero tariff list of Sri Lanka, only three are relevant for India. By contrast, of the 1351 items in the Indian zero tariff list sixty eight export items from Sri Lanka can expect to gain. Therefore, India's gain from the zero tariff lists appears to be marginal.

Overall, the distributional impact of the concessions offered under the ILFTA can be summarized as follows: of the 2907 export items from India to Sri Lanka, 21.4 per cent falls in the negative list, 0.1 per cent can be expect to benefit from zero duty rate, and 20.6 per cent could enjoy preferential tariff reduction.

On the other hand, of the 380 export items from Sri Lanka to India, 13.1 per cent are subject to the negative list, 17.9 per cent to zero duty rate and 57.4 per cent are subject to preferential treatment of fifty per cent and 11.6 per cent of export items are subject to twenty five per cent of tariffs.

By looking at data in table 3 and 4 one may tend to arrive at the conclusion that Sri Lanka is likely to gain more from the ILFTA. Initial conditions in both countries need to be compared in arriving at such conclusions. Sri Lanka has a more liberal external trade and investment regime compared to India. Nearly seventy per cent of Sri Lankan imports are subject to a nominal import tariff of ten per cent. And the country has agreed to phase out existing anomalies in tariffs over a eight year period, nearly 57.9 per cent of traded items will be freed from tariffs as a result.

Table 3 shows the distribution of concessions granted by India on the HS cording chapter basis. The majority of the products in the list are subject to fifty per cent tariff preference. In the cases of plastic and rubber products and textile articles, a significant number of export goods are subject to India's negative list. Zero tariff access has been granted to minerals, wood products, paper products and machinery and equipment. Concession on machinery and equipment, however, will have a limited gain for Sri Lanka, because it comprises only a very small proportion of exports to India. By contrast exporters of paper, mineral and wood products are likely to gain more. Over ninety per cent of total exports of these export categories to India are subject to zero duty.

Table 3: Concessions Granted by India to Sri Lankan Exports

HS Code	Chapters	No of Concessions Granted by India				% of Exports Subject to Concessions			
		-ve	0%	50%	25%	-ve	0%	50%	25%
01-05	Live animals, animal products			2				100	
06-14	Vegetable products		2	18			0.2	99.8	
15	Animal/vegetable fats and oils			3				100	
16-24	Prepared foodstuffs			28				100	
25-27	Mineral products		2	1			92.0	8.0	
28-38	Chemical Products		2	34			0.3	99.7	
39-40	Plastic and rubber products	21		10		91.4		8.6	
41-43	Leather products			4				100	
44-46	Wood products		6	1			98.1	1.9	
47-49	Paper products	2	18	3		9.3	90.4	0.3	
50-63	Textile articles	27			44	21.5			78.5
64-67	Footwear			4				100	
68-70	Stone, plaster, cement			11				100	
71	Pearls			4				100	
72-83	Base metal			37				100	
84-85	Machinery & mechanical goods		36	22			50.5	49.5	
86-89	Transport equipment			9				100	
90-92	Optical, photographic equipmen		2	8			6.5	93.5	
93	Arms & ammunition								
94-96	Misc. Manufactured articles			19				100	
97-99	Works of art								
Total		50	68	218	44	13.6	9.9	68.0	8.5

Source: Dushni Weerakoon and Wijayasiri Janaka Regional Economic Cooperation in South Asia: A Sri Lankan *Perspective*, International Economic Series No.6, Institute of Policy Studies, Colombo, 2001

Table 4: Concessions Granted by Sri Lanka vis-a-viz Indian Exports

HS Code Chapters		No of Concessions Granted by Sri Lanka				% of Exports Subject to Concessions			
		-ve	0%	50%	Other	-ve	0%	50%	Other
01-05	Live animals, animal products	25			6	17.5			82.5
06-14	Vegetable products	86			8	99.2			0.8
15	Animal/vegetable fats and oils	11			3	84.9			15.1
16-24	Prepared foodstuffs	58			5	35.4			64.6
25-27	Mineral products	8			44	74.4			25.6
28-38	Chemical Products	19		124	325	5.9		14.5	79.7
39-40	Plastic and rubber products	62			78	52.6			47.4
41-43	Leather products	6			23	61.5			38.5
44-46	Wood products	5			30	35.3			64.7
47-49	Paper products	42			49	74.3			25.7
50-63	Textile articles	16			474	1.9			98.1
64-67	Footwear	22			10	93.5			6.5
68-70	Stone, plaster, cement	33			73	75.0			25.0
71	Pearls	1			14				100
72-83	Base metal	99		162	116	25.4		56.5	18.1
84-85	Machinery & mechanical goods	61	3	312	203	18.0	0.5	50.2	31.4
86-89	Transport equipment	23			40	76.8			23.2
90-92	Optical, photographic equipmen	6			131	4.8			95.2
93	Arms & ammunition								0.0
94-96	Misc. Manufactured articles	40			49	56.0			44
97-99	Works of art				2				100
Total		623	3	598	1683	44.1	0.1	12.8	43.0

Source: Dushni Weerakoon and Wijayasiri Janaka *Regional Economic Cooperation in South Asia: A Sri Lankan Perspective*, International Economic Series No.6, Institute of Policy Studies, Colombo, 2001.

Table 4 sets out the distribution of concessions granted to Indian exports by Sri Lanka. The data in table 4 indicate that most categories of export interest to India have been subject to Sri Lanka's negative list. There are 623 traded items are in the negative list out of which eighty six items are applicable to the category of vegetable products, ninety nine items in base metals, sixty one in machinery and mechanical equipment and twenty three in transport equipment. This means that almost all exports of vegetable products from India will not enjoy any benefit from FTA as they are subject to the negative list of Sri Lanka. This is also true in the case of transport equipments. Nearly seventy seven per cent of imports fall within Sri Lanka's negative list.

The data in table 3 and 4 indicate that in the short run, a very little trade is free of import tariffs under the ILFTA. For example, out of 319 items that have been allowed to enter into the Sri Lankan market duty free only three items were of the export interest of India. And this accounts for mere 0.1 per cent of total exports to Sri Lanka.

India has removed tariffs on 1351 items under the agreement. Only sixty eight items were of the export interest to Sri Lanka, comprising nearly ten per cent of total exports to India. The items fall in the negative list of Sri Lanka account for over forty four per cent of imports from India and the Indian negative list accounted for approximately fourteen per cent of imports from Sri Lanka.

Table 5. Tariff Elimination Method adopted by ILFTA

ILFTA	Zero Duty List	Immediate tariff reduction to 0%
	50% Duty List	With reduction raised to 70, 90 and 100% in three years
	Residual List	Reduction to 0% in 3 years by India (50% reduction of tariff in 1st year, 75% in 2nd, and 100 in 3rd year) Reduction to 0% in 8 years by Sri Lanka 35% by end of 3 years, 70% by end of 6 years, and 100% by end of 8th Year
	Negative List	Not subject to tariff reduction

Source: Adopted from Dushni Weerakoon and Wijayasiri Janaka *Implication to Member States of Progession from SAPTA to SAFTA*, A Report prepared for the SAARC Secretariat, Kathmandu Nepal, Institute of Policy Studies, Colombo, 2003.

Over the medium and long term both countries will have free access to each others market (see table 5). Over two thirds of Sri Lanka's total export to India enter the market with fifty per cent preferential tariff in the first year. And 100 per cent free access will be granted at the end of three years. Similarly, Sri Lanka allow duty free access to thirteen per cent of Indian exports over the medium term, and at the end of the eight years, nearly fifty five per cent of Indian exports will gain access to Sri Lankan markets duty free.

The Achievement of the ILFTA

Sri Lanka's bilateral trade and economic relation with India have improved after the implementation of the agreement. From January to December 2005, the value of bilateral trade between India and Sri Lanka has reached the nearly $1637 million. The bilateral trade between the two countries has increased five folds during the last five years thanks to the ILFTA.

Exports from Sri Lanka to India have increased rapidly and the trade balance, which remained favorable to India, has changed from 15.7:1 in 1998 to 2.4:1 in the first ten months of 2005. India has long been a main exporter to Sri Lanka and fifteen per cent of Sri Lanka's imports came from India. Sri Lankan exports to Indian increased in many folds and now India has become the third largest export market for Sri Lankan products.

Services Sector Development

Trade in services is different than that of goods. Trade in goods takes place using the single mode of cross boarder while that of services will be supplied using four different modes such as Cross Border Supply, Consumption Abroad, Commercial Presence, and Presence of Natural Persons. Sri Lankan residents are not permitted to purchase financial services abroad freely using the first two modes of cross border supply and consumption abroad in complying with the exchange rate regulations.

Trade in financial services in particular falls within the definitions of capital accounts and both India and Sri Lanka have not liberalized their capital accounts. Therefore the liberalization of services sector has to face certain rigidities in both countries.

Table 6 shows the progress in India's joint ventures in Sri Lanka during the twenty six years. The data reveal that business services are the major avenue of cooperation in the regard. This trend is likely to change and join ventures in other areas will also emerge if the two countries implement the CEPA.

Table 6. Indian Join Ventures in Sri Lanka [Services]

Year 1978-2004			
No	*Sector*	*Board of Investment [Sri Lanka]*	*India Investment Center [India]*
1	Business Service [including software]	15	13
2	Construction and Related Engineering Services	4	3
3	Financial Services	0	6
4	Health	2	2
5	Tourism & Travel Related Services	2	5
6	Audiovisual Services	5	1
7	Transport Services	5	1
		33	31

Source: Nisha Taneja, Arpita Mukarjee, Sanath Jayanetti, and Tilani Jayawardane *Indo-Sri Lanka Trade in Services: FTA II and Beyond*, Indian Council for Research on International Economic Relations, New Delhi, 2004.

Investment Flows

Direct investment flows from India to Sri Lanka has also increased significantly in recent times and now India is the second largest direct foreign investor in Sri Lanka amounting the value of $520 million. Sri Lanka has offered attractive investment incentive packages to Indian investors willing to invest in ventures that utilize Sri Lankan resources. Board of Investment has approved $520 million investment from 150 Indian firms by the end of 2004. More than half of the Indian investment in the SAARC region has come to Sri Lanka.

The investment of $75 million by the Indian Oil Company (IOC) has been the largest in recent times next to the Apollo

Hospitals. The Sri Lankan Export Development Board has opened its first foreign branch in Bangalore, in order to attract Indian investments in Sri Lanka.

Other notable Indian investments are TATA's, Taj Hotels, VSNL, Watawala Plantations, ICICI Bank, Nicholas Bramel, Jet Airways, Sahara Airways, Indian Airlines, Ashok Leyland, and a sizable number of small-scale investors. Human resource and education and training institutions such as ICFAI, have invested in Sri Lanka.

Successful Sri Lankan investment in India includes Ceylon Biscuits, Brandix, Mas Body Line (Pvt Ltd), Damro Export Limited, John Keels and Indo Sri Lankan Stainless Steel Ltd.

Other Areas of Cooperation

Bilateral cooperation in the services sector has also been improved. Sri Lankan Airlines has increased its weekly flights to India to 109, and Indian Airlines, Jet Airways, Sahara Airways have also increased their services to Sri Lanka.

Recently after the change in leadership in Sri Lanka, steps were taken to strengthen the bilateral relationship between the two countries. India has granted initially a credit line of $100 for the Colombo Matara Railway line Project. Areas were identified for bilateral investment in the development of Eastern Sri Lanka. Development of the port town of Trincomalee and its suburbs, the establishment of a 500-megawatt thermal power plant by Ceylon Electricity Board with the collaboration of National Thermal Power Company of India are the two projects in the pipeline.

The two countries were agreed to cooperate in the revision of agriculture prices in future rounds of talks in addition to mutual cooperation in the areas of information technology, reusable energy sources etc,. Discussions were also held to seek the possibility of establishing an information technology (IT) park in Sri Lanka.

India has agreed to allocate fifty placements for Sri Lankan students who seek professional qualifications in Indian educational institutions, in addition to fifty scholarships under the Colombo Plan.

Conclusion

Sri Lanka and India have taken a bilateral initiative to establish free trade and investment regimes in the respective countries. Sri Lanka has also signed a free trade agreement with Pakistan. There are signs that other countries in the region will follow the bilateral initiative. Significant level of progress has been made in the areas of trade in goods and investment. The positive developments towards a CEPA encompassing trade and investment likely to lead more integration of the two fast moving economies in the region.

References

1. Jagdish Bhagwati, " Regionalism or Multilateralism: An Overview", in J. De Melo and A. Panagariya (eds), *New Dimesions in Regional Integration,* UK: Cambridge University Press, 1993.
2. Dushni Weerakoon and Wijayasiri Janaka, *Regional Economic Cooperation in South Asia: A Sri Lankan Perspective*, Colombo: Institute of Policy Studies, Colombo, 2001, p. 3.
3. *Ibid,* p.15.
4. Dushni Weerakoon and Janaka Wijayasiri, *Implication to Member States of Progression from SAPTA to SAFTA*, A Report prepared for the SAARC Secretariat, Kathmandu, Colombo: Institute of Policy Studies, 2003.

15

Ground Level Problems Encountered in Importing Sri Lankan Goods into India under the FTA

Somindra Kishen Hazari

The spirit and purpose of the FTA was to allow preferential access to each others markets. Unfortunately when the FTA was signed in 1998 and when the list was released in 2000 the criteria was laid down, but not the procedures. Perhaps it was envisaged there would be no ambiguity.

Whilst Indian goods have "flooded and swamped" the Sri Lankan market the access given to Sri Lankan goods is limited and there is no end to the long list of Non Tariff Barriers that confront these goods.

Most Indians are not aware of the fact that the standard of living in Sri Lanka is significantly higher than India.

As Sri Lanka opened its economy in 1977, many years before India, the Sri Lankan market has the major "brands of the world" and some of the facilities in Sri Lanka are far superior than the ones in India.

If India is perceived and seen as only a fair weather friend and that India is only for Indians it does not augur well. Furthermore, if India's dominance as a regional super power is to continue then the support of its immediate neighbours is very important. Having good trade relations which are not one way in nature will put the relationship on a firmer wicket.

Appearing below are some of the non tariff Barriers that are put up by The Indian bureaucracy.

1. The Certificate of Origin (COO) from Sri Lanka issued by the department of Commerce, government of Sri Lanka can only be issued after the shipment has been effected.
   As shipment from Sri Lanka arrive within a period of twenty four hours, the goods arrive prior to the documents. Without the essential COO which has to be certified by the local Sri Lankan High Commission there is a delay.
2. Often Indian customs doubt the Country of Origin of the goods which results in a further delay.
   There is a lack of awareness that the COO stipulates thirty five per cent for value addition.
   The computation of the value addition allows for the inclusion of profit, which is always debatable.
3. Delays at every point result in demurrage and other costs being incurred which are prohibitive.
4. Additional costs result in the cost benefit under the FTA being negated. This also very often results in the Indian importer being dissuaded from importing further consignments.
5. The classification of goods is also an ambiguous area. Whilst some goods appear on the OPEN GENERAL LICENCE (OGL) whilst when the goods arrive the importer is told that a SPECIAL IMPORT LICENCE (SIL) is required. This SIL has to be issued by the concerned ministry from Delhi, which is of course time consuming and expensive.
6. Documents are asked for which are not specified in the FTA and furthermore when documents are submitted which are in accordance with the FTA the officials communicate that these are not the proper documents and request of "other" documents.
7. Powerful local lobbies influence decisions and more important the time taken to issue these licenses, which result in additional, costs being incurred by the importer.
8. Various additional checks / certifications are ordered on the goods although they have been tested and certified by the

relevant authorities in Sri Lanka, where it is an acknowledged fact that the standards are higher than the average Indian standards. Furthermore there is no procedure stipulate for the checking which again results in disputes and of course further precious time resulting in additional costs being incurred by the importer.

9. For checking edible items the checking is done by labs situated a distance away such as imports into Chennai are sent to CFTRI Mysore and imports into Mumbai are sent to CFTRI Pune. The procedure to send frozen goods is also not specified, which is most important given the highly perishable nature of the goods. The labs in their own wisdom are rigid and choose not to adopt modern methods of communication and are still great patrons of registered post leading to further delays.

10. At times different ports in India classify the goods imported under different duties. At times customs declare that although for certain goods where there is no Basic Customs Duty but Counter Vailing Duty is applicable. The importer due to the time and cost factor pays this amount under protest and starts the ball rolling to claim this amount paid which is a very time consuming process as getting back from the government has no specified time frame.

    If imports are being made from a group company then the valuation has to be cleared by the Special Valuation Branch to ensure that there is no transfer pricing (a better word for under invoicing)

    Ignorance leads to misconceptions which lead to suspicions / doubts.

    This is against the spirit of the FTA.

11. Very often confidential cost sheets are requested for, which land up in the hands of competitors and are misused.

12. The state of Tamil Nadu imposes and additional sales tax on imported goods, which is against WTO guidelines, which results in an additional cost.

13. If there are any doubts and checks ordered by Indian customs / Authorities which result in nothing incorrect being found then let not the costs incurred resulting from these delay/s be passed onto the importer.

14. The quota set under the FTA for the import of Sri Lankan garments into India has also not been reached. The stipulation that these garments must be made from Indian fabric is not justified nor is it viable.
15. As a result of the end of the quota regime in 2005 there has been a significant investment by Sri Lankan garment manufacturers in India, which has not been acknowledged.
16. By limiting imports into India for certain goods such as for garments and tea stating "monitoring purposes" does not augur well as India is an established software super power and to formulate a programme for this "monitoring" would be a trivial job.
17. Only with effect from September 2005 could Sri Lankan nationals open simple bank accounts in India and sit on boards of private limited companies. This is because India had classified Sri Lankans in the same category as Pakistanis. As many Sri Lankans visit India for educational / shopping / religious and medical grounds and not being allowed to have a bank account was forcing them to look at other means of bringing in funds. Sri Lankans are the highest per capita shoppers in Chennai. The numbers that come to India for medical attention for Kidney / heart and other ailments is also significant.
18. The downturn in the tea industry in South India was wrongly attributed to the import of Sri Lankan tea, by some political parties / lobbies. The imports of Sri Lankan teas into India have been significant, it is no where near the quota set.

    The loss of the Russian market and the influx of cheaper teas from Vietnam and Indonesia into India where not publicized, unfortunately which were some of the reasons which affected the southern tea industry.

    There was an incorrect notion that Sri Lankan teas are cheap and they are flooding the market. Sri Lankan teas are quality teas and compete in the quality range.

    The tea board in India has to approve the imports which is time consuming as again there are no procedures laid down.
19. There has no doubt been a misuse by certain section of importers in areas such as imports of Copper and Garlic. The guilty must be condemned but one cannot paint all exports from Sri Lanka as being suspect.

20. Unfortunately some Sri Lankan companies have not displayed the best of ethics as they have requested some Indian companies to import their product/s check market the same and set up distribution of the same. These companies have then appointed other companies to distribute their products and have not compensated the earlier company which launched their product / got their product accepted by retail chains etc.
21. Indian exporters do not face any barriers when export their goods to Sri Lanka.
22. Whilst Indians do not require a visa to visit Sri Lanka up to thirty days Sri Lankans do require a visa to visit India. The longest lines for visas seekers in Sri Lanka are outside the Indian High Commission.

    It must be acknowledged that the Indian high commission in Colombo has put up sunshades for the people who line up and have improved facilities in general but a lot more improvements can be effected.

    Of course if visas can be issued on arrival it will improve trade significantly.
23. There was a perception in Sri Lanka that the FTA was designed only to benefit India but trade figures now dispel this belief, however, India is seen as a "Big Brother" and to some as a "Big Bully".

A note of caution, a few years back when the Sri Lankan army was in a difficult situation and appealed to India for assistance it was not provided. Sri Lanka then only approached Pakistan for assistance which was promptly provided. This led to Pakistan arms and military advisors being stationed just across the Palk Straits.

SECTION-VI
INDO-SRI LANKAN PARTNERSHIP

16

The *'why'*, and the *'how'* of India-Sri Lanka Partnership

N. Sathiya Moorthy

Decades down the line, the late Indian prime minister Indira Gandhi's observation is proving true in the reverse as well. Despite the end of the Cold War, the continuing US-led global war on terrorism, and the increasing economic inter-dependence of nations and peoples have made the Indian Ocean neighbourhood a strategic locale, requiring both nations to work together for their common good more than ever.

In this, the increasing role of trade and economy in shaping bilateral relations between states – and also the possibilities for India to learn from the Sri Lankan experience with economic reforms – should be acknowledged even in the global context. Yet, the collective and individual concerns over sovereignty and security continue to stay on the top of individual national agendas. This is particularly so when nations are held close to each other either by a strip of land border, or just a stream of water, as between India and Sri Lanka. The twenty-kilometre stretch of the Palk Strait between India and Sri Lanka means that they have a shared strategic concern in their shared Indian Ocean neighbourhood. India is the only nation to be called an 'immediate neighbour' of and by Sri Lanka. In turn, it is a geographical reality that Sri Lanka is also the 'strategic gateway' to India on the Ocean front.

India-Sri Lanka Strategic Relationship

Great powers have emerged by 'managing' their regional neighbourhood, be it in the traditional American way of 'making friends and influencing peoples', or the failed 'Soviet way' of walking over them on heavy boots. While aspiring to grow out of its traditional role and image as a regional power, India needs to revive confidence in the neighbourhood. There is no better way than to get increasingly engaged with Sri Lanka, which has constantly sought its help and cooperation in all matters of politics, economics and security. There is no other country in the neighbourhood whose external policy and internal economy are linked to domestic politics as in Sri Lanka, and there is no other nation that can address all these issues better than India.

India has the political and economic muscle to push genuine Sri Lankan interests in the international arena without having to involve militarily. New Delhi's ability and willingness to rush the Indian navy and air force at a very short notice for relief work when the 'Boxer Day' tsunami struck Sri Lanka without notice in 2004 demonstrated precisely as much. It erased individual Sri Lankan apprehensions, if any, of India wanting a permanent military presence in Sri Lanka – at the same time, would have tempted predators, with or without a flotilla, to consider seeking a 'base-facility' of some kind as and when the environment so evolved.

The Way Ahead...

There however seems to be some confusion in the Indian mind as to the quantum, if not direction, of possible Indian involvement – not intervention — in the current and future Sri Lankan affairs, starting with the stalled peace process between the Colombo government and the LTTE. This confusion often flows from the past behaviour of Sri Lanka, the present political situation in the two nations, and the Rajiv Gandhi assassination case in which LTTE leader Velupillai Prabhakaran is the main accused before the Indian courts. Today when the peace process has provided the entry-point for non-littoral nations to seek a role in Sri Lankan affairs, India whose legitimate right and duty it has been, has stayed away after substantive deliberations, internally:

1) New Delhi should now dismiss Colombo's decision to offer refueling facilities for the Pakistan air force during the Bangladesh War as part of the Cold War mindset, and flowing

from possible Sri Lankan apprehensions about Indian designs – to which subsequent developments did lend some credence.

2) Like the US overcoming the Vietnam psyche through introspection, the Indian establishment and polity should re-visit the IPKF experience when that generation is still around, for strategic, diplomatic and military lessons for the future, without letting it tie New Delhi down to the past.

3) Given the near-permanency of coalition politics in India, New Delhi has to create institutional mechanisms, for instance, to educate regional politicians as in Tamil Nadu on the long-term strategic imperatives of foreign policy, working into the scheme, their own legitimate concerns and compulsions – without allowing one to hold the other, hostage. (In the current context, for instance, the Tamil Nadu polity now wanting India not to get involved, may have a different view if the recent trickle of 'Sri Lankan refugees' became a flood – the like of which had led to their demand, and subsequent 'Indian involvement' in the early eighties.)

4) The Indian polity and diplomacy also have to concede such domestic compulsions to the Sinhala polity in Sri Lanka in evolving a southern consensus to the peace process, and appreciate the same likewise. (For its part, the Sri Lankan government too may have to constantly educate the Sinhala polity and society on the imperatives for peace, and of the peace process).

5) While LTTE leader Prabhakaran's continued status as the main accused in the Rajiv Gandhi assassination case continues, India needs to prepare for the possible reality of the peace process conferring legitimacy on the leader and the organization. Neither the Sri Lankan public opinion, nor the international community's views would countenance any tough posture by New Delhi.

6) Likewise, India has to strategize for the possibility of the Sri Lankan government conferring legitimacy on the LTTE militia, including the Sea Tigers and the infant Air Tigers (?), and their induction into the established structures of the Sri Lankan security apparatus, either at the national or provincial-level, as and when a negotiated settlement is arrived at. New Delhi cannot afford to be caught napping, nor could it

sent out a discordant note, citing the otherwise justified strategic and security concerns to such induction, if and when it came about. (Even New Delhi's reservations, if any, need to be pushed hard at every stage, and more directly, requiring greater Indian involvement with the various stake-holders in Sri Lanka).

7) India cannot hope to reclaim the lost ground in bilateral equations with Sri Lanka after letting non-littoral players to take a greater initiative in the peace process, in which the island-nation's administration, polity and people want greater Indian presence and contribution. He who pays the piper would then call the tune.

In this background, India should re-look at the current position of benevolent indifference to events in Sri Lanka, and should share a seat on the Tokyo Donors' Conference, like the US (which too has banned the LTTE, and has refused to talk directly with the organization), and the EU (which even while being an American ally has displayed a mind, if not course, of its own).

Power-Devolution and the Indian Model

Going beyond the long-term strategic inter-dependence of the two nations, India is also being favoured for the peace-facilitation role as much by the Sinhala south as by the various streams of Tamil and Muslim political and societal opinion in the north and the east from time to time. Prabhakaran's much-publicized news conference of 10 April 2002 reflected this sentiment from the LTTE side. Starting off late to study independent India's continual engagement with insurgency, the Sinhala polity seems to have concluded that any peace proposal having New Delhi's blessings would not compromise the sovereignty and territorial integrity of the island-nation, and would at the same time draw from the rich Indian experience in power-devolution, benefiting the nation as a whole.

The Indian experience with political demands/insurgency is rich, varied and successful — diluting the cause (Telangana agitation), bringing around the protestors by addressing their legitimate concerns (Assam and Gorkhaland agitations), tiring out the rebel (Mizo National Front), or putting down terrorism and engaging moderates in a negotiated settlement at the same time (Punjab). Political Sri Lanka can also draw inspiration from the

Indian constitutional scheme, which has inherent provisions for addressing the ever-increasing aspirations of an evolving socio-economic community – and also from India's greater ability to succeed as a nation-state, overcoming the equally inherent deficiencies of religion and language, caste and creed, economic differences and social hierarchy.

The Indian model is possibly the only one of its kind, more so in South Asia, which is both 'unitary' and 'federal' in parts – and is thus capable of addressing the real and not-so-real concerns of the southern Sinhala polity in Sri Lanka, as also the legitimate aspirations of the Tamils. A power-devolution package based on the Indian model could thus involve Sri Lankan provinces being empowered with the rights and responsibilities for maintaining law and order, and controlling crime (policing powers), food, healthcare and education – and discharged by the provinces without confusion or irresponsibility of any kind. The 'subordinate legislative powers' conferred on the state legislatures by the Indian parliament in this regard are clear and complete. So are the constitutionally mandated finance commission, the provision for the grant of royalty for mineral wealth to the states to the centre, and evolution of local self-government institutions, or *panchayati raj*, at the lower end of the trickle-down process of power-devolution.

At the ground level, the inherent provisions and vibrancy of the Indian constitutional scheme has contributed to the creation of new states reflecting newer regional aspirations, that too through simple-majority resolutions of parliament. This included the wholesale linguistic reorganization of states, redrawing borders in most cases, only six years after the constitution came into being. Though controversial at the political-level until very recently, the Indian ingenuity of granting a separate constitution for the northern state of Jammu and Kashmir is worthy of emulation in distinctively difficult circumstances of the kind.

There is also the political process, which effortlessly took care of such issues as re-naming Madras state as Tamil Nadu, and later acceding to the state's request for the chief minister to unfurl the national flag on Independence Day — the governors continue to do the honours elsewhere – and allowing the state police to have a separate standard of its own. At the national-level, the evolving political process has set the healthy tradition of the president and prime minister often coming from two regions of the country – with one of them possibly representing the minority communities. So much so, now India has a president in Abdul Kalam, and prime minister in Manmohan Singh, both of whom come from two different minority communities in the country – with no questions asked.

Going beyond in-built democratic scheme of checks-and-balances, the Indian judiciary has often guided the evolutionary process through constant intervention and corrective steps. Even while continuously upholding the centre's constitutional authority to disband errant state governments, the higher judiciary in India, has drawn a clear distinction from political abuse of such power through landmark verdicts in the Bommai case, and more recently, the Bihar assembly dissolution case. The supreme court verdict in the Mandal case and the judicial introduction of the creamy layer concept likewise meant a re-look at the constitutionally-mandated 'reservations' in jobs and higher education when the society had become upwardly mobile and the political abuse of the provision needed to be halted.

The Indian political and constitutional scheme, its application and experience are object lessons in creating an internal agenda for nation-building in the twentieth century, particularly so in the Third World. As and when permanent peace returned to Sri Lanka, the nation would have to address internal contradictions on the socio-economic front down to the last man, his expectations and aspirations, the failure of which in the past had contributed greatly to the emergence of Sinhala and Tamil militancy, separately but around the same time. This was also an inevitable factor in the Karuna rebellion within the LTTE when temporary peace had returned to the Tamil areas in the light of the Cease-fire Agreement (CFA).

Economic Reforms: Learning from the Sri Lankan Experience

If it is on politics and the political scheme that India may have something to offer contemporary Sri Lanka, it is on the evolving economic scheme in the country that political India may have something to learn from the Sri Lankan experience, in turn. As used to be the case with socialism, India has been learning while growing with the economic reforms, too. The slogan, 'reforms with a human face' is a product of this learning process, and already some Indian states, if not the union government, have either applied brakes on their reformist zeal, or reversed it in toto after their non-populist administrative decisions had contributed to electoral reverses for the party in power.

Apart from the eternal sense of job-security, high pay, and terminal benefits attaching to government jobs, the reforms regimen in India has also hit at education and healthcare at all levels. The segregation of education from pre-primary to professional levels, thanks to increased privatization and higher fee-structure in state institutions with the very first signs of reforms, has frustrated the ambitions of an emerging generation, particularly in the rural areas. The high cost of medical education and the simultaneous fall in the healthcare standards in the state sector may soon begin ailing the society and polity as a whole.

There is also an increasing feeling that the human face part of the reforms, if at all, could lead only to the marginalization of the beneficiary class, and not their empowerment, unlike in the past, and contributing to the emergence of newer vote-banks of the old and the infirm, both neglected by the families and the state alike, the forgotten farmer and the under-employed urban youth. Sri Lanka, under similar circumstances, had recorded militancy of the left-leaning JVP in the Sinhala south and west, and the Tamil nationalist militancy of the LTTE kind in the north and the east. There may be a lesson in it for reformist India to have a re-look at the process in particularly in the context of fast-paced Naxalite growth and expansion.

For Sri Lanka, in turn, a return of permanent peace could cut open festering wounds left behind by the military handling of the socio-economic problem by the nation's Ivy League political class, which did not have the benefit of a *Swadeshi*-like call as in India before independence. The nation has already been denied the contributions of a thinking generation of over 100,000 slain youth of the Sinhala-JVP and Tamil-LTTE varieties. The face of the Tamil polity has already been changed, and with the passage of time, it is changing also on the Sinhala side. As and when there is ethnic peace, together and separately, these factors could re-set the political clock on the reforms regimen. There again India may have some lessons to learn.

Independent of such a broad-spectrum approach, a closer look at Sri Lanka would also raise questions about the outright success of the reforms regimen in alien cultures, polity and society.

While the high literacy rate has been a Sri Lankan hallmark even before the days of economic reforms, education in the country has stagnated mostly at the higher-secondary level. Hardly one per cent of those passing out of the A-Level — equivalent to the Plus-Two in India – can dream of admission for higher education, which is confined to the university campuses that are few and far between.

The urban centres, of which the reforms regimen has not produced any, have eighteen-year-olds eking out a living from modestly paid jobs, even for which they would have been under-qualified otherwise. Their rural brethren are left only to fret and fume, what with even traditional agricultural and dairy products getting increasingly imported from outside the country, to fill the shop-shelves in Colombo and the few other cities dotting the landscape.

In a way, Sri Lanka may be sitting on a socio-economic powder keg, whose tendency and potency might become known as and when permanent peace returned to the island-nation. For, that would also be when the internal contradictions of the kind could get increasingly exposed as a part of a re-emerging internal agenda, now what with the national focus and energies being consumed entirely by the conflict in the north-east first, and the national desire for restoration of permanent peace, since. If it came to that, this could well have the potency to upset the socio-political equilibrium in India – particularly southern India, going beyond the traditional 'Tamil bonding'.

Economy, Growth and Development

Notwithstanding the reforms-related lessons that both India and Sri Lanka can learn from each other, there are immediate and more direct issues of greater economic and developmental activity between the two nations. Sri Lanka is a 'dependent nation' as for as the economic affairs of the people and the government goes as a whole, and this does not seem to have been fully understood in India. New Delhi thus may have to begin practicing 'economic diplomacy' with greater vigour and purpose, if it is not to be left behind on the politico-strategic front.

While seeking to increase bilateral trade through SAFTA and the pending economic cooperation between the two nations, India and Sri Lanka can initiate specific measures:

i. Sri Lanka may need to facilitate greater FDI through land and duty concessions in non-traditional areas as healthcare, medical education, and other streams of professional education. Indian private investment and expertise in professional education would help Sri Lanka grow at a faster pace, by equipping the future generations for better overseas employment, going beyond the current crop of trained housemaids. This in turn will ensure an increased flow of foreign remittances, particularly *per capita* forex remittance.

ii. Any Indian private/public investment in the higher education sector in Sri Lanka would also directly help in the country making large forex savings, as ambitious aspirants with affordability often migrate to the West, Australia, New Zealand and Singapore for doing such courses – and often to settle down in those countries, subsequently, leading to brain-drain (which again had afflicted India until a decade or so ago).

iii. Indian involvement in the medical education sector, even if individual cost of acquisition could be prohibitive initially, could serve the cause of healthcare through the teaching hospitals attached to such educational institutions. A healthy nation alone can aspire to become a wealthy nation, as well.

iv. Given the spending-vibrancy in the Sri Lankan economy, Indian manufacturers of domestic and luxury goods stand to benefit by expanding their market network, and thus market-share in Sri Lanka. Imaginative and strategic marketing could help them, as India now has an island-wide reputation for a world-class manufacturing base for all goods, including automobiles. The Indian industry can do well to pass on the high savings in manufacturing and transportation costs *viz a viz* their competitors from other parts of the world operating in the Sri Lankan market, to the customer, thus benefiting all parties.

v. Given the inherent problems attaching to fishing in the Palk Strait and also the socio-political sensitivities involved, the two nations could help their traditional fishermen to set up common cooperatives to promote fishing in the region – and also consider the 'mother ship' concept for high-sea fishing.

vi. The setting up of a petroleum ministry, and the subsequent appointment of a petroleum minister in Sri Lanka for the first time in 2005 has expanded the scope for cooperation between the two nations in matters of oil exploration and refining in the Gulf of Mannar region. Given the vast downstream manufacturing potential of such facilities, a streamlined approach could also help improve employment potential in both nations, particularly for the coastal fishermen along the two shores of the Palk Strait.

Economic Development

i. Given the vast, untapped and often untrained labour available in Sri Lanka, select Indian industries could be encouraged through incentives, to consider the setting up of bases in the island, for manufacturing goods, both for the domestic market and for the regional and global markets. India can learn from Sri Lanka in matters of faster port-handling, shipment-clearance, etc, as has often been pointed out.
ii. The early restoration of the ferry service between Sri Lanka and Tamil Nadu (Tuticorin) in Tamil Nadu, and the early commencement of the proposed ferry service to Vizhijam in south Kerala, would help promote bilateral trade, tourism, understanding and dependence.
iii. The proposed land bridge connecting the two nations could also help promote tourism and trade between the two countries, and also further facilitate the growth of Colombo as a container port capable of handling large vessels and larger traffic even after the completion of work on the Sethusamudram Project. The land bridge would link Sri Lanka not only to southern India and the rest of India, but in times of peace and greater regional and global cooperation, to the Eurasian landmass as a whole.
iv. In matters of science and technology impacting on better communication facilities and consequent improvement in bilateral trade and relations, the two nations can explore the possibility of Sri Lanka being allocated transponders in Indian satellites. This could also be used to study the weather patterns, and the facility extended to other SAARC nations over time.

Culture and Education

India gave Buddhism to Sri Lanka, and this is widely acknowledged across the nation. The cultural and historic linkages between the Tamil areas of Sri Lanka and southern Tamil Nadu are also well documented. So is the traditional linkages between the Muslim communities in the two nations, who, however, seem to have maintained those contacts, mainly because of better economic status and business relations. Across the island, Gandhiji and Jawaharlal Nehru, particularly for the older generation continue to be the inspiration for the limited Sri Lankan national movement.

In turn, the national symbol of the Indian state, the 'Sarnath Lion', and also the 'Dharma Chakra' at the centre of the national flag, are contributions of Buddhism to India. Gandhiji also adopted the non-violent *Ahimsa* form of protest also from Buddhist percept. Yet, the average Indian does not know that Buddhists in Sri Lanka, including their monks, are traditionally non-vegetarians in their eating habits. In turn, even Buddhist monks in Sri Lanka often refuse to believe that vegetarianism for instance is a creed attributed to the religion in the land of its founder.

In this background, there is still a lot that each can learn from the other, in terms of education and culture, tradition and tourism:

a) Education

India's present-day success as a regional power poised to become a global power impinges on the scientific temperament carefully nurtured from the early years of independence. The setting up of CSIR (Council for Scientific and Industrial Research), the IITs and IIMs, the nation's early forays into space and nuclear technologies against heavy odds, nearer home and afar, have paid off since. A 'new Sri Lanka' – or, any other nation in the neighbourhood – has to develop such a temperament and purpose if it has to grow, and also get counted. The Indian experience and expertise can help.

i. Sri Lanka has to upgrade the educational standards of the younger generation if they have to contribute substantially to nation-building, and the nation itself has to live down the image of a 'dependent economy'. The Indian experience can help, while the Indian standards could become the touchstone. As part of the growing mutual dependence and exchanges among SAARC nations, Indian universities could allocate quotas for students from individual SAARC members.

ii. In the case of Sri Lanka, it can be accompanied by 'scholarships' for 'Plantation Tamil' students of Indian origin. The government of India should also consider setting up higher educational facilities for the 'Plantation Tamils' in their immediate vicinity, which could also benefit their Sinhala brethren in the neighbourhood.

iii. A stage may soon come, if it has not already happened, when India may have another segment of the society getting ready to climb up the social and economic ladder. Like their brethren of the sixties and the seventies (whose progenies have since become successful professionals earning in millions), the new-layer aspirants would require to be equipped in skilled and semi-skilled trades that could fetch them substantial salaries in the overseas job market. The reality may soon be donning that in most Indian states there are now more professional educational institutions than the forgotten polytechnics, which used to equip educated youth in various skilled and semi-skilled trades. India could well turn to Sri Lanka for such expertise, as the nation is known to have specific programmes for training housemaids for the overseas job-markets, but whose progenies are now financially-equipped to take up serious professional education, which could equip them for better-paid jobs, nearer home and afar.

b) Culture

There is a need and opportunity to diversify Indian interest in Sri Lankan cultural and heritage sites, and *vice versa*, laying greater stress on the traditional Indian linkages to Buddhism, particularly in southern India – and the increasing Sri Lankan (Tamil and Sinhala) interest in the Hindu temples at Sabarimala and Guruvayoor in Kerala, Tiruchendur and Madurai in Tamil Nadu, and Puttaparthi in Andhra Pradesh. India may, however, need to modify procedures for issuance of visas, as at present Sri Lanka follows a visa-on-arrival principle, and this contradiction leaves a bad taste in the average Sri Lankan from whatever religion and region.

i. On contemporary culture front, there is now a greater fan following for Hindi films and Tamil film songs among the Sinhala youth than is discernible in India. A greater appreciation of this emerging trend could help modify perceptions in India, Tamil Nadu in particular. This could bring people closer, and deflect from the Tamil Nadu-centric approach to bilateral affairs.

ii. Apart from the policy, business and promotional aspects of education, particularly professional education, there may now be a need to study the commonality between the languages being spoken in the two countries. Such studies could, and should, go beyond the known linkages between Tamil language and culture in the two nations. There is a lot in common between Sinhala language and culture on the one hand, and those of various Indian states, notably southern India, on the other.

iii. Academics from both countries could also be encouraged to study the structure and usage-patterns between Sinhala and Tamil language as spoken in Sri Lanka.

iv. The commonality in the dialect of Tamil spoken in Sri Lanka and southern coastal Tamil Nadu too need a closer study and appreciation, given that the rhythmic pattern of 'spoken Tamil' across Sri Lanka has a shade in common with that of the coastal population in the southern Tamil Nadu district of Kanyakumari, which in turn had formed a part of Kerala state until re-organization in 1956.

c) Tourism

Given that Indians rank first among foreign tourists visiting Sri Lanka, and also the scope for improving Sri Lankan tourist inflow into India, there is need for facilitating direct 'rupee-rupee exchange' at airports in both countries:

i. While Sri Lanka is generally accepted as a better 'tourist manager' among the South Asian nations, it can boost its travel and tourism-related income by the government/private operators taking a leaf out of the Indian example in meeting the demands 'budget tourists'. State-run Tourism Development Corporations in most Indian states and also at the centre thus have 'budget packages' by their own buses to various tourist destinations, where they have also budget-accommodation. In Sri Lanka, the Tourism Development Board stops with training and accrediting tourist operators, instead.

ii. In matters of eco-tourism and ecology-supportive tourism, Sri Lanka has a lot to teach in terms of preserving the pristine nature of the nation's flora for the foreigner to admire. India in particular can also take lessons in creating a mindset among the local population, which while fighting for space with the wild elephants in their immediate neighbourhood, has not produced any 'Veerappan-like' poacher, who kills the animal for the tusk, with which he could make a killing in the illegal international market for ivory.

Sharing and Caring....

The growing 'global village' has made sharing and caring between nations and peoples understandable and inevitable – and even more possible than in the past, near and distant. It is only the political will that is now required to make dreams such as that of the Tamil poet-patriot, Subramania Bharati, a reality.

Writing in the early years of the twentieth century, Bharati, an eternal optimist, dreamt of a land bridge connecting India and Sri Lanka. Like the Sethusamudram Project, which has taken over a century to fruition now, Bharati's dream, *"Sinhala theevinu-kkore paalam amaip-pom, Sethu-vai meedu-ruthi veedhi samaip-pom'* too needs to be given a physical form and shape.

Maybe, there is light at the end of the horizon, signaling the dawn of a new morn!

17

Indo-Sri Lanka Cooperation in Education

Santasilan Kadirgamar

The close and intimate ties between Sri Lanka and India stretching back to centuries before recorded history have left their impact on every aspect of life. Geographical proximity and cultural identities including shared habits, customs, ways of life, and values firmly grounded on the four main religions, and the humanistic and rational movements of recent times, have bound us irretrievably together over the centuries.

Shared experiences under European imperialism with its economic, political and cultural oppression created a sense of solidarity in the first half of the twentieth century. The legacy of European imperialism had its negative as well as positive dimensions. Among the positive dimensions was the development of a modern educational system, though not without its faults.

One may add that among other factors such as the development of infrastructure consisting of a reasonably well-developed system of transportation consisting roads and railways leading to mobility, the characteristics of an open and democratic society evolved from the mid-decades of the nineteenth century. The establishment of legislative councils and the final evolution of a representative system enabled both countries to successfully work the parliamentary system from the time of independence. Noteworthy is the fact that both countries have had the rare and proud distinction in Asia and the rest of the third World, of having changed governments through the peaceful exercise of the ballot from as early as the mid-1950s. Though imperfect, and often marred by the eruption of communal violence, frequent declarations of a state of emergency, prolonged conflict, and the consequent violations of democratic and human rights, representative institutions and related institutions of civil society have survived and are today deeply rooted in both countries. This commitment to democratic rights was reaffirmed in Article 20 of the Joint Statement issued by India and Sri Lanka at the end of the president Mahinda Rajapakse's state visit in December 2005. The president of Sri Lanka and the prime minister of India noted that both countries have a record of unbroken commitment to the free and fair exercise of the franchise, and to democratic governance.

The long and remarkable non-violent struggle for independence in India, the assertion of the 'Indian-ness of India', resurgence and cultural revival, together with the liberal values imparted under the system of education that evolved from the early decades of the nineteenth century laid the foundations for this achievement. This naturally had its impact on Sri Lanka.

India has had a longer history than Sri Lanka in the field of college and university education. The Universities of Bombay, Calcutta and Madras were established in 1856, and thereafter several other Universities came into existence. In the post-independence era tertiary education expanded rapidly, which has today reached degrees of excellence comparable to the best in the world. Sri Lanka's achievements have been in achieving high literacy rates through a well-organized school system that reaches to much of the remotest and most backward areas of the island, though as pointed out below there are serious discrepancies and inequalities. This has survived the destruction, instability and brain drain resulting from conflict and war. This together with universal health care provided free by the state enabled Sri Lanka to achieve comparatively low infant mortality rates and high life expectancy in the third World. Population growth rate stabilized and today the population stands at a manageable twenty million.

But we have failed in building upwards from this remarkable achievement. In the field of tertiary education the country has not kept up with India and is fast ceasing to be competitive with several countries in Asia, especially in Southeast Asia. Singapore and

Malaysia in the 1960s employed University of Ceylon graduates and lecturers to build up their respective universities. Today while some faculties in some of the Sri Lankan universities are able to maintain standards and compete, on the average Sri Lanka is lagging behind. One may even say that the university system in the country is in deep crisis. Some of the causes for this are discussed below. Cooperation with India is one if not the most practicable way out.

Civic institutions and civil society derive strength and are firmly founded in our school system and institutions of tertiary education, in particular the colleges and universities. A healthy and vibrant press and today the electronic media depend a great deal on the quality of young people produced by our schools and universities. In fact education is the bedrock on which society survives.

A Hundred Years of Educational Links with India

The cooperation envisaged is nothing new. From the mid-decades of the nineteenth century India and the Ceylon of that time had strong bonds in the field of education. Until recent years the Jaffna district in northern Lanka - the cultural center and the most densely populated Tamil district,-was one of the most advanced educationally and second only to that of Colombo, if not on par with Colombo. Literacy in the English language was higher than in most parts of the country. This in contemporary times had far-reaching political consequences leading to the present conflict, the causes and results of which are beyond the scope of this paper.[1]

The advances made in education in Jaffna are often attributed to the large number of schools established by the American Ceylon Mission, in addition to that by other Christian denominations and the Hindu Board of Education. While this is to a large extent true, the quality of education imparted owed a great deal to the links with India.

The first graduates of the Madras University were C.W.Thamotherampillai and Harold Viswanathapillai, both from the Batticotta Seminary founded in Jaffna in 1822 by the A.C.M. In the second half of the nineteenth century Jaffna College (founded in 1872 and successor to the Batticotta Seminary) was affiliated to the Calcutta University during 1891-1907.[2]

Sinhalese students from the other districts in country also used this facility, but in ratio to their respective populations more Tamils than Sinhalese came to India for educational purposes. Ties of language (Tamil) and religion (Hinduism) made India, especially south India a homely place. But then Jaffna students did not confine themselves to Tamil Nadu. From the late 1940s to the early 60s they went to several cities in other parts of India, wherever opportunities were available.

Another dimension in these intimate relations with India was the presence of a large number of teachers, particularly from Kerala, in Jaffna and the rest of the island. This began in the early 1920s. The University College and the subsequent University of Ceylon founded in 1942 did not produce the required teachers in a rapidly expanding school system in the country. The introduction of free and compulsory education in 1944, and the growing demand for instruction in the sciences, that is Mathematics, Physics, Chemistry, Botany and Zoology made it imperative to bring in teachers from India. Once again ties of language and adaptability to the culture and environment, simple life style and low cost of living that prevailed in Jaffna, made this district an attractive proposition. The Ceylon rupee was strong, one Ceylon rupee being equivalent to two Indian rupees at that time.

Jaffna College in 1947 had founded an Undergraduate department and was preparing students leading to the B.A. and B.Sc external examinations of the University of London. It had been transformed after 1908 into a leading secondary school. By the 1950s twenty per cent of the Jaffna College secondary school teachers were from India and in the Undergraduate Department several lecturers were Indians.

The advancement of education in Jaffna in the mid-decades of the twentieth century owes much to the strong bonds that we had with India from the mid-nineteenth century, in particular to the contribution made by competent teachers from India who made a major contribution to this development. It is a tribute to the principals of schools in Jaffna, administrators and the management included, that they had the vision to tap the resources available in India at a crucial period in our history. This was reciprocated by the Tamil community in integrating hundreds of these teachers into our society. The teachers from India, mostly from Kerala adapted themselves speedily to life in Jaffna, including the use of the Tamil language and cultural norms prevalent here. We have to acknowledge the debt of gratitude we owe to India and the teachers concerned. We also have to recognize the fundamental reality that restoring the bonds with India is a paramount necessity if we are to regain the educational eminence we once enjoyed, devastated by twenty-five years of war. This will require the recruitment of teachers from India in all fields, especially to teach in the English medium and also to teach English as a second language. The objective is education in its fullest sense; such as we had in our times, which was the envy and pattern for many others far and near.[4]

The newly founded University of Ceylon too in its early years had several lecturers and professors from India. In 1964 a rigid policy of Ceylonisation came into effect and with that ended nearly a century of cooperation with India in the field of education. These changes were partly due to the rise in unemployed graduates, especially in the humanities and social sciences. Equally damaging had been the shortsighted decision by the government to terminate the holding of the University of London external examinations in the country. While some students sat for these exams through private study, Jaffna College and Aquinas University College in Colombo had established themselves as popular institutions where students enrolled for the London degree courses.

1956 Nationalism and its consequences

This year 2006 we observe fifty years of Sinhala only, and hence is an opportune moment look back and see what went wrong. Any evaluation of post-1956 changes is likely to be controversial. Sinhalese and Tamil nationalism and more recently the emerging Muslim nationalism command considerable allegiance in the country. The decision to make Sinhala and Tamil the media of instruction in schools in the1940s was the correct decision. The decision in 1956 to make Sinhalese the official language for the Sinhalese people was also the right decision. The fundamental error was in not recognizing the legitimate rights of the Tamil people and in not making Tamil also an official language. This created a climate of unrest, leading to conflict, violence, the resort to arms and the predicament we are in today. The prospects of a peaceful evolution of a post-colonial society changed, with disastrous consequences to the political, social and economic life of the country.

In making Sinhalese and Tamil the media of instruction adequate plans were not initiated to retain English as an effective second language and a link language. In fact the Sinhalese and to a lesser extent the Tamils mind set was anti-English. This was further aggravated when in haste and without any planning the media of instruction in the then four university campuses were changed to Sinhalese and Tamil. English if not thrown out was utterly neglected in our educational institutions from the kindergarten right up to the university. The nationalization of denominational schools took place at the same time in the early 1960s, leaving just about fifty private schools that had to be non-fee levying – a practical impossibility. Most of the denominational schools had been managed by Christians, both Roman Catholic and Non-Roman Catholic. It was about the same time that the London exams were terminated. Both Jaffna College and Aquinas University College were both Christian Colleges. With the rapidly expanding demand for a university education, universities were established in haste without even the required buildings and no planning of courses of study. The result was an over-production of graduates in the humanities and social sciences without knowledge of English and the skills that go with it leading to unemployment. The unemployed and under-employed fuelled unrest. The country got trapped in a vicious circle.

Several generations of students have paid a heavy price for the hasty and ill-considered decisions made within a space of ten to fifteen years from 1956. The two major parties that have ruled the country share responsibility for the disastrous consequences. In the context of education all communities were affected. The frequent changes of government and the lack of consensus have further aggravated the situation. Some realization has taken place and an effort is being made to restore English as the media of instruction in the schools. This in the view of some is to begin at the wrong end. The country does not have the teachers to do this on a national scale. There are not enough competent teachers to teach English as a language leave alone teach mathematics, chemistry or economics in English.

This is where the Indian experience becomes meaningful. Other countries like Malaysia have committed similar blunders like Lanka in adopting a monolingual approach. In Japan, which is often cited as an example by mono-lingual nationalists, in the Meiji era 1868-1912 and the first half of the twentieth century when the foundations for a highly developed educational system were laid, faculty members and students in universities were proficient in English or another European language. To this day English is given the utmost importance from middle school to the university. Recently Japan has initiated a policy of recruiting hundreds of English teachers from abroad to teach English and has encouraged the teaching of oral English in primary schools. The teaching of English is much more important for a small country like Sri Lanka with its limited resources.

Secondly education in Sri Lanka has been the monopoly of the state. Education should be the responsibility of the state and but by no means its monopoly. Unlike in India all our universities are state universities without providing space for private initiative. Private universities and colleges have come into existence in Malaysia catering to tertiary education. The Indian community in Malaysia has established a full-fledged university in northern Malaysia, though it is not meant exclusively for the Indians. Any attempt at initiating Indo-Sri Lanka cooperation in education must begin with self-criticism and a study of the Indian experience in education in the last five decades.

Beyond Parochial Images and Political Boundaries

Recommendations and planning must come from experts in the field and those vested with the responsibility for education – that is administrators, heads of institutions, and the teachers in service. Public discussion of proposals and reforms is vital. Over politicisation, the bane of Sri Lankan politics is undesirable. The time has come for consensus not only in education but also in several other areas such as the economy, and most of all pertaining to the national question. There is no way forward in the country without a resolution of this burning issue.

In both India and Sri Lanka there is a growing consciousness and awareness for fundamental changes in how we have approached problems that confront the country and the acute need for cooperation with India.

For too long, we have looked at each other's region as the other region, the other language and the other religion. We have been busy for rather unfortunate historical reasons and political expediency imagining parochial images and situations about the other region. But this is a larger issue. Especially in south India, due to the ethnic (problem), and historical reasons and the attempt to see each other in different cultural categories, we have not tried to reach out or relate to each other.

We have come to realize that, as both the processes of globalisation and historical conditions demand, we cannot live in watertight compartments any more. We have to think beyond political boundaries. We have to think not only in terms of the South Asian region but the Indian Ocean Rim. We have to look at the best of human aspirations, and intellectual and cultural elements, and how we can draw upon those human achievements, celebrating both diversity and humanity. Looked at from that point of view, the entire purpose of this gathering is to organise a focal point for coming together.

The other point is that so far we have not looked at the commonalities and the shared culture we have. We have been re-looking at the whole region. The area south of the Deccan is so much part of the Sri Lankan history as it is north of the Vindhya region. Buddhism and Jainism came to Sri Lanka from north of the Vindhya region. Various cultural elements from the Gangetic plains came to Sri Lanka. An entire spectrum of technological, spiritual, cultural and linguistic aspects came from south India, including the states of Orissa, Andhra Pradesh, Maharashtra, Kerala and Tamil Nadu.

If we take the problems that have been dominant in Sri Lankan politics in colonial and post-colonial periods and even in the pre-colonial period, the baggage of labels - our history has always been about south Indian invasions; then we have the estate Tamils' situation; then the emergence of the Tamil problem, which is connected to south India. We have historical evidence that throughout history, small groups of people, communities and culture have come to Sri Lanka from peninsular India. There has been close cultural interaction between Orissa and Sri Lanka, including a lot of art forms from Orissa, and the Mahayana Tantric situations.

There was close interaction between Andhra Pradesh and Sri Lanka both in terms of philosophy and the movement of people from Andhra Pradesh to Sri Lanka. Then we have Tamil Nadu: movement of people, culture, political campaigns, and so on. Also Kerala. This whole composite region has had both positive and negative relationships, which have been recognised by the respective governments in New Delhi and Colombo as a vital factor in the relationship between the two countries. As such, there is now an overt feeling that we must have closer working relationship and greater understanding. Into that agenda, you have to write in the peninsular India-Sri Lankan greater understanding process as a critical factor. It does not get filled in merely by students from Sri Lanka to India, occasional researches, cultural troops coming and going. This has to be a sustained, self-perpetuating programme. At the end of the sessions, the agreement was that this cannot be an *ad hoc* programme and it has to be recognised by policy makers in both the countries.

In the context of Seneviratne's contention[5] that we must have a closer working relationship and that this has to be recognized by policy makers in both countries. We here note article 13 in the recently concluded joint statement mentioned above:

The two sides reiterated their desire to accelerate their cooperation in the field of human resource development, and in the fashioning of educational policies appropriate for developing within the national workforces, the skills and capacities required by the twenty first Century. Towards this end, it was agreed that the joint Working group under the India-Sri Lanka MOU on the Education Exchange Programme would be operationalized at the earliest possible. Several measures funded by India to enhance cooperation in the field of education and training were also agreed upon. These include the Mahatma Gandhi scholarship scheme for 100 deserving Sri Lankan students every year, the upgradation of libraries and science laboratories in the Upcountry areas, the setting up of a Chair in Contemporary Indian studies in Peradeniya University and commissioning of a field study on vocational training centers.[6]

Identifying Areas for Action

While welcoming the joint statement referred to above, as Seneviratne has pointed out we have to go beyond ad hoc programmes to a sustained self-perpetuating programmes.

We need programmes recognized and implemented by policymakers. Here are some specific proposals. The development of every facet of education in the broadest terms will necessarily require greater cooperation with India.

(1) Restore the free flow of students and teachers that prevailed prior to the 1960s, by relaxing visa and foreign exchange regulations, and a liberal grant of scholarships based on foreign

aid. Any effort to restore communicative skills in English will require hundreds of teachers from India. Information Technology is another area where cooperation and assistance will be required and this is intrinsically related to skills in the English language. If we are serious about English as the medium of instruction on an island wide scale, and in the sciences in particular, we will need teachers from India just as we did in the 1940s to the early 60s. Exchange of students and teachers at all levels will enrich both countries, lead to mutual respect and greater understanding. Youth in Sri Lanka in particular need such exposure on an all-island scale and not merely confined to Colombo.

(2) Re-introduce the affiliated college system (state and private) with universities in India. This will require a bold initiative by the Sri Lankan government based on consensus among the major political parties. To begin with there could be one or two colleges in every one of the twenty two districts. Some of these could be affiliated to universities in India conforming to standards determined by the authorities there. Proliferation of colleges in the western province and other advanced districts should be avoided. Only eleven per cent of the eligible student population takes to tertiary education (including three per cent admitted to university education). The affiliated college degrees could be three years, and in some cases two years post A-level or three-years post O-level. In Japan there are a variety of such schools and colleges, called junior Colleges and Senmon Gakko (special schools). In our part of the world have not broken away from the traditional disciplines. Efforts should be made to train self-employed farmers and those in the fishing industry.

As suggested by Kumar David[7], we must move away from fields that are already flooded with local graduates and topics that are not economically productive and generative of employment and self-employment. The move all over the world is to a variety of educational topics, which are geared to productive activity. The emphasis must be on practical employable skills. Examples are Hotel & Tourism, Computer Hardware Technicians, Software Support Service, Electrical & Electronic Technician, Printing and allied trades, Automotive Technology, and numerous other fields not necessarily technology only; such as food and beverage; business, book-keeping and legal support services; off-shore communications and software help persons like in India. We will need teachers from India to supplement the local ones since there are not enough numbers and not enough variety locally. To correct a half a century of destructive nationalism we need at least one college exclusively for English instruction in every district each enrolling hundreds of students. Apparently the Mahinda Rajapakse government is committed to the English for all idea. We have to so strike hard while the iron is hot.

(3) Any programme aimed at Indo-Sri Lankan cooperation in education will have to give special attention to the workers in the plantation sector, often referred to as Tamils of Indian origin, and also as up-country Tamils. Muttiah has coined a new term "Indo-Lankans."[8] Rendered stateless by the Citizenship Acts of 1948, after years of controversy regarding their status, their destiny was finally determined on the basis of the Indo-Ceylon agreements of 1966 and 1972 by the then governments of India and Ceylon, without their participation or consent of these people or their representatives. Fifty per cent of these workers were repatriated to India and the balance was assured of Sri Lankan citizenship, a painfully slow process that has now been concluded. Today Sri Lanka=s plantation Tamils constitute around five per cent of the country=s population, numbering just under a million in a total population of twenty million

Among developing countries as indicated above, Sri Lanka has an impressive record in literacy achievements. But the educational indicators in the plantations are significantly lower than the national benchmarks on literacy, school participation and school retention. The gender gaps are also considerably wider in the plantations in comparison to the rest of the country. The proportion of children without schooling is twenty two (compared to seven per cent nationally), fifteen per cent male and forty per cent female. Female school retention rates are also significantly low. About sixty per cent of boys and girls enter grade one, but only six per cent of girls continue until grade ten compared to twenty one per cent of boys.[9]

(4) Sri Lankan students like their counterparts in India have the aptitude and aspirations for a successful career in the several disciplines available in the field of engineering. Affiliated Institutions to several Indian Institutes of Technology, which in turn were established with international cooperation, or similar institutes set up with Indian aid would be a major contribution to Sri Lanka, and

a healthy example of South Asian cooperation. In the private sector we already have a branch of the Apollo hospital in Colombo with highly qualified Indian doctors working together with Sri Lankan doctors. Though expensive, this is yet cheaper than for patients to go all the way to Chennai for treatment. This enterprise fulfils a vital need and illustrates the space available for cooperation.

Obviously there are likely to be many other areas where cooperation will be possible. The above four suggestions are highlighted as matter of urgent concern that should be addressed in the next decade. The first and fundamental step to achieve comprehensive human security leading to a higher quality of life for all is education. Exchange of teachers and students, and the experience of living and learning together is a vial element in building pluralist and multi-cultural societies respecting identity and promoting unity in diversity.

References

1 The writer had his education at Jaffna College and the University of Ceylon. The views expressed in this paper are written in the context of his experiences as student and later lecturer in the Undergraduate Department of Jaffna College, the Universities of Colombo and Jaffna and seventeen years of teaching experience in Japan where he had a valuable exposure to the system of education prevalent in that country.

2 In Lanka secondary schools are called Colleges. This is a wrong usage of the word but for historical reasons is still used. Jaffna College aspired to provide College level courses and had limited successes in this effort, but today has once again been reduced to the status of a mere secondary school.

3 J.V.Chelliah, *A Century of English Education, the Story of the Batticotta Seminary and Jaffna college,* Jaffna college: Vaddukoddai, Reprinted 1984, (First Published in 1922).

4 Silan Kadirgamar, "The Indian Contribution to Education at Jaffna College", in Satha Wijeyanayagam (ed), *Reflections 2005,* Ontario: Jubilee Publication of the Jaffna College Alumni Association, 2005, pp. 66-68.

5 Sudarshan Seneviratne, "We have to think beyond political boundaries", in interview given to T.S.Subramaniam, *Frontline,* vol.22, no.8, 12 –25 March 2005.

6 Joint statement issued by India and Sri Lanka on Friday 30 December 2005 at end of president Mahinda Rajapakse's state visit.

7 Kumar David in response to the writer's request for some suggestions for this paper. He is Chair Professor of Electrical Engineering, South China University of Technology Guanzhou, China andHonorary Fellow, ISE Department Hong Kong Polytechnic University, Hung Hom, Kowloon, Hong Kong.

8 S.Muttiah, *The Indo-Lankans: Their 200-Year Saga*, Colombo: Indian Heritage Foundation, 2003

9 Amali Philips in response to request for data based on her research provides these facts based on the following references: Swarna Jayaweera, "Gender, Education and Development in Sri Lanka", in Christine Heward and Sheila Bunwaree (ed), *Gender, Education and Development: Beyond Access to Empowerment*, London and New York: Zed Press, 1999, pp. 173-188; Angela Little, *Labouring to Learn: Towards a Political Economy of Plantations, People and Education in Sri Lanka*, New York: St. Martins Press, 1999; Daniel Atkin, "Gender and the Tea Woman, *Voice of Women*", Colombo, 1995, pp. 7-9.

18

Sustaining Tourism Through Cultural Cooperation

G.S. Rao & Shailesh Sikha

Introduction

Tourism, an industry with significant contribution to the economies, has evolved out of the need of the people to travel and the need of people to associate with the purpose of travel. The travel of people and the resultant effects have provided linkages between cultures. Considering the case of religions, there are cultural linkages associated with travel. Be it the case of the flow of Buddhist Philosophy to Sri Lanka or the relative reference of Lanka as being an important part of the epic Ramayana, travel from centuries, has had significant influence on cultures of both the countries. The synonymous natures of cultures are a case of sustainable practices on the cultural front wherein importance is on cooperation. Can there be an influence of tourism cultures of similar nature based on the best practices evident across tourism sectors in India and Sri Lanka. The paper seeks to explore, the cases of best practices in tourism; the influence of each of the countries on other in adaptation of the practices and proposes a cultural cooperation model for tourism education. The relevant model proposed is conceived as a conceptual 'Indo-Sri Lanka School of Cooperative Tourism Practices.'

Travel and tourism is recognised as one the world's highest priority industries, with the travel and tourism economy world over contributing for 10.6% of the global GDP in 2005. Over the next ten years, the economic activity is expected to register a growth of 4.6% per annum in real terms.[1] Sustainability of economic development, through tourism, depends on a variety of capital(s) that have *'capacity to produce flows of economically desirable outputs'*. In this context, five kinds of capital[2] need to be maintained – *'financial, natural, produced, human, and social'*. In terms of contribution of tourism, in numbers, the essential economic activities towards sustainability of capital include production, consumption and distribution. These must be supplemented by 'resource maintenance'.

Capital for Sustainable Development

In the above background, it would be in order to examine different types of capital, their origin and growth, an investment for productive output, in terms of return on investment, constitutes the *Financial Capita;* a financial stock is expected to lead to an investment in activities resulting in better outputs. World Travel and Tourism Council forecasts travel and tourism to be *'...a catalyst for construction and manufacturing.'* In terms of capital investment, World Travel and Tourism Council estimate that travel and tourism would have contributed 9.4% of the total investment in 2005. Total capital investment in travel and tourism is estimated to be ten per cent of the total investments in 2015. With increase in awareness on balance of relationship between human economies and nature, total natural environments are being considered as *Natural Capital. 'The stocks of clean water and air, as well as forests, fisheries, and the ever evolving systems that support them ...etc constitute natural capital.'* Apart from the natural capital, the other type of physical capital, 'the produced capital' represents *'physical assets that are generated by applying human productive activities to natural capital, and that are used to provide a flow of goods or services...'*

To ensure the desired flow of services, one needs to apply *'human productive activities / capabilities'*; these can be related to knowledge, education, training, skills, behavioural habits, levels of energy, physical and mental health. While some of the characteristics are inherited, others may be created and enhanced through nurturance, education and experience.

Physical capital outlined, natural and produced, in the context of tourism reflects the heritage. Heritage may be natural, built and cultural. While natural and produced heritage are significant, *'the traditional artistic heritage developed and maintained by a community of a country… consists of 'verbal expressions', such as folk tales, folk poetry and riddles; 'musical expressions', such as folk songs and instrumental music; 'expressions by action', such as folk dances, plays and artistic forms of rituals whether or not reduced to a material form; and 'tangible expressions' such as productions of folk art, in particular, drawings, paintings, carvings, sculptures, pottery, terracotta, mosaic, woodwork, metal-ware, jewellery, basket weaving, needlework, textiles, carpets, costumes; musical instruments; and architectural forms'* may be termed as 'expressions of folklore / traditional cultural expressions.'[3]

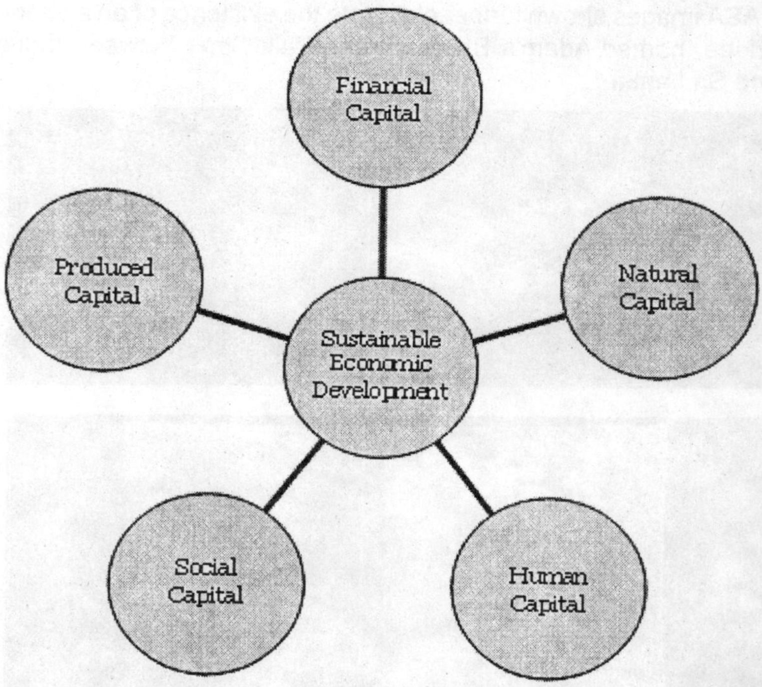

Source: Adapted from Neva R. Goodwin, "Five Kinds of Capital: Useful Concepts for Sustainable Development", http://ase.tufts.edu/gdae, 1 January 2006.

While it may be relevant to create capital stocks, social coordination of economic activity is necessary to encourage cooperation amongst groups of people to achieve the goal of efficient production. *'The stock of trust, mutual understanding, shared values, and socially held knowledge that facilitates the social coordination of economic activity'* may be referred to as *Social Capital.* The important components of social capital are 'norms and networks'.

Indo – Sri Lanka: Linkages

Social cooperation of economic activity is essential for achieving efficiency of social capital; the linkage between India and Sri Lanka reflects this aspect amply. Two hundred thousand years ago, Sri Lanka was considered to be an extension of the Indian subcontinent. Archaeological finds relate to such a linkage.[4] NASA images shown further elaborate the existence of an ancient bridge, named Adam's Bridge, in the Palk Strait between India and Sri Lanka.[5]

Source: NASA Digital Image Collection at www.lankalibrary.com

Adam's bridge made of chain of shoals (thirty kilometers long) with unique curvature and compositions is supposed to be man-made. The human habitation in Sri Lanka dates back to about 1,750,000 years, with the bridge's age being nearly equivalent. It is interesting to note that Ramayana epic is supposed to have taken place in '*Tretha Yuga*', about 1,700,000 years ago. A mention of the bridge between Rameshwaram (India) and Sri Lankan coast, under the supervision of Lord Rama, may perhaps be a linking factor between ancient history and Indian mythology.

Text 22 of *'Srimad Bhagavatham'* describes the event as
"nara-devatvam apannah
sura-karya-cikirsaya
samudra-nigrahadini
cakre viryani atah param"

English Translation to the Sanskrit verse:

"In the eighteenth incarnation (of Lord Krishna), the Lord appeared as King Rama. In order to perform some pleasing work for the demigods, He exhibited superhuman powers by controlling the Indian Ocean and then eliminated the atheist King Ravana, who was on the other side of the sea"

(Source: www.lankalibrary.com)

The shared historical and cultural legacy of South India and Sri Lanka can be specifically quoted.[6] Further, Buddhism is considered to be the *'social transformatory force'* which linked Indian subcontinent and Sri Lanka through religion, trade and politics. Further, technological, cultural and subsistence patterns at some of the sites from Mesolithic period, around 30,000 B.C., in Sri Lanka are similar to sites in Tirunelveli district, reflecting the possibility of movement of community to Sri Lanka from south India. Further there is flow of north Indian ideologies, Buddhism and Jainism, into south India and Sri Lanka. Archaeological evidence from Amaravathi (Andhra Pradesh – India) suggests such intrusions prior to Mauryan period in the form of items such as the Northern Black Polished Ware reflecting the southern trade route *(Dakshinapatha)*. There are inscriptions by *Settis*, the merchant bankers, in Amaravati. Unlike in India, Buddhist monasteries ran huge establishments and carried on trade providing for sustenance and thereby earning the patronage of the state.

Ethical Travel

Applicability of concepts of various types of capital relates to the concept of sustainability of a destination. However, scope exists for promoting sustainability from the perspective of the traveller. *Ethical Travel* is a concept wherein *'traveller experiences environmental beauty and cultural immersion while actually contributing to the ecological preservation and social development of the host country'.*[7]

In a study conducted for arriving at a list of ethical destinations in the developing world for the American tourists, 'ethicalness of destinations' was investigated in three categories: *eco-tourism practices, environmental standards, and socio-development indicators.* The concept of ecotourism was outlined on the basis of key principles of conservation of the natural environment, low visitor impact, and benefit to the local population. Bhutan is one of two best-known ecotourism destinations, the other being Peru, with 'low volume, high quality' visitors paying handsome amounts for visiting the pristine Himalayan kingdom. Ecotourism provided for the direct linkage between the local environment and the communities and hence, contributed for 'ethical travel.' However, the category of social development does not reflect such a standing for Bhutan.

The second category of ethicalness relates to evaluation of the environment with six factors – 'Carbon dioxide emissions, energy efficiency, percentage of protected land, percentage of mammals under threat, the environmental sustainability index, and the number of major international environmental treaties ratified.' Seven countries – Argentina, Bhutan, Brazil, Costa Rica, Peru, Sri Lanka, and Uruguay, have earned very high environmental ratings. The practices relate to apart from eco-tourism industry, 'how serious, a country is protecting its environment.' The countries with the highest percentage of threatened wildlife (above twenty per cent), include India, a case for concern.

The third category of ethicalness relates to social development reflecting the commitment of government towards the citizens. Sri Lanka figures prominently in terms of high social development with low levels of inequality, better health of citizens and better women status.

Sustainable Tourism Development Model

With best practices cited for 'Ethical Travel' available in the SAARC neighbours – Sri Lanka and Bhutan, and capital required for sustainable development identified, a model of sustainable tourism, involving development through capital outcomes and feedback through ethicalness of destinations, can be as follows:

Sustainable Tourism =	**Tourism Development**	**+**	**Feedback on Destinations**
	(Creation of Capital -Financial -Natural -Produced -Human -Social)		(Ethicalness of Destination)

For example, if museum presentation can be considered as one of the short falls in Sri Lanka, as in Indian museum,[8] a 'walk tour' through historical phases providing understanding of way of life is suggested as a part of the cultural tourism. While these factors can reduce the ethicalness of a destination, there is a case wherein apparent strength of India on the cultural front can be combined with the best practices reflected by Sri Lanka for a collaborative approach for development of ethical destinations. Further, *in tune with aspects reflecting the concepts of capital for tourism and ethicalness of such of the capital, a collaborative educational venture can be helpful for arriving at the factors necessary for development and sustenance*.

Establishment of a 'Centre of Excellence' in Tourism Practices

Tourism is identified as a key sector in world economy. We can achieve sustainable economic development through creation of five types of capital – financial, natural, produced, human and social. With social capital necessary for economic efficiency, norms and networks assume significance. Such of linkages have existed earlier between India and Sri Lanka. Geographically, historically and culturally, a legacy is shared between our two countries. A route for flow of ideologies, trade and culture in relation of history to mythology is already established. Further, the importance of Sri Lanka as a case of best practice, for promotion of 'Ethical Travel' and the related categories of strength are significant parameters for cooperation between India and Sri Lanka for promotion of ideology of 'ethical travel destination'. A sustainable tourism development model is proposed and a need for collaborative partnership for establishing a 'centre of excellence' is felt.

References

1 See World Travel and Tourism Council, "India: Travel and Tourism – The 2005 Travel & Tourism Economic Research", http://www.wttc.org, 1 January 2006.

2. Neva R. goodwin, " Five Kinds of Capital: Useful Concepts for Sustaintable Development", http:// ase.tuffs.edu./gdae, 1 January 2006

3 P.V. Vatsala G. Kutty, "National Experiences with the Protection of Expressions of Folklore / Traditional Cultural Expressions: India, Indonesia and the Philippines", http://www.wipo.int/tk/en/studies/cultural/expressions/study/kutty.pdf, 26 December 2005.

4 S.U. Deranyagila, "Prehistoric basis for the rise of civilization in Sri Lanka and southern India", http://www.lankalibrary.com, 15 January 2006.

5 Lankalibrary, "NASA Images Find 1,750,000 Year Old Man-Made Bridge between India and Sri Lanka", www.lankalibrary.com, 15 January 2006.

6 Sudharshan Seneviratne, "Conserving a shared legacy", http://www.flonnet.com/fl2012/stories/20030620002009200, 15 January 2006.

7 Jeff Greenwald and Kiran Auerbach, "Ethical Travel – What it Means, and Where to Go: The World's Best Ethical Travel Destinations", http://ethicaltraveler.com/destinations.php, 27 December 2005.

8 See Seniviratne, n.6.

Appendix 1

Delimitation of the Gulf of Mannar and Palk Strait, 25th October 1921

Copy of the letter from C. W. E. Cotton, Esq., CYE, ICS, dated the 25th October 1921.

I have the honour to submit herewith a copy of the report of the delegates of the Government of Madras and Ceylon on the delimitation of Palk Strait, and the Gulf of Mannar, which was signed this morning. The delegation met at Council Chamber, Ceylon, at 2.30 p.m. yesterday, and, after a little preliminary fencing, the Hon'ble Mr. Horsburgh on behalf of the Ceylon delegation proposed for our consideration that the delimitation should follow the median line, subject to an incursion beyond that line so as to include the islet of Kachchativu and three miles to the westward, Mr. Horsburgh maintained that this islet belongs to Ceylon and quoted from correspondence with the Government of India in which possession was definitely claimed, and, it was to be inferred, acquiesced in. We were entirely unprepared for this and had received no instructions either to consent or admit such a claim. For all we know, the Madras Government or the Government of India is in possession of documentary evidence, which conclusively rebuts Mr Horsburgh's contentions. Mr. Leach informed the meeting that the Rajah of Ramand asserts that Kachchativu is within his Zamindari, that it forms part of the original area on which Poishoush was calculated, that it had been leased to the father of the present lessee by a former Setupati and that he is receiving rent there from, but Mr. Horsburgh retorted that if the territorial claim of the Ceylon Government to this islet was disputed by us, the conference must dissolve. It may be recalled that at the preliminary meeting held at Fort St. George the line proposed to be adopted by us ran only about a mile to the eastward of Kachchativu, which indicated that its neighbourhood was not considered of any importance from a fisheries point of view and having again obtained assurance from Mr. Hornell on this point, we unanimously decided that the delimitation of the new jurisdictions for fishing purposes could be decided independently of the question of territoriality. The delimitation line was accordingly fixed, with our concurrence 3 miles west of Kachchativu and the Ceylon representatives thereupon agreed to a more orderly alignment south of the island than they had originally proposed, so that important chank beds in that area should fall entirely within the Madras sphere of influence. The line where it crosses Adam's Bridge was fixed exactly half way between Dhanushkodi and Talaimannar, an arrangement agreeable to both parties in view of the contingency that the cost of a bridge along this natural causeway is likely to be appointed according to such division. The remainder of the line was accepted without discussion and a draft report was then prepared and agreed to. To this report, it will be seen that we have added a rider, so as not to prejudice any territorial claim which the Government of Madras or the Government of India may wish to prefer in respect of this islet of Kachchativu, but I am to explain that we consider that even if such a claim should be pressed and prevail, there is no necessity, so far as the valuable pearl and chank fisheries are concerned for any consequential modification being demanded of the delimitation line which the Conference has unanimously approved. We are inclined to regard the Ceylon claim to this islet as sentimental rather than practical, and consider that the advantage gained elsewhere more that compensate the Government of Madras for the loss of any fishing rights in its immediate neighbourhood. The other member of the delegation have seen and concur in this report.

After some discussion, it was unanimously agreed that the line of delimitation of Palk's Strait and the Gulf of Mannar between the Government of India and the Government of Ceylon should run as follows:

Starting from a point in Palk's Strait.

A.	Long	80° 3' E.
	Lat.	10° 05' N.
	To a point B.	
B.	Long	79° 35' E.
	Lat.	9° 57' N.
	To a point C.	
C.	Long	79° 21' E.

	Lat.	9° 38' N.
	To a point D.	
D.	Long	79° 32' E.
	Lat.	9° 13' N.
	To a point E.	
E.	Long	79° 32' E.
	Lat.	9° 6' N.

On Adam's Bridge, and hence in the Gulf of Mannar by a line due S.W. true from
Long. 79° 32' E.
Lat 9° 6' N.
To the parallel of Lat. S.N.

C. W. E. Cotton	:	Representing the Government of Madras
G. H. Finnis	:	
James Hornell	:	
A. G. Leach	:	
B. Horsburgh	:	Representing the Government of Ceylon.
B. Constantine	:	
W. C. S. Inoles	:	
Dr. J. Pear son	:	

The above is signed by us, representative of the Government of Madras, without prejudice to any territorial claim which may be made by the Government of India to the island of Kachchativu.

C. W. E. Cotton
G. H. Finnis
James Hornell
A. G. Leach

Colombo, 25th October 1921.

Appendix 2

Agreement between Sri Lanka and India on the Boundary in Historic Waters between the two Countries and Related Matters, 26 and 28 June 1974

The Government of the Republic of Sri Lanka and the Government of the Republic of India,

Desiring to determine the boundary line in the historic waters between Sri Lanka and India and to settle the related matters in a manner, which is fair and equitable to both sides,

Having examined the entire question from all angles and taken into account the historical and other evidence and legal aspects thereof,

Have agreed as follows:

Article 1

The boundary between Sri Lanka and India in the waters from Palk Strait to Adam's Bridge shall be arcs of Great Circles between the following positions, in the sequence given below, defined by latitude and longitude:

Position 1: 10° 05' North, 80° 03' East
Position 2: 09° 57' North, 79° 35' East
Position 3: 09° 40.15' North, 79° 22.60' East
Position 4: 09° 21.80' North, 79° 30.70' East
Position 5: 09° 13' North, 79° 32' East
Position 6: 09° 06' North, 79° 32' East

Article 2

The co-ordinates of the positions specified in Article 1 are geographical co-ordinates and the straight lines connecting them are indicated in the chart annexed hereto which has been signed by the surveyors authorized by the two Governments, respectively.

Article 3

The actual location of the aforementioned positions at sea and on the sea-bed shall be determined by a method to be mutually agreed upon by the surveyors authorized for the purpose by the two Governments, respectively.

Article 4

Each country shall have sovereignty and exclusive jurisdiction and control over the waters, the islands, the continental shelf and the subsoil thereof, falling on its own side of the aforesaid boundary.

Article 5

Subject to the foregoing, Indian fishermen and pilgrims will enjoy access to visit Kachchativu as hitherto, and will not be required by Sri Lanka to obtain travel documents or visas for these purposes.

Article 6

The vessels of Sri Lanka and India will enjoy in each other's waters such rights as they have traditionally enjoyed therein.

Article 7

If any single geological petroleum or natural gas structure or field, or any single geological structure or field of any other mineral deposit, including sand or gravel, extends across the boundary referred to in Article 1 and the part of such structure or field which is situated on one side of the boundary is exploited, in whole or in part, from the other side of the boundary, the two countries shall seek to reach agreement as to the manner in which the structure or field shall be most effectively exploited and the manner in which the proceeds deriving there from shall be apportioned.

Article 8

This Agreement shall be subject to ratification. It shall enter into force on the date of exchange of the instruments of ratification, which will take place as soon as possible.

For the Government of the Republic of India	For the Government of the Republic of Sri Lanka
Sd/-Indira Gandhi	Sd/- Sirimavo R. D. Bandaranaike

Appendix 3

Agreement between Sri Lanka and India on the Maritime Boundary between the two countries in the Gulf of Mannar and the Bay of Bengal and Related Matters, 23 March 1976

23 March 1976

The Government of the Republic of Sri Lanka and the Government of the Republic of India,

Recalling that the boundary in the Palk Strait has been settled by the Agreement between the Republic of Sri Lanka and the Republic of India on the Boundary in Historic Waters between the Two Countries and Related Matters, signed on 26/28 June 1974,

And desiring to extend that boundary by determining the maritime boundary between the two countries in the Gulf of Mannar and the Bay of Bengal,

Have agreed as follows:

Article 1

The maritime boundary between Sri Lanka and India in the Gulf of Mannar shall be arcs of great circles between the following positions, in the sequence given below, defined by latitude and longitude:

Position 1 m: 09° 06'.0 N
79° 32'.0 E
Position 2 m: 09° 00'.0 N
79° 31'.3 E
Position 3 m: 08° 53'.8 N
79° 29'.3 E
Position 4 m: 08° 40'.0 N
79° 18'.2 N

Position 5 m: 08° 37'.2 N
79° 13'.0 E
Position 6 m: 08° 31'.2 N
79° 04'.7 E
Position 7 m: 08° 22'.2 N
78° 55'.4 E
Position 8 m: 08° 12'.2 N
78° 53'.7 E
Position 9 m: 07° 35'.3 N
78° 45'.7 E
Position 10 m: 07° 21'.0 N
78° 38'.8 E
Position 11 m: 06° 30'.8 N
78° 12'.2 E
Position 12 m: 05° 53'.9 N
77° 50'.7 E
Position 13 m: 05° 00'.0 N
77° 10'.6 E

The extension of the boundary beyond position 13 m will be done subsequently.

Article 2

The maritime boundary between Sri Lanka and India in the Bay of Bengal shall be arcs of great circles between the following positions, in the sequence given below, defined by latitude and longitude:

Position 1 b:
10° 05'.0 N 80° 03'.0 E
Position 1 ba: 10° 05'.8 N 80° 05'.0 E
Position 1 bb: 10° 08'.4 N 80° 09'.5 E
Position 2 b:
10° 33' 0 N 80° 46'.0 E
Position 3 b:
10° 41'.7 N 81° 02'.5 E
Position 4 b:
11° 02'.7 N 81° 56'.0 E
Position 5 b:
11° 16'.0 N 82° 24'.4 E
Position 6 b:
11° 26'.6 N 83° 22'.0 E

Article 3

The coordinates of the positions specified in Articles I and II are geographical coordinates and the straight lines connecting them are indicated in the chart annexed hereto, which has been signed by the surveyors duly authorised by the two Governments respectively.

Article 4

The actual location at sea and on the sea-bed of the positions specified in Articles 1 and 2 shall be determined by a method to be mutually agreed upon by the surveyors authorised for the purpose by the two Governments, respectively.

Article 5

(1) Each Party shall have sovereignty over the historic waters and territorial sea, as well as over the islands, falling on its side of the aforesaid boundary.

(2) Each Party shall have sovereign rights and exclusive jurisdiction over the continental shelf and the exclusive economic zone as well as over their resources, whether living or non-living, falling on its side of the aforesaid boundary.

(3) Each Party shall respect rights of navigation through its territorial sea and exclusive economic zone in accordance with its laws and regulations and the rules of international law.

Article 6

If any single geological petroleum or natural gas structure or field, or any single geological structure or field of any mineral deposit, including sand or gravel, extends across the boundary referred to in Articles 1 and 2 and the part of such structure or field which is situated on one side of the boundary is exploited, in whole or in part, from the other side of the boundary, the two countries shall seek to reach agreement as to the manner in which the structure or field shall be most effectively exploited and the manner in which the proceeds deriving there from shall be apportioned.

Article 7

The Agreement shall be subject to ratification. It shall enter into force on the date of exchange of instruments of ratification, which shall take place as soon as possible.

New Delhi, 23rd March 1976.

Appendix 4

Supplementary Agreement between Sri Lanka and India on the Extension of the Maritime Boundary between the two Countries in the Gulf of Mannar from Position 13 m to the Trijunction Point between Sri Lanka, India and Maldives (Point T) 22 November 1976

The Government of the Republic of Sri Lanka and the Government of the Republic of India

Recalling the Agreement between Sri Lanka and India on the Maritime Boundary between the two countries in the Gulf of Mannar and the Bay of Bengal and related matters, which was signed in March 1976 (a copy of which is annexed hereto marked Annex I), and which, in Article I, provides that "the extension of the boundary beyond position 13 m will be done subsequently",

Recalling the Agreement between Sri Lanka, India and Maldives concerning the determination of the trijunction point between the three countries in the Gulf of Mannar, which was signed by the representatives of the three Governments in July 1976 (copy of which is annexed hereto marked Annex II),

And desiring to extend the maritime boundary between Sri Lanka and India in the Gulf of Mannar from position 13 m to the trijunction point (point T),

Have agreed as follows:

Article 1

The maritime boundary between Sri Lanka and India in the Gulf of Mannar beyond position 13 m, defined in the Maritime Boundary Agreement of March 1976 (Annex I), up to the trijunction point (point T) defined in the trilateral agreement of July 1976 (Annex II) shall be arcs of great circles between the following positions, defined by latitude and longitude:

Position 13 m: 05° 00'.0 N 77° 10'.6 E
Point T: 04° 47'.04 N 77° 01'.40 E

Article 2

The provisions of Article III to Article VII of the Maritime Boundary Agreement of March 1976 (Annex I) shall apply, mutatis mutandis, to this Agreement, as if this Agreement were supplementary to and an integral part of that Agreement.

Colombo, 22nd November 1976.

Appendix 5

Indo-Sri Lanka Agreement to Establish Peace and Normalcy in Sri Lanka, 1987

Indo-Sri Lanka Agreement to Establish Peace and Normalcy in Sri Lanka

The Prime Minister of the Republic of India, His Excellency Mr. Rajiv Gandhi and the President of the Democratic Republic of Sri Lanka, Mr. J. R. Jayawardene having met at Colombo on 29 July 1987,

Attaching utmost importance to nurturing, intensifying and strengthening the traditional friendship of India and Sri Lanka and acknowledging the imperative need of resolving the ethnic problem of Sri Lanka, and the consequent violence, and for the safety, well-being and prosperity of people belonging to all communities of Sri Lanka,

Having this day entered into the following agreement to fulfill this objective,

1.1 desiring to preserve the unity, sovereignty and territorial integrity of Sri Lanka;

1.2 acknowledging that Sri Lanka is a multi-ethnic and multi-lingual plural society consisting, inter-alia, of Sinhalese, Tamils, Muslims (Moors) and Burgers;

1.3 recognising that each ethnic group has a distinct cultural and linguistic identity which has to be carefully nurtured;

1.4 also recognising that the Northern and the Eastern provinces have been areas of historical habitation of Sri Lankan Tamil speaking peoples, who have at all times hitherto lived together in this territory with other ethnic groups;

1.5 conscious of the necessity of strengthening the forces contributing to the unity, sovereignty and territorial integrity of Sri Lanka, and preserving its character as a multi-ethnic, multi-lingual and multi- religious plural society, in which all citizens can live in equality, safety and harmony, and prosper and fulfil their aspirations;

2. Resolve that:

2.1 Since the Government of Sri Lanka proposes to permit adjoining Provinces to join to form one administrative unit and also by a Referendum to separate as may be permitted to the Northern and Eastern provinces as outlined below:

2.2 During the period, which shall be considered an interim period (i.e. from the date of the elections to the provincial council, as specified in para 2.8 to the date of the Referendum as specified in para 2.3), the Northern and Eastern provinces as now constituted, will form one administrative unit, having one elected Provincial Council. Such a unit will have one Governor, one Chief Minister and one Board of Ministers.

2.3 There will be a referendum on or before 31st December 1988 to enable the people of the Eastern Province to decide whether:

(A) The Eastern province should remain linked with the Northern province as one administrative unit, and continue to be governed together with the Northern Province as specified in para 2.2 or:

(B) The Eastern Province should constitute a separate administrative unit having its own distinct provincial council with a separate governor, chief minister and board of ministers. The president may, at his discretion, decide to postpone such a referendum.

2.4 All persons, who have been displaced due to ethnic violence or other reasons, will have the right to vote in such a Referendum. Necessary conditions to enable them to return to areas from where they were displaced will be created.

2.5 The Referendum, when held, will be monitored by a committee headed by the Chief Justice, a member appointed by the President, nominated by the Government of Sri Lanka, and a member appointed by the President, nominated by the representatives of the Tamil speaking people of the Eastern province.

2.6 A simple majority will be sufficient to determine the result of the Referendum.

2.7 Meetings and other forms of propaganda, permissible within the laws of the country, will be allowed before the Referendum.

2.8 Elections to Provincial Councils will be held within the next three months, in any event before 31st December 1987. Indian observers will be invited for elections to the Provincial Council of the North and East.

2.9 The emergency will be lifted in the Eastern and Northern provinces by 15 August 1987. A cessation of hostilities will come into effect all over the Island within 48 hours of signing of this Agreement. All arms presently held by militant groups will be surrendered in accordance with an agreed procedure to authorities to be designated by the Government of Sri Lanka. Consequent to the cessation of hostilities and the surrender of arms by militant groups, the army and other security personnel will be confined to barracks in camps as on 25 May 1987. The process of surrendering arms and the confining of security personnel moving back to barracks shall be completed within 72 hours of the cessation of hostilities coming into effect.

2.10 The Government of Sri Lanka will utilise for the purpose of law enforcement and maintenance of security in the Northern and Eastern Provinces the same organizations and mechanisms of Government as are used in the rest of the country.

2.11 The President of Sri Lanka will grant a general amnesty to political and other prisoners now held in custody under the Prevention of Terrorism Act and other emergency laws, and to combatants, as well as to those persons accused, charged and/or convicted under these laws. The Government of Sri Lanka will make special efforts to rehabilitate militant youth with a view to bringing them back into the mainstream of national life. India will cooperate in the process.

2.12 The Government of Sri Lanka will accept and abide by the above provisions and expect all others to do likewise.

2.13 If the framework for the resolutions is accepted, the Government of Sri Lanka will implement the relevant proposals forthwith.

2.14 The Government of India will underwrite and guarantee the resolutions, and cooperate in the implementation of these proposals.

2.15 These proposals are conditional to an acceptance of proposals negotiated from 4.5.1986 to 19.12.1986. Residual matters not finalised during the above negotiations shall be resolved between India and Sri Lanka within a period of six weeks of signing this agreement. These proposals are also conditional to the Government of India cooperating directly with the Government of Sri Lanka in their implementation.

2.16 These proposals are also conditional to the Government of India taking the following actions if any militant groups operating in Sri Lanka do not accept this framework of proposals for a settlement, namely:

(A) India will take all necessary steps to ensure that Indian territory is not used for activities prejudicial to the unity, integrity and security of Sri Lanka

(B) The Indian Navy/Coast Guard will cooperate with the Sri Lankan navy in preventing Tamil militant activities from affecting Sri Lanka.

(C) In the event that the Government of Sri Lanka requests the Government of India to afford military assistance to implement these proposals the Government of India will cooperate by giving to the Government of Sri Lanka such military assistance as and when requested.

(D) The Government of India will expedite repatriation from Sri Lanka of Indian citizens to India who are resident there concurrently with the repatriation of Sri Lankan refugees from Tamil Nadu.

(E) The Governments of Sri Lanka and India will cooperate in ensuring the physical security and safety of all communities inhabiting the Northern and Eastern Provinces.

2.17 The Government of Sri Lanka shall ensure free, full and fair participation of voters from all communities in the Northern and Eastern Provinces in electoral processes envisaged in this Agreement. The Government of India will extend full cooperation to the Government of Sri Lanka in this regard.

2.18 The official language of Sri Lanka shall be Sinhala. Tamil and English will also be official languages.

3. This agreement and the annexure thereto shall come into force upon signature.

In witness whereof, we have set our hands and seals hereunto. Done in Colombo, Sri Lanka, on this the twenty-ninth day of July of the year one thousand nine hundred and eighty seven, in duplicate, both texts being equally authentic.

Sd/-
Rajiv Gandhi
Prime Minister of the
Republic of India

Sd/-
Junius Richard Jayawardene
President of the Democratic
Socialist Republic of Sri Lanka

Annexure to the Agreement

1. His Excellency the President of Sri Lanka and the Prime Minister of India agree that the Referendum mentioned in paragraph 2 and its sub-paragraphs of the Agreement will be observed by a representative of the Election Commission of India to be invited by His Excellency the President of Sri Lanka.
2. Similarly, both heads of Government agree that the elections to the Provincial Council mentioned in paragraph 2.8 of the Agreement will be observed by a representative of the Government of India to be invited by His Excellency the President of Sri Lanka.
3. His Excellency the President of Sri Lanka agrees that the Home guards would be disbanded and all paramilitary personnel will be withdrawn from the Eastern and Northern Provinces with a view to creating conditions conducive to fair elections to the Council.
   The President, in his discretion, shall absorb such paramilitary forces, which came into being due to ethnic violence, into the regular security forces of Sri Lanka.
4. The President of Sri Lanka and the Prime Minister of India agree that the Tamil militants shall surrender their arms to authorities agreed upon to be designated by the President of Sri Lanka. The surrender shall take place in the presence of one senior representative each of the Sri Lankan Red Cross and the Indian Red Cross.
5. The President of Sri Lanka and the Prime Minister of India agree that a joint Indo-Sri Lankan observer group consisting of qualified representatives of the Government of India and the Government of Sri Lanka would monitor the cessation of hostilities from 31 July 1987.

6. The Prime Minister of India and the President of Sri Lanka also agree that in the terms of paragraph 2.14 and paragraph 2.16(c) of the Agreement, an Indian Peace Keeping contingent may be invited by the President of Sri Lanka to guarantee and enforce the cessation of hostilities, if so required.

Exchange of Letters Between the Prime Minister of India and the President of Sri Lanka

Prime Minister of India
New Delhi
29 July 1987
Excellency,

Conscious of the friendship between our two countries stretching over two millennia and more, and recognizing the importance of nurturing this traditional friendship, it is imperative that both Sri Lanka and India reaffirm the decision not to allow our respective territories to be used for activities prejudicial to each other's unity, territorial integrity and security.

In this spirit, you had, in the course of our discussions agreed to meet some of India's concerns as follows:

i. Your Excellency and myself will reach an early understanding about the relevance and employment of foreign military and intelligence personnel with a view to ensuring that such presences will not prejudice Indo-Sri Lankan relations.
ii. Trincomalee or any other ports in Sri Lanka will not be made available for military use by any country in a manner prejudicial to India's interests.
iii. The work of restoring and operating the Trincomalee oil tank farm will be undertaken as a joint venture between India and Sri Lanka.
iv. Sri Lanka's agreements with foreign broadcasting organizations will be reviewed to ensure that any facilities set up by them in Sri Lanka are used solely as public broadcasting facilities and not for any military or intelligence purposes.

In the same spirit India will:

i. Deport all Sri Lankan citizens who are found to be engaging in terrorist activities or advocating separatism or secessionism.

ii. Provide training facilities and military supplies for Sri Lankan forces.

India and Sri Lanka have agreed to set up a joint consultative mechanism to continuously review matters of common concern in the light of the objectives stated in para 1 and specifically to monitor the implementation of other matters contained in this letter.

Kindly confirm, Excellency, that the above correctly sets out the agreement reached between us. Please accept, Excellency, the assurances of my highest consideration.

Yours sincerely,

Sd/-
(Rajiv Gandhi)

His Excellency
Mr. J. R. Jayawardene
President of Sri Lanka
29 July 1987
Excellency,

Please refer to your letter dated 29th of July 1987, which reads as follows:

1. Conscious of the friendship between our two countries stretching over two millennia and more, and recognizing the importance of nurturing this traditional friendship, it is imperative that both Sri Lanka and India reaffirm the decision not to allow our respective territories to be used for activities prejudicial to each other's unity, territorial integrity and security.
2. In this spirit, you had, in the course of our discussions agreed to meet some of India's concerns as follows:
   (i) Your Excellency and myself will reach an early understanding about the relevance and employment of foreign military and intelligence personnel with a view to ensuring that such presences will not prejudice Indo-Sri Lankan relations.
   (ii) Trincomalee or any other ports in Sri Lanka will not be made available for military use by any country in a manner prejudicial to India's interests.
   (iii) The work of restoring and operating the Trincomalee oil tank farm will be undertaken as a joint venture between India and Sri Lanka.

(iv) Sri Lanka's agreements with foreign broadcasting organizations will be reviewed to ensure that any facilities set up by them in Sri Lanka are used solely as public broadcasting facilities and not for any military or intelligence purposes.

3. In the same spirit India will:

(i) Deport all Sri Lankan citizens who are found to be engaging in terrorist activities or advocating separatism or secessionism

(ii) Provide training facilities and military supplies for Sri Lankan forces.

4. India and Sri Lanka have agreed to set up a joint consultative mechanism to continuously review matters of common concern in the light of the objectives stated in para 1 and specifically to monitor the implementation of other matters contained in this letter.

5. Kindly confirm, Excellency, that the above correctly sets out the agreement reached between us. Please accept, Excellency, the assurances of my highest consideration.

Yours sincerely,

Sd/-
(Rajiv Gandhi)

His Excellency
Mr. J. R. Jayawardene
President of the democratic Republic of Sri Lanka, Colombo
This is to confirm that the above correctly sets out the understanding reached between us. Please accept, Excellency, the assurances of my highest consideration.
(J. R. Jayawardene)
President

Appendix 6

Free Trade Agreement between the Republic of India and the Democratic Socialist Republic of Sri Lanka

Preamble

The Government of the Republic of India and the Government of the Democratic Socialist Republic of Sri Lanka, (hereinafter referred to as the "Contracting Parties").

CONSIDERING that the expansion of their domestic markets, through economic integration, is a vital prerequisite for accelerating their processes of economic development.

BEARING in mind the desire to promote mutually beneficial bilateral trade.

CONVINCED of the need to establish and promote free trade arrangements for strengthening intra-regional economic cooperation and the development of national economies.

FURTHER RECOGNIZING that progressive reductions and elimination of obstacles to bilateral trade through a bilateral free trade agreement (hereinafter referred to as "The Agreement") would contribute to the expansion of world trade.

HAVE agreed as follows:

Article I

Objectives

1. The Contracting Parties shall establish a Free Trade Area in accordance with the provisions of this Agreement and in conformity with relevant provisions of the General Agreement on Tariff and Trade, 1994.
2. The objectives of this Agreement are:
   (i) To promote through the expansion of trade the harmonious development of the economic relations between India and Sri Lanka.
   (ii) To provide fair conditions of competition for trade between India and Sri Lanka

(iii) In the implementation of this Agreement the Contracting Parties shall pay due regard to the principle of reciprocity

(iv) To contribute in this way, by the removal of barriers to trade, to the harmonious development and expansion of world trade

Article II

Definitions

For the purpose of this agreement:

1. "Tariffs" means basic customs duties included in the national schedules of the Contracting Parties.

2. "Products" means all products including manufactures and commodities in their raw, semi-processed and processed forms.

3. "Preferential Treatment" means any concession or privilege granted under this Agreement by a Contracting Party through the elimination of tariffs on the movement of goods.

4. "The Committee" means the Joint Committee referred to in Article XI.

5. "Serious Injury" means significant damage to domestic producers, of like or similar products resulting from a substantial increase of preferential imports in situations which cause substantial losses in terms of earnings, production or employment unsustainable in the short term. The examination of the impact on the domestic industry concerned shall also include an evaluation of other relevant economic factors and indices having a bearing on the state of the domestic industry of that product.

6. "Threat of serious injury" means a situation in which a substantial increase of preferential imports is of a nature so as to cause "Serious injury" to domestic producers, and that such injury, although not yet existing is clearly imminent. A determination of threat of serious injury shall be based on facts and not on more allegation, conjecture, or remote or hypothetical possibility.

7. "Critical circumstances" means the emergence of an exceptional situation where massive preferential imports are causing or threatening to cause "serious injury" difficult to repair and which calls for immediate action.

Article III
Elimination of Tariffs

The Contracting Parties hereby agree to establish a Free Trade Area for the purpose of free movement of goods between their countries through elimination of tariffs on the movement of goods in accordance with the provisions of Annexures A and B which shall form an integral part of this Agreement.

Article IV
General Exceptions

Nothing in this Agreement shall prevent any Contracting Party from taking action and adopting measures, which it considers necessary for the protection of its national security, the protection of public morals, the protection of human, animal or plant life and health, and the protection of articles of artistic, historic and archaeological value, as is provided for in Articles XX and XXI of the General Agreement on Tariff and Trade, 1994.

Article V
National Treatment

The Contracting Parties affirm their commitment to the principles enshrined in Article III of GATT 1994.

Article VI
State Trading Enterprises

1. Nothing in this Agreement shall be construed to prevent a Contracting Party from maintaining or establishing a state trading enterprise as understood in Article XVII of General Agreement on Tariff and Trade, 1994.
2. Each Contracting Party shall ensure that any state enterprise that it maintains or establishes acts in a manner that is not inconsistent with the obligations of the Contracting Parties, under this Agreement and accords non-discriminatory treatment in the import from and export to the other Contracting Party.

Article VII
Rules of Origin

1. Products covered by the provisions of this Agreement shall be eligible for preferential treatment provided they satisfy

the Rules of Origin as set out in Annexure C to this Agreement which shall form an integral part of this Agreement.

2. For the development of specific sectors of the industry of either Contracting Party, lower value addition norms for the products manufactured or produced by those sectors may be considered through mutual negotiations.

Article VIII
Safeguard Measures

1. If any product, which is the subject of preferential treatment under this Agreement, is imported into the territory of a Contracting Party in such a manner or in such quantities as to cause or threaten to cause, serious injury in the importing Contracting Party, the importing Contracting Party may, with prior consultations except in critical circumstances, suspend provisionally without discrimination the preferential treatment accorded under the Agreement.

2. When action has been taken by either Contracting Party in terms of paragraph I of this Article, it shall simultaneously notify the other Contracting Party and the Joint Committee established in terms of Article XI. The Committee shall enter into consultations with the concerned Contracting Party and endeavor to reach mutually acceptable agreement to remedy the situation. Should the consultations in the Committee fail to resolve the issue within sixty days, the party affected by such action shall have the right to withdraw the preferential treatment.

Article IX
Domestic Legislation

The Contracting Parties shall be free to apply their domestic legislation to restrict imports, in cases where prices are influenced by unfair trade practices like subsidies or dumping. Subsidies and dumping shall be understood to have the same meaning as in the General Agreement on Tariff and Trade, 1994 and the relevant WTO Agreements.

Article X
Balance of Payment Measures

1. Notwithstanding the provisions of this Agreement, any Contracting Party facing balance of payments difficulties may

suspend provisionally the preferential treatment as to the quantity and value of merchandise permitted to be imported under the Agreement. When such action has taken place, the Contracting Party, which initiates such action shall simultaneously notify the other Contracting Party.

2. Any Contracting Party, which takes action according to paragraph 1 of this Article, shall afford, upon request from the other Contracting Party, adequate opportunities for consultations with a view to preserving the stability of the preferential treatment provided under this Agreement.

Article XI
Joint Committee

1. A Joint Committee shall be established at Ministerial level. The Committee shall meet at least once a year to review the progress made in the implementation of this Agreement and to ensure that benefits of trade expansion emanating from this Agreement accrue to both Contracting Parties equitably. The Committee may set up Sub-Committees and/or Working Groups as considered necessary.
2. In order to facilitate cooperation in customs matters, the Contracting Parties agree to establish a Working Group on customs related issues including harmonization of tariff headings. The Working Group shall meet as often as required and shall report to the Committee on its deliberations.
3. The Committee shall accord adequate opportunities for consultation on representations made by any Contracting Party with respect to any matter affecting the implementation of the Agreement. The Committee shall adopt appropriate measures for settling any matter arising from such representations within 6 months of the representation being made. Each Contracting Party shall implement such measures immediately.
4. The Committee shall nominate one apex chamber of trade and industry in each country as the nodal chamber to represent the views of the trade and industry on matters relating to this Agreement.

Article XII
Consultations

1. Each Contracting Party shall accord sympathetic consideration to and shall afford adequate opportunity for,

consultations regarding such representations as may be made by the other Contracting Party with respect to any matter affecting the operation of this Agreement.

2. The Committee may meet at the request of a Contracting Party to consider any matter for which it has not been possible to find a satisfactory solution through consultations under paragraph 1 above.

Article XIII
Settlement of Disputes

1. Any dispute that may arise between commercial entities of the Contracting Parties shall be referred for amicable settlement to the nodal apex chambers. Such references shall, as far as possible, be settled through mutual consultations by the Chambers. In the event of an amicable solution not being found, the matter shall be referred to an Arbitral Tribunal for a binding decision. The Tribunal shall be constituted the Joint Committee in consultation with the relevant Arbitration Bodies in the two countries.
2. Any dispute between the Contracting Parties regarding the interpretation and application of the provisions of this Agreement or any instrument adopted within its framework shall be amicably settled through negotiations failing which a notification may be made to the Committee by any one of the Contracting Parties.

Article XIV

Duration and Termination of Agreement

This Agreement shall remain in force until either Contracting Party terminates this Agreement by giving six months written notice to the other of its intention to terminate the Agreement.

Article XV
Amendments

The Agreement may be modified or amended through mutual agreement of the Contracting Parties. Proposals for such modifications or amendments shall be submitted to the Joint Committee and upon acceptance by the Joint Committee, shall be approved in accordance with the applicable legal procedures of each Contracting Party. Such modifications or amendments shall become effective when confirmed through an exchange of diplomatic notes and shall constitute an integral part of the Agreement. Provided however that in emergency situations, proposals for modifications may be considered by the Contracting Parties and if agreed, given effect to through an exchange of diplomatic notes.

Article XVI
Annexures to be finalized.

Annexure D(i) and D(ii) (Negative Lists of India and Sri Lanka respectively), E (Items on which India has undertaken to give 100% tariff concession on coming into force of the Agreement) and F (Items on which Sri Lanka has undertaken to give 100% tariff concession on the coming into force of the Agreement) shall be finalised within a period of 60 days of the signing of this Agreement. All the Annexures shall form an integral part of the Agreement.

Article XVII
Entry into Force

The Agreement shall enter into force on the thirtieth day after the Contracting Parties hereto have notified each other that their respective constitutional requirements and procedures have been completed.

In witness where of the undersigned, duly authorised thereto by their respective Governments have signed this Agreement.

Done in duplicate at New Delhi this 28th day of December 1998 in two originals in the English language.

Sd/-
For the Government of the Republic of India

Sd/-
For the Government of the Democratic Socialist Republic of Sri Lanka

Annexure - 'A'
Concession offered by India

The Government of India shall grant duty free access to all exports from Sri Lanka in respect of items freely importable into India, except on items listed in Annex D of this Agreement, in accordance with the phase out schedule detailed below:

1. Upon entry into force of the Agreement :-
   a. Zero duty access for the items in Annexure 'E'
   b. 50% margin of preference on the remaining items except on items listed in Annexure D. Concessions on items in Chapters 51 to 56, 58 to 60 and 63 shall be restricted to 25%.
2. The margin of preference on the items mentioned in (b) above shall be increased to 100% in two stages within three years of the coming into force of the Agreement, except for the textiles items referred to in 1(b) above.

Annexure - 'B'

Concession offered by Sri Lanka Government of Sri Lanka shall provide tariff concessions on exports from India to Sri Lanka in respect of items freely importable into Sri Lanka, as detailed below:-

1. Zero duty for the items in Annex 'F' - I, upon entering into force of the Agreement.
2. 50% margin of preference for the items in Annex 'F' - II, upon coming into force of the Agreement. The margin of preference in respect of these items shall be deepened to 70%, 90% and 100%, respectively, at the end of the first, second and third year of the entry into force of the Agreement.
3. For the remaining items except those in Annex 'D', the tariffs shall be brought down by not less than 35% before the expiry of three years and 70% before the expiry of the sixth year and 100% before the expiry of eight years, from the date of entry into force of the Agreement.

CONCESSION OFFERED BY SRI LANKA

Annexure - 'C'

RULES OF ORIGIN

1. Short title/commencement

   These rules may be called the rules of Determination of Origin of Goods under the Free Trade Agreement between the Democratic Socialistic Republic of Sri Lanka and the Republic of India.

2. Application

   These rules shall apply to products consigned from the territory of either of the Contracting Parties.

3. Determination of Origin

No product shall be deemed to be the produce or manufacture of either country unless the conditions specified in these rules are complied with in relation to such products, to the satisfaction of the appropriate Authority.

4. Claim at the time of importation

The importer of the product shall, at the time of importation:

a. make a claim that the products are the produce or manufacture of the country from which they are imported and such products are eligible for preferential treatment under the Agreement, and

b. produce the evidence specified in these rules.

5. Originating products

Products covered by the Agreement imported into the territory of a Contracting Party from another Contracting Party which are consigned directly within the meaning of rule 9 hereof, shall be eligible for preferential treatment if they conform to the origin requirement under any one of the following conditions:

a. Products wholly produced or obtained in the territory of the exporting Contracting Party as defined in rule 6; or

b. Products not wholly produced or obtained in the territory of the exporting Contracting Party, provided that the said products are eligible under rule 7 or rule 8.

6. Wholly produced or obtained

Within the meaning of rule 5(a), the following shall be considered as wholly produced or obtained in the territory of the exporting Contracting Party:

a. raw or mineral products extracted from its soil, its water or its seabed;

b. vegetable products harvested there;

c. animals born and raised there;

d. products obtained from animals referred to in clause (c) above;

e. products obtained by hunting or fishing conducted there;

f. products of sea fishing and other marine products from the high seas by its vessels3,4;

g. products processed and/or made on board its factory ships exclusively from products referred to in clause (f) above 4, 5;

h. used articles collected there, fit only for the recovery of raw materials;

i. waste and scrap resulting from manufacturing operations conducted there;

j. products extracted from the seabed or below seabed which is situated outside its territorial waters, provided that it has exclusive exploitation rights;

k. goods produced there exclusively from the products referred to in clauses (a) to (j) above.

7. Not wholly produced or obtained

a. Within the meaning of rule 5(b), products worked on or processed as a result of which the total value of the materials, parts or produce originating from countries other than the Contracting Parties or of undetermined origin used does not exceed 65% of the f.o.b. value of the products produced or obtained and the final process of manufacture is performed within the territory of the exporting Contracting Party shall be eligible for preferential treatment, subject to the provisions of clauses (b), (c), (d) and (e) of rule 7 and rule 8.

b. Non-originating materials shall be considered to be sufficiently worked or processed when the product obtained is classified in a heading, at the four digit level, of the Harmonised Commodity Description and Coding System different from those in which all the non-originating materials used in its manufacture are classified.

c. In order to determine whether a product originates in the territory of a Contracting Party, it shall not be necessary to establish whether the power and fuel, plant and equipment, and machines and tools used to obtain such products originate in third countries or not.

d. The following shall in any event be considered as insufficient working or processing to confer the status of originating products, whether or not there is a change of heading:

1. Operations to ensure the preservation of products in good condition during transport and storage (ventilation, spreading out, drying, chilling, placing in salt, sulphur dioxide or other aqueous solutions, removal of damaged parts, and like operations).

2. Simple operations consisting of removal of dust, sifting or screening, sorting, classifying, matching (including the making-up of sets of articles), washing, painting, cutting up;

3. (i) changes of packing and breaking up and assembly of consignments,
(ii) simple slicing, cutting and repacking or placing in bottles, flasks, bags, boxes, fixing on cards or boards, etc., and all other simple packing operations.
4. the affixing of marks, labels or other like distinguishing signs on products or their packaging;
5. simple mixing of products, whether or not of different kinds, where one or more components of the mixture do not meet the conditions laid down in these Rules to enable them to be considered as originating products;
6. simple assembly of parts of products to constitute a complete product;
7. a combination of two or more operations specified in (a) to (f);
8. slaughter of animals.
e. The value of the non-originating materials, parts or produce shall be:
i. The c.i.f. value at the time of importation of the materials, parts or produce where this can be proven; or
ii. The earliest ascertainable price paid for the materials, parts or produce of undetermined origin in the territory of the Contracting Parties where the working or processing takes place.
8. Cumulative rules of origin
In respect of a product, which complies with the origin requirements provided in rule 5(b) and is exported by any Contracting Party and which has used material, parts or products originating in the territory of the other Contracting Party, the value addition in the territory of the exporting Contracting Party shall be not less than 25 per cent of the f.o.b. value of the product under export subject to the condition that the aggregate value addition in the territories of the Contracting Parties is not less than 35 per cent of the f.o.b. value of the product under export.
9. Direct consignment
The following shall be considered to be directly consigned from the exporting country to the importing country:
a. if the products are transported without passing through the territory of any country other than the countries of the Contracting Parties.

b. The products whose transport involves transit through one or more intermediate countries with or without transhipment or temporary storage in such countries; provided that

i. the transit entry is justified for geographical reason or by considerations related exclusively to transport requirements;

ii. the products have not entered into trade or consumption there; and

iii. the products have not undergone any operation there other than unloading and reloading or any operation required to keep them in good condition.

10. Treatment of packing

When determining the origin of products, packing should be considered as forming a whole with the product it contains. However, packing may be treated separately if the national legislation so requires.

11. Certificate of origin

Products eligible for a Certificate of origin in the form annexed shall support preferential treatment issued by an authority designated by the Government of the exporting country and notified to the other country in accordance with the certification procedures to be devised and approved by both the Contracting Parties.

12. Prohibitions

Either country may prohibit importation of products containing any inputs originating from States with which it does not have economic and commercial relations;

13. Co-operation between contracting parties

a. The Contracting Parties will do their best to co-operate in order to specify origin of inputs in the Certificate of origin.

b. The Contracting Parties will take measures necessary to address, to investigate and, where appropriate, to take legal and/or administrative action to prevent circumvention of this Agreement through false declaration concerning country of origin or falsification of original documents.

c. Both the Contracting Parties will co-operate fully, consistent with their domestic laws and procedures, in instances of circumvention or alleged circumvention of the Agreement to address problems arising from circumvention including facilitation of joint plant visits and contacts by representatives of both Contracting Parties upon request and on a case-by-case basis.

d. If either Party believes that the rules of origin are being circumvented, it may request consultation to address the matter or matters concerned with a view to seeking a mutually satisfactory solution. Each party will hold such consultations promptly.

15. Review

These rules may be reviewed as and when necessary upon request of either Contracting Party and may be open to such modifications as may be agreed upon.

Notes:

1. Includes mineral fuels, lubricants and related materials as well as mineral or metal ores
2. Includes agricultural and forestry products
3. "Vessels" shall refer to fishing vessels engaged in commercial fishing, registered in the country of the Contracting Party and operated by a citizen or citizens of the Contracting Party or partnership, corporation or association, duly registered in such country, at least 60 per cent of equity of which is owned by a citizen or citizens and/or Government of such Contracting Party or 75 per cent by citizens and/or Governments of the Contracting Parties. However, the products taken from vessels, engaged in commercial fishing under Bilateral Agreements which provide for chartering/leasing of such vessels and/or sharing of catch between Contracting Party will also be eligible or preferential treatment.
4. In respect of vessels or factory ships operated by Government agencies, the requirements of flying the flag of the Contracting Party does not apply.
5. For the purpose of this Agreement, the term "factory ship" means any vessel, as defined, used for processing and/or making on board products exclusively from those products referred to in clause (f) of Rule 6.
6. Cumulation as implied by Rule 8 means that only products which have acquired originating status in the territory of one Contracting Party may be taken into account when used as inputs for a finished product eligible for preferential treatment in the territory of the other Contracting Party.

CERTIFICATE OF ORIGIN

<table>
<tr><td colspan="3">1. Goods consigned from (Exporters' Business Name, Address, Country)</td><td colspan="3">Reference No.
INDO-SRI LANKA FREE TRADE AGREEMENT (ISFTA) (Combined declaration and certificate)
Issued in (Country) (See notes)</td></tr>
<tr><td colspan="3">2. Goods consigned to (Consignee's Name, Address, Country)</td><td colspan="3" rowspan="2">4. For Official use</td></tr>
<tr><td colspan="3">3. Means of transport and route (as far as known)</td></tr>
<tr><td>5. Tariff item number</td><td>6. Marks and numbers of packages</td><td>7. Number and kind of packages: description of goods</td><td>8. Origin criterion (see Notes)</td><td>9. Gross weight or other quantity</td><td>10. Number and date of invoice</td></tr>
<tr><td colspan="3">11. Declaration by the Exporter
The undersigned hereby declares that the above details and statements are correct; That all the goods were produced in(Country)and that they comply with the origin requirements specified for those goods in ISFTA for goods exported to (Importing Country)
Place and date, signature of the authorised signatory</td><td colspan="3">12. Certificate:
It is hereby certified, on the basis of control carried out that the declaration by the exporter is correct.
Place and date, signature and stamp of certifying authority.</td></tr>
</table>

(Contd.)

(Contd. Certificate of Origin)

I. To qualify for preference, products must:

* fall within a description of products eligible for concessions in the country of destination under this agreement.

* comply with ISFTA Rules of Origin. Each Articie in a consignment must qualify separately in its own right; and

* comply with the consignment conditions specified by the ISFTA Rules of Origin. In general products must be consigned directly within the meaning of Rule 9 hereof from the country of exportation to the country of destination.

II. Entries to be made in Box 8

Preference products must be wholly produced or obtained in the exporting Contracting Party in accordance with Rule 6 of the ISFTA Rule of Origin, or where not wholly produced or obtained in the exporting Contracting Party must be eligible under Rule 7 or Rule 8

Products wholly produced or obtained enter the letter 'A' in box 8.

Products not wholly produced or obtained; the entry in box 8 should be as follows:

8. Enter letter 'B' in box 8 for products, which meet the origin criterion according to Rule

7. Entry of letter would be followed by the sum of the value of materials, parts or produce originating from non-contracting parties or undetermined origin used, expressed as a percentage of the f.o.b. value of the products; (example B ( ) percent).

9. Enter letter 'C' in box 8 for products, which meet the origin criteria according to Rule 8. Entry of letter 'C' would be followed by the sum of the aggregate content originating in the territory of the exporting Contracting Party expressed as a percentage of the f.o.b. value of the exported product: (example 'C' ( ) per cent).

Bibliography

Articles:

Alling, Greg, "Economic Liberalization and Separatist Nationalism: The Cases of Sri Lanka and Tibet," *Journal of International Affairs*, vol.51, no.1, Summer 1997, pp.117-45.

Burger, Angela S. "Policing a Communal Society: The Case of Sri Lanka," *Asian Survey*, vol.27, no.7, July 1987, pp.822-33.

Canagaretna, Sujit M. "Nation Building in a Multiethnic Setting: The Sri Lankan Case," *Asian Affairs*, vol.14, no.1, Spring 1987, pp.1-19.

Crossette, Barbara, "Sri Lanka: In the Shadow of the Indian Elephant," *World Policy Journal*, vol.19, no.1, Spring 2002, pp.25-36.

Dash, Kishore C., "The Political Economy of Regional Cooperation in South Asia," *Pacific Affairs*, vol.69, no.2, 1999, pp.185-209.

De Mel, N., "Body Politics: (Re)cognizing the Female Suicide Bomber in Sri Lanka," *Indian Journal of Gender Studies,* vol.11, no.1, 2004, pp.76-91.

DeVotta, Neil "Control Democracy, Institutional Decay, and the Quest for Eelam: Explaining Ethnic Conflict in Sri Lanka," *Pacific Affairs*, vol.73, no.1, Spring 2000, pp.55-77.

———, "Sri Lanka's Structural Adjustment Program and Its Impact on Indo-Lanka Relations," *Asian Survey*, vol.38, no.5, May 1998, pp.457-73.

Embree, Ainslie, "Statehood in South Asia," Journal of International Affairs, vol.51, no.1, Summer 1997, pp.1-19.

Gokhale, Balkrishna Govind, "The Ravada Buddhism and Modernization," *Journal of Asian and African Studies*, v.34, no.1, February 1999, pp.33-45.

Gooneratne, John, "Maritime Neighbours," *Himal*, January 2004, pp.66-67.

Hennayake, Shantha K., "The Peace Accord and the Tamils in Sri Lanka," *Asian Survey,* vol.29, no.4, April 1989, p.401-15.

Isham, Jonathan and Kahkonen, Satu, "Institutional Determinants of the Impact of Community-Based Water Services: Evidence from Sri Lanka and India," *Economic Development and Cultural Change*, vol.50, no.3, April 2002, pp.667-91.

Jayasuriya, Sisira and Dushni Weerakoon, "India-Sri Lanka Trade and Investment Links" in P. Shome (ed), *India and Economic Cooperation in South Asia*, New Delhi: Indian Council for Research on International Economic Relations, New Delhi, 2001.

Jayawardane, Amal, "The Soviet Attitude Towards the Indo-Sri Lankan Problem," *Pacific Affairs*, vol.64, no.2, Summer 1991, pp.194-207.

Kearney, Robert N., "Language and the Rise of Tamil Separatism in Sri Lanka," *Asian Survey*, vol.18, no.5, May 1978, pp.521-34.

Kearney, Robert N. and Miller, D.B., "The Spiral of Suicide and Social Change in Sri Lanka," *Journal of Asian Studies,* vol.2, no.1, 1985, pp.81-101.

Kelegama, Saman, "Sri Lanka Exports to India: Impact of Free Trade Agreement," *Economic and Political Weekly*, vol.37, no.30, July 2003, pp.3153-54.

Knutsen, Hege M., "Globalisation and the Garment Industry in Sri Lanka," *Journal of Contemporary Asia,* vol.33, no.2, May 2003, pp.225-51.

Kodikara, Shelton U., "The Continuing Crisis in Sri Lanka: the JVP, the Indian Troops, and Tamil Politics," *Asian Survey*, vol.29, no.7, Jul 1989, pp.716-24.

Krishna, Sankaran, "India and Sri Lanka: A Fatal Convergence," *Studies in Conflict and Terrorism*, vol.15, no.4, October 1992, pp.267-81.

Langford, Christopher and Storey, Pamela, "Sex Differentials in Mortality Early in the Twentieth Century: Sri Lanka and India Compared," *Population and Development Review*, vol.19, no.2, June 1993, pp.263-82.

McGowan, William, "India's Quagmire in Sri Lanka," *The Nation*, vol.246, no.25, Jun 1988, pp.896-99.

Mahendran, Arjuna and Rajive Casie Chitty, "Hanuman's Bridge: Facilitating Trade and Investment between Śri Lanka and Southern India," *South Asian Survey*, vol.7, no.1, 2000, pp.25-35.

Matthews, Bruce, "Sri Lanka in 1988: Seeds of Accord," *Asian Survey*, vol.29, no.2, February 1989, pp.229-35.

Mujtaba, Syed Ali, "India: Fishing for Trouble," *Himal*, October 2003, pp.9-11.

Mukherjee, I.N. "Indo-Sri Lanka Trade and Investment Linkages with Special Reference to SAPTA and Free Trade," *South Asia Economic Journal*, March 2000.

Muni, S. D., "Kachchativu Settlement: Befriending Neighbouring Regimes," *Economic and Political Weekly*, vol.9, no.28, July 1974, pp.1119-122.

Nadarajah, Suthaharan and Sriskandarajah, Dhananjayan, "Liberation Struggle or Terrorism? The Politics of Naming the LTTE," *Third World Quarterly*, vol.26, no.1, 2005, pp.87-100.

Nair, Ravi, "Refugee Protection in South Asia," *Journal of International Affairs*, vol.51, no.1, Summer 1997, pp.201-20.

Nuruzzaman, M.D., "SAARC and Subregional Co-operation: Domestic Politics and Foreign Policies in South Asia," *Contemporary South Asia*, vol.8, no.3, November 1999, pp.311-23.

Oberst, Robert C., "Political Decay in Sri Lanka," *Current History*, vol.88, no.542, December 1989, p.425-30.

Pfaffenberger, Bryan, "Sri Lanka in 1987: Indian Intervention and Resurgence of the JVP," *Asian Survey*, vol.28, no.2, February 1988, pp.137-47.

Phadnis, Urmila, "Ethnicity and Nation-Building in South Asia: A Case Study of Sri Lanka," *India Quarterly*, vol.35, no.3, July-September 1979, pp.329-50.

Premdas, Ralph R., and S.W.R. de A Samarasinghe, "Sri Lanka's Ethnic Conflict: The Indo-Lanka Peace Accord," *Asian Survey*, vol.28, no.6, June 1988, p.676-90.

Raju, A. Subramanyam, "Sethusamudram Ship Canal Project: Problems and Prospects," *Indian Ocean Survey*, vol.1, no.2, July-December 2005, pp.105-08.

———, "Energy Cooperation in South Asia," in Dennis Rumely and Sanjay Chaturvedi (eds), *Energy Security and the Indian Ocean,* New Delhi: South Asian Publishers, 2005, pp. 190-203.

———, "Fishermen (In) Security in Indo-Sri Lankan Waters", in Santishree Pandit (ed), *Human Security in India-Conflict in the New Age of Insecurity* (forthcoming).

———, "India's Security in the Palk Straits", in Gopalji Malviya (ed), *Security Dimensions of Peninsular India,* Chennai: Centre for Security Analysis, 2005, pp.63-79.

———, "Maritime Issues in South Asia," in A. Subramanyam Raju (ed), *Reconstructing South Asia: An Agenda,* New Delhi: Gyan Publishing House, 2007.

Rakodi, Carole, " Getting the Pipe Laid is One Matter and Getting the Water Flowing through the Pipes is Another': User Views on Public-Sector Urban Water Provision in Zimbabwe, Sri Lanka, Ghana and India," *International Planning Studies*, vol.5, no.3, October 2000, pp.365-92.

Rao, P. Venkateshwar, "Ethnic Conflict in Sri Lanka: India's Role and Perception," *Asian Survey*, vol.28, no.4, April 1988, pp.419-36.

Reed, Ananya Mukherjee, "Regionalization in South Asia: Theory and Praxis," *Pacific Affairs*, vol.70, no.2, Summer 1997, p.235-51.

Roberts, M., "Filial Devotion in Tamil Culture and the Tiger Cult of Martyrdom", *Contribution to Indian Sociology*, vol.31, no.2, 1996, pp.245-72.

Sahadevan, P., "Failure of Peace Process in Sri Lanka," *Mainstream*, vol.31, no.10, January 1993, p.25.

Sambandan, V.S., "The LTTE's Blueprint," *Frontline,* vol.20, no.23, November 2003, pp.12-14.

Samarasinghe, S.W.R. De A and Kamala Liyanage, "Friends and Foes of the Indo-Sri Lanka Accord," in K.M. de Silva and S.W.R. de A. Samarasinghe (ed.), *Peace Accords and Ethnic Conflict*, New York: Pinter; and St. Martin's Press, 1993.

Sarvananthan, Muttukrishna, "Contraband Trade Between India and Sri Lanka," *Journal of Contemporary Asia*, vol.31, no.1, 2001, pp.31-57.

———, "Contraband Trade and Unofficial Capital Transfers between Sri Lanka and India", *Economic and Political Weekly,* vol.29, no.30, July 1994, pp.1948-56.

———, "Indo-Sri Lanka Free Trade: Hype and Reality, *Economic and Political Weekly*, April 2000, pp.1-7.

————, "The Nature, Causes and Effects of Contraband Trade and Capital Between India and Sri Lanka," *Contemporary South Asia*, vol.8, no.2, July 1999, pp.211-18.

Silva, K.T., and Pushpakumara, W.D.N.R., "Love, Hate and the Upsurge in Youth Suicide in Sri Lanka: Suicide Trends in a Mahaweli New Settlement," *Sri Lanka Journal of Social Sciences,* vol.19, nos.1&2, 1996, pp.73-92.

Singh, K.R., "Sri Lanka-Evolution of Naval Strategy," *Journal of Indian Ocean Studies*, vol.10, no.1, April 2002, pp.91-99.

Somasundaram, D.J & Rajadurai, S.,"War and Suicide in Northern Sri Lanka," *Acta Psychiatrica,* vol.91, no.1, 1995, pp.1-4.

Suryanarayan, V.," Stepping Stone to a Separate State," *Frontline,* 21 November 2003, p.15

Viswam, S., "India-Sri Lanka Agreement: Triumph of Statesmanship," *Indian Foreign Review,* vol.24, September 1987, pp. 4-30.

Vivekanandan, V., "Crossing Maritime Borders: The Problem and Solution in the Indo-Sri Lankan Context," in K.G. Kumar (ed), *Forging Unity: Coastal Communities and the Indian Ocean's Future,* Chennai: International Collective in Support of Fishworkers, 2003, pp.76-89.

Books

Akhtar, Shaheen, *Geo-Strategic Dynamics of Indo-Sri Lanka Relations*, Colombo: Bandaranaike Centre for International Studies, 1996.

Austin, Dennis, *Democracy and Violence in India and Sri Lanka,* London: Royal Institute of International Affairs, 1994.

Bhasin, Avtar Singh, (ed.), *India-Sri Lanka Relations and Sri Lanka's Ethnic Conflict: Documents: 1947-2000,* 5 vols., New Delhi: India Research Press, 2001.

Bose, Sumantra, *States, Nations, Sovereignty, Sri Lanka, India and the Tamil Eelam Movemen,* New Delhi: Sage Publications, 1994.

Bullion, Alan J, *India, Sri Lanka and the Tamil Crisis 1976-1994: An International Perspective,* London: Pinter, 1995.

Chari PR, Joseph Mallika and Subha Chandran (eds.) *Missing Boundaries, Migrants, Settlers and Internally Displaced Persons of South Asia,* Delhi: Manohar Publishers, 2003.

Coelho, Vincent, *Across the Palk Straits: India-Sri Lanka Relations,* New Delhi: Palit and Palit Publishers,1976.

Dagmar, Hellman-Rajanayagam, *Peace Initiatives towards Reconciliation and Nation Building in Sri Lanka: An International Perspective,* Kuala Lumpur: Malaysian Ceylonese Congress, 2002.

Deraniyagala, Siran Upendra, *Pre-Historic Basis for the Rise of Civilization in Sri Lanka and South India,* Chennai: Second Vesak Memorial Lecture, 2004.

Dar, Gulam Mohammad, *The Ethnic Conflict in Sri-Lanka: Impact on Indo-Sri-Lanka Relations,* New Delhi: Dilpreet Publishing House, 2005.

De Silva, K.M, *Regional Powers and Small State Security. India and Sri Lanka, 1977-1990,* Washington DC,: Woodrow Wilson Center Press, 1995.

De Silva, K.M., G H Peiris & S W R de A Samarasinghe (eds.), *Corruption in South Asia: India, Pakistan and Sri Lanka*, Kandy: International Centre for Ethnic Studies, 2002.

Douglas Allen (ed), *Religion and Political Conflict in South Asia: India, Pakistan, and Sri Lanka,* Westport, Connecticut: Greenwood Press, 1992.

Dubey, R.K., *Indo-Sri Lankan Relationships with Special Reference to the Tamil Problem*, Delhi: Deep and Deep Publications, 1989.

Ghosh, Partha S, *Ethnicity versus Nationalism: The Devolution Discourse in Sri Lanka,* New Delhi: Sage Publishers, 2003.

Gunarathna, Rohan, *Indian Intervention in Sri Lanka: The Role of India's Intelligence Agencies,* Colombo: South Asian Network on Conflict Research, 1993.

Jagota, S.P., *Maritime Boundary,* London: Martinus Nijhoff Publishers, 1985.

Jayewardene, Hiran W, *The Regime of Islands in International Law,* London: Martinus Nijhoff Publishers, 1988.

Jayasinghe, W.T., *The Indo-Ceylon Problem: The Politics of Immigrant Labour,* Colombo:Staford Lake Publications, 2002.

———, *Kachchativu and the Maritime Boundary of Sri Lanka,* Colombo: Stamford Lake Publication, 2003.

Kadian, Rajesh. *India's Sri Lanka Fiasco: Peace Keepers at War,* New Delhi: Vision Books, 1990.

Kodikara, Shelton U., *Indo-Ceylon Relations since Independence,* Colombo: Ceylon Institute of World Affairs, 1965.

——— (ed), *South Asian Strategic Issues: Sri Lankan Perspectives,* New Delhi: Sage, 1990.

Malviya, Gopalji, *Security Dimensions of Peninsular India,* Chennai: Centre for Security Analysis, 2005.

Morell, B. James, *The Law of the Sea*, Jefferson, Missouri: McFarland, 1992.

Muni, S.D, *Pangs of proximity: India and Sri Lanka's Ethnic Crisis,* New Delhi: Sage, 1993.

Narayan Swamy M.R, *The Tigers of Sri Lanka: From Boys to Guerrillas*, Delhi: Konark Publishers Pvt Ltd, 1994.

Nishida, T and Sivasubramaniam K, *Atlas of Deep Water Demersal Fishing Resources in the Bay of Bengal (BOBP/WP/53)*, Chennai: Bay of Bengal Programme, n.d.

Panikkar, K. M., *India and the Indian Ocean,* Bombay: George Allen Unwin, 1945.

Phadnis, Urmila, *Ethnicity and Nation-building in South Asia,* New Delhi: Sage Publications, 1989.

Pillai, Somasundaram *A, Sri Lanka: Fisheries Exploitation and Development,* Wattala: Ambalam Publications, 2002.

Raju, A.Subramanyam & S. Keethaponchalan, *Maritime Cooperation Between India and Sri Lanka*, New Delhi: Manohar Publishers, 2006.

Raju, A. Subramanyam (ed), *Reconstructing South Asia: An Agenda* (forthcoming)

——— (ed), *Terrorism in South Asia: Views from India*, New Delhi: India Research Press, Singapore: Marshall Cavendish Academic, 2004.

Ramaswamy, P, *New Delhi and Sri Lanka: Four Decades of Politics and Diplomacy*, New Delhi: Allied Publishers Pvt Ltd, 1987.

Rao, P.V., ed., *India and the Indian Ocean: In the Twilight of the Millennium,* New Delhi: South Asian Publishers, 2003.

Rothberg, Robert I., *Creating Peace in Sri Lanka: Civil War and Reconciliation,* Brookings Institutuion, 1999.

Sahadevan, P, *India and Overseas Indians: the Case of Sri Lanka.* Delhi: Kalinga Publications, 1995

——— (ed), *Conflict and Peace Making in South Asia,* New Delhi: Lancers Books, 2001.

Sankaran, Krishna, *India's Role in Sri Lanka's Ethnic Conflict*, Colombo: Marga Institute, Colombo, 2001.

———, *Postcolonial Insecurities: India, Sri Lanka, and the Question of Nationhood*, Minneapolis, MN: University of Minnesota Press, 1999.

Seevaratnam, N, *The Tamil National Question and the Indo Sri Lanka Peace Accord*, Delhi: Konark Publications, 1989.

Sharma, R.N, *The Archaeology of the Indian Subcontinent and Sri Lanka: A Selected Bibliography*, Westport, Connecticut: Greenwoodpress, 2000.

Simmondes, Kenneth R., *New Directions in the Law of the Sea*, London: Oceana Publications, 1988.

Suryanarayan, V, *Kachchativu and Problems of Indian Fishermen in the Palk Bay Region*, Madras: TR Publications, 1994.

Conflict Over Fisheries in the Palk Bay Region, New Delhi: Lancer Publishers, 2005.

———and Sudarsen, V, *Between Fear and Hope: Sri Lankan Refugees in Tamil Nadu*, Madras: TR Publications, 2002.

Swami, M.R.N., *Tigers of Lanka: From Boys to Guerrillas,* New Delhi: Konark, 1994.

United Nations, *The Law of the Sea: United Nations Convention on the Law of the Sea,* New York: United Nations, 1983.

Index

T